Deliberative Systems in Theory and Practice

Deliberative democracy is a growing branch of democratic theory that is also influential in contemporary political practice. Deliberation involves a process of mutual justification where participants offer reasons for their positions, listen to the views of others, and reconsider their preferences in the light of new information and arguments. More recently, deliberative democracy has taken a systemic turn opening up a new way of thinking about public deliberation in contemporary democracies. The deliberative system approach suggests understanding deliberation as a communicative activity that occurs in a diversity of spaces, and emphasizes the need for interconnection between these spaces. It offers promising solutions to some of the long-standing theoretical issues in the deliberative democracy literature such as legitimation, inclusion, representation, as well as the interaction and interconnection between public opinion formation and decision-making sites more generally. Despite its conceptual and practical appeal, however, the concept of deliberative systems also entails potential problems and raises several important questions. These include questions around the deliberative and democratic credentials of the system as a whole, the prospects of its institutionalization, and various issues related to its empirical analysis. The deliberative systems approach therefore requires greater theoretical critical scrutiny, and empirical investigation. This book contributes to this endeavor by bringing together cutting edge research on the theory and practice of deliberative systems. It identifies the key challenges against the concept to enhance understanding of both its prospects and problems promoting its refinement accordingly.

The chapters in this book were originally published as two special issues of *Critical Policy Studies*.

Stephen Elstub is a Lecturer in British Politics at the School of Geography, Politics and Sociology, Newcastle University, United Kindgom. His main research interests are in public opinion, political communication, civil society and political participation, all viewed through the lens of deliberative democracy.

Selen A. Ercan is an Associate Professor of Politics at the Centre for Deliberative Democracy and Global Governance, Institute for Governance and Policy Analysis, University of Canberra, Australia. She works in the area of deliberative democracy focusing particularly on the capacity of this approach in addressing irreconcilable value conflicts in contemporary polities.

Ricardo Fabrino Mendonça is an Associate Professor at the Department of Political Science, Federal University of Minas Gerais, Brazil. He researches democratic theory, critical theory, politics of recognition, social movements and political communication.

Deliberative Systems in Theory and Practice

Edited by
Stephen Elstub, Selen A. Ercan and
Ricardo Fabrino Mendonça

LONDON AND NEW YORK

First published 2018
by Routledge
2 Park Square, Milton Park, Abingdon, Oxon, OX14 4RN, UK

and by Routledge
711 Third Avenue, New York, NY 10017, USA

Routledge is an imprint of the Taylor & Francis Group, an informa business

© 2018 Institute of Local Government Studies, University of Birmingham

All rights reserved. No part of this book may be reprinted or reproduced or utilised in any form or by any electronic, mechanical, or other means, now known or hereafter invented, including photocopying and recording, or in any information storage or retrieval system, without permission in writing from the publishers.

Trademark notice: Product or corporate names may be trademarks or registered trademarks, and are used only for identification and explanation without intent to infringe.

British Library Cataloguing in Publication Data
A catalogue record for this book is available from the British Library

ISBN 13: 978-0-8153-9613-0

Typeset in Minion Pro
by RefineCatch Limited, Bungay, Suffolk

Publisher's Note
The publisher accepts responsibility for any inconsistencies that may have arisen during the conversion of this book from journal articles to book chapters, namely the possible inclusion of journal terminology.

Disclaimer
Every effort has been made to contact copyright holders for their permission to reprint material in this book. The publishers would be grateful to hear from any copyright holder who is not here acknowledged and will undertake to rectify any errors or omissions in future editions of this book.

Contents

Citation Information vii
Notes on Contributors ix

1. The fourth generation of deliberative democracy 1
   Stephen Elstub, Selen A. Ercan and Ricardo Fabrino Mendonça

Section I: Deliberative systems in theory

2. The boundaries of a deliberative system: the case of disruptive protest 14
   William Smith

3. Mitigating systemic dangers: the role of connectivity inducers in a deliberative system 33
   Ricardo Fabrino Mendonça

4. Deliberative elitism? Distributed deliberation and the organization of epistemic inequality 53
   Alfred Moore

5. Reflections on the theory of deliberative systems 71
   John S. Dryzek

Section II: Deliberative systems in practice

6. Message received? Examining transmission in deliberative systems 78
   John Boswell, Carolyn M. Hendriks and Selen A. Ercan

7. Brazilian Social Assistance Policy: an empirical test of the concept of deliberative systems 99
   Debora Rezende de Almeida and Eleonora Schettini Cunha

8. Deliberative networks 120
   Andrew Knops

9. Reflections on how to empirically ground the deliberative system's theory 140
   Leonardo Avritzer

Index 145

Citation Information

The following chapters were originally published in *Critical Policy Studies*, volume 10, issue 2 (July 2016). When citing this material, please use the original page numbering for each article, as follows:

Chapter 1
The fourth generation of deliberative democracy
Stephen Elstub, Selen A. Ercan and Ricardo Fabrino Mendonça
Critical Policy Studies, volume 10, issue 2 (July 2016), pp. 139–151

Chapter 2
The boundaries of a deliberative system: the case of disruptive protest
William Smith
Critical Policy Studies, volume 10, issue 2 (July 2016), pp. 152–170

Chapter 3
Mitigating systemic dangers: the role of connectivity inducers in a deliberative system
Ricardo Fabrino Mendonça
Critical Policy Studies, volume 10, issue 2 (July 2016), pp. 171–190

Chapter 4
Deliberative elitism? Distributed deliberation and the organization of epistemic inequality
Alfred Moore
Critical Policy Studies, volume 10, issue 2 (July 2016), pp. 191–208

Chapter 5
Reflections on the theory of deliberative systems
John S. Dryzek
Critical Policy Studies, volume 10, issue 2 (July 2016), pp. 209–215

The following chapters were originally published in *Critical Policy Studies*, volume 10, issue 3 (October 2016). When citing this material, please use the original page numbering for each article, as follows:

Chapter 6
Message received? Examining transmission in deliberative systems
John Boswell, Carolyn M. Hendriks and Selen A. Ercan
Critical Policy Studies, volume 10, issue 3 (October 2016), pp. 263–283

Chapter 7
Brazilian Social Assistance Policy: an empirical test of the concept of deliberative systems
Debora Rezende de Almeida and Eleonora Schettini Cunha
Critical Policy Studies, volume 10, issue 3 (October 2016), pp. 284–304

Chapter 8
Deliberative networks
Andrew Knops
Critical Policy Studies, volume 10, issue 3 (October 2016), pp. 305–324

Chapter 9
Reflections on how to empirically ground the deliberative system's theory
Leonardo Avritzer
Critical Policy Studies, volume 10, issue 3 (October 2016), pp. 325–329

For any permission-related enquiries please visit:
http://www.tandfonline.com/page/help/permissions

Notes on Contributors

Leonardo Avritzer is a Professor at the Federal University of Minas Gerais, Brazil. He has published numerous books, book chapters, and articles in the area of democracy and citizen participation in Brazil and South America.

John Boswell is an Associate Professor in Politics at the University of Southampton, UK. His expertise is on the boundary of political theory and public policy, and centres around contemporary issues and themes in democratic governance. He is the author of *The Real War on Obesity: Contesting Knowledge and Meaning in a Public Health Crisis* (2016).

Eleonora Schettini Cunha is a Professor in the Department of Political Science at the Federal University of Minas Gerais, Brazil. Among her published books are *Democracia e reinvenção do Estado: lições do Brasil e da Índia* (2007) and *Efetividade deliberativa de conselhos de Assistência Social* (2009). She has also published on political participation, deliberation and democratic theory in Brazilian and other journals.

Debora Rezende de Almeida is a Professor in the Department of Political Science at the University of Brasília, where she leads a research group on the Relationship Between Civil Society and the State (RESOCIE).

John S. Dryzek is ARC Laureate Fellow and Centenary Professor in the Centre for Deliberative Democracy and Global Governance, University of Canberra, Australia. Working in both political theory and empirical social science, he is best known for his contributions in the areas of democratic theory and practice and environmental politics.

Stephen Elstub is a Lecturer in British Politics at the School of Geography, Politics and Sociology, Newcastle University, UK. His main research interests are in public opinion, political communication, civil society and political participation, all viewed through the lens of deliberative democracy.

Selen A. Ercan is an Associate Professor of Politics at the Centre for Deliberative Democracy and Global Governance, Institute for Governance and Policy Analysis, University of Canberra, Australia. She works in the area of deliberative democracy focusing particularly on the capacity of this approach in addressing irreconcilable value conflicts in contemporary polities.

Ricardo Fabrino Mendonça is an Associate Professor at the Federal University of Minas Gerais, Brazil. He is a CNPq (National Council for Scientific and Technological Development) and a Fapemig Researcher. He researches democratic theory, critical theory, politics of recognition, social movements and political communication.

NOTES ON CONTRIBUTORS

Carolyn M. Hendriks is an Associate Professor at the Crawford School of Public Policy at the Australian National University. She has taught and published on deliberative forms of citizen engagement and her research has covered democratic innovation, public deliberation, alternative forms of political participation and environmental politics.

Andrew Knops is a Lecturer in the Department of Political Science and International Studies at the University of Birmingham, UK. He has written widely on deliberation, democracy and decision-making processes in, among others, the *Journal of Political Philosophy*, *Political Theory* and the *Journal of Theoretical Politics*.

Alfred Moore is a Lecturer in Political Theory in the Department of Politics at the University of York, UK. He works on contemporary political theory, and is the author of *Critical Elitism: Deliberation, Democracy, and the Politics of Expertise* (2017, Cambridge University Press).

William Smith is an Associate Professor in the Department of Government and Public Administration at The Chinese University of Hong Kong. His research is in the field of contemporary political theory, with a particular focus on issues related to deliberative democracy, civil disobedience and international political thought.

The fourth generation of deliberative democracy

Stephen Elstub, Selen A. Ercan and Ricardo Fabrino Mendonça

ABSTRACT
This editorial introduction presents an overview of the themes explored in the symposium on 'Deliberative Systems in Theory and Practice'. The concept of 'deliberative system' has gained renewed attention among deliberative democrats. A systemic approach to deliberative democracy opens up a new way of thinking about public deliberation. However, as the key protagonists responsible for the systemic resurgence acknowledge, the framework requires greater theoretical critical scrutiny and empirical investigation. The symposium will contribute to this endeavor by bringing together cutting edge research on the theory and practice of deliberative systems. This introduction offers a brief outline and review of the existing systemic approaches to deliberation, articulating the overlaps and differences and reflecting on the prospects and problems of each. In doing so, we take a generational approach that delineates the development of deliberative democracy into three generations, and argue that the focus on deliberative systems has implications that are so significant for the examination of theory and practice that it heralds a fourth generation for deliberative democracy. We conclude this introduction by providing a brief synopsis of each paper and highlighting the significance of the debates for critical policy studies.

In recent years, the concept of 'deliberative system' has gained renewed attention among deliberative democrats (Thompson 2008; Dryzek 2010a; Parkinson and Mansbridge 2012). The concept of deliberative system refers to an understanding of deliberation as a communicative activity that occurs in multiple, diverse yet partly overlapping spaces, and emphasizes the need for interconnection between these spaces. On this account, deliberation is not confined to the structured forums, which have been the focal point of attention for the scholars of deliberative democracy since the 'deliberative turn' in democratic theory in 1990s (Dryzek 2000). The deliberative systems approach entails three closely related ideas that, together, differentiate it from the prevailing notions of deliberation. The first is that it is an approach that conceives and promotes deliberation on a mass scale, the second is the special focus this approach places on a division of labor within a system, and the third is the idea of seeking criteria for 'deliberation' across this myriad of institutions and processes of contemporary polities.

The growing body of literature on deliberative systems outlines various merits of this concept in both theory and practice. It is claimed to offer promising solutions to some of the long-standing theoretical issues in the deliberative democracy literature. For example, it offers a way of scaling up legitimation, inclusion, and representation (Parkinson 2006; Mendonça 2008), and opens up a new way of conceptualizing the interaction between public opinion and decision-making moments of deliberation (Dryzek 2010b; Elstub and McLaverty 2013). Besides its various theoretical merits, the deliberative systems approach also provides a new way of studying the practice of deliberation in contemporary democracies. It offers fresh answers to some of the prevailing questions, including how to understand and study the relationship between mini-publics and the broader system (Warren 2007; Hendriks 2004; Dodge 2009; Niemeyer 2014; Ercan, Hendriks, and Boswell 2015), how to conceptualize the connections and transmission across different sites of deliberative activity (Boswell 2015), and which standards to employ when assessing the deliberative quality of a system as a whole (Dryzek 2009; O'Flynn and Curato 2015).

Despite its conceptual and practical appeal, the concept of deliberative systems also entails potential problems and raises several questions that require attention. The most recent scholarly debates around this concept entail the relationship between the parts and the whole of the deliberative system (Owen and Smith 2015), the prospects of its institutionalization, and the methodological difficulties related to its empirical analysis (Ercan, Hendriks, and Boswell 2015). As the rejuvenated focus on deliberative systems is proving crucial for current developments in this field, the concept merits greater scrutiny and empirical investigation. This special double issue on deliberative systems will contribute to this endeavor by bringing together cutting edge conceptual and empirical research on the theory and practice of deliberative systems. It will seek to identify the key challenges against the concept and contribute toward its refinement.

The purpose of this editorial introduction piece is twofold. First, it seeks to present an overview of the themes explored in both issues emphasizing the promises and limitations associated with the deliberative systems approach. Second, we seek to situate the deliberative systems approach within the broader deliberative democracy scholarship, which we believe is crucial for capturing the distinctive features of this approach. In doing so, we build on the generational argument made by Elstub (2010) that delineates the development of deliberative democracy into three generations. This enables us to demonstrate why the interest in the ideas of the deliberative system has developed in response to the previous generations' perceived limitations. Furthermore, we argue that the focus on deliberative systems has implications that are so significant for the examination of theory and practice that it heralds a fourth generation. While we appreciate these ramifications for bringing prospects with respect to conceiving deliberative democracy on the mass scale, we also draw attention to possible problems that this achievement could lead to, based on excessive concept stretching on what constitutes deliberation (Ercan and Dryzek 2015). We conclude this introduction by providing a brief synopsis of each article included in this symposium.

The transformation of deliberative democracy across generations

Deliberative democracy has never been a unified theory. Moreover, 'as deliberative theory has developed and matured, it has also become more internally differentiated' (Neblo 2007, 530). Deliberative democrats differ on the questions of what sorts of communication count as deliberative, where deliberation should take place, who should deliberate and how, and what should be the expected outcome of deliberation (Dryzek 2000; Chambers 2003; Gutmann and Thompson 2004; Thompson 2008). Besides significant philosophical differences among different deliberative democrats, there are also variations in terms of *foci* throughout time, which allow us to consider the developments in this field in terms of four generations, at least for analytical purposes.[1] By identifying 'discrete generational cohorts' in deliberative democracy, we aim to highlight their 'distinctive constituent elements', while avoiding the establishment of 'artificial and divisive cleavages' (Dean 2009). There are indeed considerable overlaps between the different generations, and as new generations emerge, this does not mean that previous generations become redundant. In addition, by generation, we do not mean to separate specific sets of scholars across time. Many deliberative democrats have been part of more than one of these generations. The use of the term simply aims at distinguishing important trends in diverse moments. A generational analysis enables us to detail the considerations that have led to the recent focus on deliberative systems.

The first-generation scholars of deliberative democracy can be best described through their emphasis on normative theorizing. Habermas (1996) had a very prominent role at this initial wave of thinking about deliberative democracy. He argued that legitimate decisions in a democratic polity could emerge only through a discursive procedure that allows all affected to have a say in the making of collective decisions. The normative theorizing was also central in Cohen's (1989) approach to democratic legitimacy, and in the early work of Dryzek (1990), which advanced a radical conception of discursive democracy allowing the projection of a transnational and non-anthropocentric view of democracy. These scholars articulated the need for deliberative democracy to occur on a mass/system-wide level. Nevertheless, they offered a largely normatively driven vision of deliberative democracy that the current generation of system theorists perceive as practically impossible to achieve on a mass scale as they paid insufficient attention to the challenges that contemporary complexity posed to the practice of deliberation. For example, some first-generation scholars conceptualized exchange of reasons as the only applicable form of communication resulting in uniform preference change. This rather limited notion of deliberation was directly challenged by the rise of the second generation of deliberative democracy, which sought to offer 'new and distinct interpretations of reason giving, preference change, consensus and compromise, and applicable forms of communication' (Elstub 2010, 298).

The scholars of the second generation such as Dryzek (2000), Deveaux (2003), and Young (1996) expanded the definition of deliberation in order to make it more sensitive to the increasing plurality and complexity in contemporary democracies. They problematized the consensus and rational argument requirements of deliberation and brought deliberative democratic theory in close connection with several other fields including feminism, multiculturalism, and environmental politics. Deveaux (2003), for instance, developed a deliberative approach to conflicts of culture. Dryzek (2000) challenged the liberal tone pervading deliberative scholarship influenced by Habermas and developed a critical conception of deliberation, grounded on the idea of a contestation of discourses in the public sphere. Young (1996) offered a powerful criticism of the speech styles advocated by first-generation deliberative scholars, arguing that besides rational argumentation, deliberation should allow storytelling, rhetoric, and greetings as legitimate forms of communication to enable greater inclusivity.

The second generation has acknowledged the normative nature of deliberative theory as well, yet the theoretical questions they have raised, particularly with respect to the capacity of deliberative theory to accommodate diversity and plurality in contemporary democracies, have helped to sharpen the critical edge of deliberative theory. In particular, it raised issues with potential inequalities within discursive processes and paid attention to the possibility of instrumentalization or strategic use of deliberation by powerful actors. In doing so, these scholars brought deliberative democracy closer to 'real-world' conflicts and dilemmas. Neblo (2007, 537) praised this orientation in deliberative theory arguing that these theorists 'deserve enormous credit for making deliberation a more workable and fully developed ideal' (see also Elstub 2010, 298, for a similar discussion).

However, the scholars of the second generation usually refrained from engaging in the specifics of detailed institutional design and empirical analysis of deliberative practices. The third generation emerged to correct this failing by promoting and researching the capacity of a number of institutional mechanisms that may be able to foster actual deliberation. It is, nonetheless, the revised, more practice orientated, theory of the second generation that they sought to institutionalize (Elstub 2010). After all, feasible deliberation required institutions that could cope with a variety of 'real-world' issues such as cultural pluralism, self-interests, and social inequalities.

Therefore, the dominant trend within the third generation of investigations in deliberative democracy has focused on its feasibility, namely the design of deliberative institutions and the empirical analysis of these. In doing so, the scholars of the third generation drew particularly on the growing body of literature on various participatory practices such as Citizens' Juries, Planning Cells, Consensus Conferences, and Participatory Budgeting. In the 1990s, Fishkin (1995) advanced the idea of the deliberative polls, as a new way to conduct public opinion research. The debate, then, blossomed around the notion of mini-publics and their potential to foster deliberative practice (Ackerman and Fishkin 2003; Fung 2003; Fung and Wright 2003; Gastil and Levine 2005; Avritzer 2009; Elstub 2014; Grönlund, Bächtiger, and Setälä 2014). Besides their strong interest in implementing deliberation in the context of 'real-life' politics, the third-generation scholars have also sought for suitable methods enabling the systematic and close investigation of deliberative processes and to determine the required parameters for institutional design (Sulkin and Simon 2001). In doing so, however, the third generation adopted mainly a micro approach to deliberation that isolated mini-publics and other institutions from the broader discursive environment and macro context within which they operate (Thompson 2008; Chambers 2009; Dryzek 2010b; Mansbridge et al. 2012).

It is precisely in this context that the scholars of deliberative democracy have begun to pay renewed attention to the concept of deliberative systems. The starting point of the systems approach is the need to understand deliberation beyond isolated deliberative practices and to examine not only the relationship between different deliberative sites, but also 'the relationship between deliberative and non-deliberative practices in the political system as a whole and over time' (Thompson 2008, 500). Overall, the systemic turn in deliberative democracy can be characterized as an attempt to reconcile the insights gained from three preceding generations, namely the strong normative premises, institutional feasibility, and empirical results. As such, the deliberative system approach offers a new way of thinking about the theory and practice of deliberation, and the emerging research can be seen as heralding the fourth generation of deliberative democracy.

The systemic turn and the fourth generation of deliberative democracy

The term *deliberative system* was first coined by Mansbridge at the end of the 1990s. In her seminal article, Mansbridge (1999) argues that deliberation should be understood through broad lenses capable of grasping the complexities of discursive flows in contemporary societies. Such a conception of deliberation, she notes, not only promises to be more inclusive but also draws attention to the conditions that help enhance the quality of public deliberation. Moreover, deliberation should not be reduced to face-to-face dialogue, but understood in terms of a wider discursive process. This impetus represents a significant change from some more traditional conceptions of deliberative democracy, where deliberation occurs in close proximity to binding collective decision-making (Cohen 2007).

The idea of a 'system' involving the interrelation of parts for the constitution of a deliberative process is not completely new. It had already been employed by several advocates of the deliberative turn. Most notably, the idea goes back to Habermas' (1996) notion of dual-track model of deliberation. According to Habermas, deliberative politics depends on a complex system with a nucleus that needs to be open to the peripheries of discursive production. The wild communicative flows of the broad public sphere may be filtered so as to constitute a communicative power, which can be translated through laws into administrative power (Habermas 2005, 388). The idea of a broad *clash of discourses* is also at the heart of the work of Dryzek (1990) who has advocated an approach that is not centered on individuals, but focuses on the public contestation of discourses and its influence on decision-making. In his later work, Dryzek (2010a, 2010b, 2011) has focused on the normative conditions of deliberative quality at a system level, and suggested evaluating the deliberative system in its entirety. More recently, Mansbridge et al. (2012) outline the basic functions of deliberative systems, namely the epistemic, the ethical, and the democratic function. Denying the *naïveté* of the approach, the authors present some pathologies recurrent in real-world systems, such as the tight coupling of arenas, the decoupling of discursive spheres, and the domination of the system.

Overall, the deliberative systems approach has three core notions that we think have been particularly important in terms of the evolution of deliberative democracy. The first is an attempt to conceive and promote deliberation on a mass scale, the second is the increasing focus on a division of labor within a system, and the third is an introduction of a continuum of criteria for 'deliberation' across this myriad of institutions and processes. When seen together, these attempts are sufficiently discrete from the previous generations, to represent a fourth generation of deliberative democracy. It certainly seems to be the case that systems theorists themselves believe their approach represents something like a new generation of deliberative democracy: 'Our aim is to articulate an over-arching approach to deliberation that could signal a new and we think exciting direction for deliberative theory, but which is not itself a free standing theory of deliberative democracy' (Mansbridge et al. 2012, 4). A nuanced analysis of this move, however, indicates various practical and methodological challenges. This is particularly true with respect to the relaxation of the criteria of deliberation, which may result in rendering it undistinguishable from other forms of communication, and consequently dampen the critical orientation that was at the core of the original, first generation, conceptions of deliberative democracy. To make this case, we now consider each of the distinctive notions of the deliberative system in turn.

The aim to secure the norms of deliberative democracy on a mass scale and the understanding that we need to consider broader discursive structures to achieve this is the first way that the systems approach demonstrates a break from the third generation, where the focus was on how specific and micro institutions and processes can promote democratic deliberation and advocating measures to improve this. As Chambers (2012, 54) explains it 'rather than focusing on single instances, institutions, or even spheres, this approach looks at the connections between instances, institutions, and spheres'. Similarly, Parkinson (2012, 152) indicates that the systemic turn seeks to address the democratic deficit of isolated mini-publics. This impetus alone does not indicate that the systems approach represents a fourth generation of deliberative democracy, as the normative ideal of the first was also to have democratic deliberation on a mass scale. In this sense, the fourth generation takes deliberative democracy full circle and back to its origins. Nevertheless, the renewed focus on deliberative systems does still indicate a departure from the third generation, while also being affected by the changes advanced by the second and third generations. The fourth generation is not, hence, simply a return to the premises advocated by the first.

The second crucial element on recent deliberative systems research is the increasing focus on a need for a division of labor. Accordingly, 'the criterion for good deliberation should not be that every interaction in the system exhibit mutual respect, consistency, acknowledgement, open mindedness, and moral economy, but that the larger system reflect those goals' (Mansbridge 1999, 224). The suggestion is that different parts of the system can supplement and correct the failings of other parts to form a mutually enhancing relationship (Mansbridge et al. 2012, 2f.). For example, Parkinson (2006) claims that different sites and different moments offer diverse contributions to public deliberation. In his approach, therefore, both the dimensions of time and space are essential if one is to understand the modus operandi of deliberative systems. At different phases of a policy process, diverse actors and various venues may have distinct virtues and contrasting limitations. In all of these phases, informal, formal, and intermediate discursive settings should be considered (Parkinson 2006, 168). Utilizing a similar perspective, Goodin (2005, 2008) argues for a *sequencing of deliberative moments*, claiming that the deliberative task should be distributed. This division of labor helps in the thinking of deliberation as a totality. In the sequential approach, each arena has its virtues and the way to organize the sequence of deliberative moments matters, to ensure these deliberative virtues proceed in an appropriate order. Relatedly, Hendriks (2011) advocates an integrated model of deliberation, capable of hosting a multiplicity of arenas including macro informal debate, micro formal arenas, and hybrid (or mixed) mini-publics.

In some instances of current systems theorizing, the division of labor is extended to such an extent that parts of a system that meet none of the deliberative criteria when viewed in isolation are seen to fulfill vital deliberative roles in the system (Dryzek 2011; Mansbridge et al. 2012; Bohman 2012). In turn, highly deliberative parts of the system can have detrimental effects on deliberation in the system as a whole. The existing institutions, Dryzek (2009, 1388) argues, 'can constitute, and interact within, a deliberative system in intricate and variable ways. Seemingly low deliberative quality in one location (say corporatist state institutions) may be compensated by, or even inspire, higher deliberative quality in another location (say, a flourishing public sphere). Conversely, high deliberative quality in one location may undermine deliberative quality in another.' We must, therefore, consider and evaluate an entire deliberative system rather than simply the constituent parts (Dryzek 2011, 226–227).

Owen and Smith (2015) are concerned that we could consequently have a 'deliberative system' where no deliberation actually takes place. Chambers anticipates this critique and argues that although the division of labor is required, it should not be excessive as this could be dysfunctional. We, therefore, support Thompson's (2008, 502) contention that the key is to 'treat these other activities as part of a larger democratic process, rather than as instances of deliberation per se.' This means they might be considered external to a deliberative system too. If this is accepted, then considerably more empirical evidence is required to establish that non-deliberative parts of the system do bring deliberative benefits to the system as a whole. Furthermore, we need to establish the 'appropriate normative criteria for determining when deviations from deliberative norms are legitimate' (Owen and Smith 2015, 225).

The third, more crucial, and perhaps concerning, impetus in the systems approach is the relaxation and more ecumenical view of what constitutes 'deliberation' and particularly 'democratic deliberation', to an even greater extent than was evidenced by the third generation. For example, Chambers (2012, 52) suggests that only a systemic approach to deliberative democracy can ensure mass democracy and that this 'requires that we rethink some standard definitions of deliberation and deliberative democracy.' In fact a 'capacious' definition of deliberation must be embraced. For Mansbridge (1999, 227) there is a spectrum of venues for deliberation, including representative assemblies, public assemblies, the public sphere, and everyday talk, and 'moving along this range entails moving along a similar range, from formal to informal, within the same standards for good deliberation.' Therefore, all instances of deliberation should still be judged on the criteria of reciprocity, publicity, and accountability, for example, while not expecting the same level of the criteria in each venue (Mansbridge 1999, 213). It is precisely at this point that we find the seeds of the fourth generation of deliberative democracy as the notion of what constitutes deliberation is broadened and its criteria relaxed. Neblo argues that this need not take definitions of deliberative democracy 'to the point of vacuity' as we should still view everything through 'the lens of deliberative theory' (Neblo 2005, 11; see Thompson 2008, 513, 515 for a similar stance).

This seems to be an acceptable response; however, it is not clear that all approaches to deliberative systems do employ a deliberative lens in this manner. For example, for Parkinson (2012, 154), the key to utilizing a division of labor in the system is to increase 'the pool of perspectives, claims, narratives, and reasons', but 'whether those perspectives, are generated deliberatively or not is neither here nor there.' Owen and Smith (2015, 221) rightly critique this suggestion as it ignores the fact that authentic (see Dryzek 2010b, 23) 'perspectives, claims, narratives, and reasons' in a deliberative perspective do not already exist, but must be formed and tested by running the gauntlet of public reasoning. Parkinson (2012, 159) nevertheless maintains that 'deliberation on this account still has some analytical bite- it is not all things to all people.' However, Neblo (2007, 529) acknowledges 'that there is a danger in extending a concept to the point of vacuity. If deliberation and deliberative theory are to have any cutting power they must be contrasted with other forms of political interaction' (see also Bächtiger et al. 2010, 48 for a similar suggestion).

Elstub (2010) has raised similar concerns about the danger of concept stretching within the deliberative literature. If the systemic approach makes deliberative democracy more practical and easier to achieve (through the division of labor between parts; the acceptance that all the norms of deliberative democracy will not be enacted in one place; the contention that some parts do not need to embody any elements of deliberation; the suggestion that processes that are detrimental to deliberative quality can still be essential features of the system, and the overall loosening of the criteria of what counts as deliberation), it is also important to keep in mind that deliberative democracy is a regulative ideal (Ercan and Dryzek 2015). It should, hence, be employed to critique practice, as Mendonça and Cunha (2014) have claimed. For Neblo (2007, 536), 'realism, per se, is hardly a virtue in a regulative ideal. A too realistic ideal is merely an apology for the status quo.' In other words, deliberative systems do not necessarily imply an accommodation to reality and must still work as a regulative ideal. Therefore, although a continuum of deliberative standards for assessing the parts of the system is inevitable, the standards to judge deliberative democracy at the system level need to be kept normatively robust and stringent.

In summary, the fourth generation of thought within deliberative democracy scholarship brings great potential and crucial problems to the theory and practice of deliberation. There is need of robust empirical evidence that establishes the claim that non-deliberative parts can fulfill vital systemic functions more effectively than deliberative ones. Moreover, an overly capacious set of deliberative criteria employed in the systems continuum might easily lead deliberative democracy toward vacuity and render it indistinguishable to any other approaches. The challenge then is to carefully consider, and empirically investigate, how deliberation on a mass level can be conceived and practically implemented, without excessively watering down the key tenets of deliberative democracy. The articles in this double symposium represent some important developments on this journey.

The main focus of the first symposium issue is the investigation of the implications of the systemic turn for deliberative theory. While all three articles welcome the move toward a more expansive approach to deliberation, they draw attention to various theoretical dilemmas that this approach faces. William Smith's article addresses one of the key problems highlighted here, the suggestion that non-deliberative processes are integral to deliberative systems. For Smith, this creates a boundary problem, as it becomes fuzzy as to which processes are internal and external to the system and this is hindering the normative and empirical development of the deliberative systems approach. In response, Smith offers an account of the constitutive features of a deliberative system based upon 'deliberative action'. The utility of this for drawing clear boundaries to the deliberative system is illuminated through an application to disruptive protest.

Similarly, Ricardo Mendonça draws attention to several 'systemic dangers'. He argues that the idea of deliberative systems may reinforce rather than alleviate political asymmetries, increase decision makers' discretionary powers, and cover, rather than reveal, possible incompatibilities among different discourses. Having laid out each of these dangers in detail, he then considers how they might be mitigated. According to Mendonça, the key lies in establishing and strengthening connections across different discursive arenas. This goal makes three types of actors particularly relevant for the idea of deliberative systems: bureaucrats, media, and activists. He shows how each of them can serve as inducers of connectivity in the deliberative system and help mitigate the risks previously discussed.

The third and final article of the first issue of the symposium addresses the division of labor issue that we raised above, that is central to all conceptions of the deliberative system. Alfred Moore particularly focuses on the problems a division of labor can create for democratic equality by focusing on the issue of expertise. For Moore, epistemic, and indeed all, divisions of labor in a deliberative system must be subject to meta-deliberation, and he particularly highlights how epistemic communities, the public sphere, and mini-publics can promote and enable public judgment on expertise in deliberative systems. The first issue of the symposium on deliberative systems theory is concluded with insightful critical commentary of the papers by John Dryzek, who suggests that together their critiques could represent the seeds of a fifth generation of deliberative democracy, while also calling for more empirical studies of deliberative systems to assist in overcoming some of the problems of the theory highlighted by the papers.

Drawing on rich and original empirical material, the articles in the second issue do just that and engage with several issues that confront the deliberative systems approach in practice. In this contribution, John Boswell, Carolyn Hendriks, and Selen Ercan unpack the meaning of transmission within a deliberative system and present examples of different transmission mechanisms at play. This analysis reveals how institutional and discursive context in a given society may foster or hinder transmission across different sites, and emphasizes the need for a contextualized comprehension of different processes if we are to take the agenda of scaling up deliberation forward.

The focus on connection continues to the second article of the practice special issue. Eleonora Cuhna and Debora Almeida consider how civil society can enhance representation through the interconnection of different discursive spheres in deliberative systems. Using the Brazilian social assistance system, which promotes many participatory and deliberative institutions and processes, as a case study, Cuhna and Almeida suggest that it is institutional design and the circulation of participants that were vital to promoting interconnection between discursive spheres in this context. However, they also highlight that their effects can be contradictory.

Drawing on the insights suggested by the network approach, Andrew Knops develops a normative framework to navigate the complexity of real-world policy processes and assess the deliberativeness of these processes. Given that no single real-world deliberative exchange alone can cover all the issues faced by complex policy issues, Knops suggests understanding deliberation in terms of a 'network of deliberative exchanges'. Provided that each network is grounded in deliberative principle, he argues, the network model demonstrates that it is possible to scale up deliberation and make it relevant for the real-world decision-making processes. By using the concept of the network of deliberative exchanges as a benchmark, Knops discusses the poor deliberative quality of the key stages in the Thatcher government's decision to adopt a poll tax in the UK. The second issue of the symposium on deliberative systems in practice is concluded with astute critical commentary of the papers by Leonardo Avritzer. He highlights the common themes of connection and transmission, and advocates the integration of the empirical frameworks, across the three papers.

Together, these articles advance the agenda of research on deliberative systems in theory and practice, and deliberative democracy in general. Given their focus on a variety of controversial policy issues and process problems, the articles also have relevance for the study of policy making and the practices of policy analysis in contemporary democracies. For the scholars of public policy, the deliberative systems approach offers most notably a new normative angle to capture and evaluate the democratic quality of debates on controversial policy issues and to analyze the veracity of the policy process. It suggests a new way of mapping the sites and actors of policy processes by paying particular attention to the broader context of such processes. As such, it is our hope that the articles in this symposium will also further the conversation and cross-fertilization across different subfields of political science, including critical policy studies.

Notes

1. We use the term 'generations' here as an umbrella term that provides a narrative of change in deliberative democracy that is not linear, similar to the 'wave' metaphor in feminism. Our purpose is to bring a coherence and unity to a diversity of approaches to deliberative democracy.

Disclosure statement

No potential conflict of interest was reported by the authors.

ORCID

Selen Ercan http://orcid.org/0000-0002-3649-2882

References

Ackerman, B., and J. Fishkin. 2003. "Deliberation Day." In *Debating Deliberative Democracy*, edited by J. Fishkin and P. Laslett, 07–30. Malden: Blackwell.

Avritzer, L. 2009. *Participatory Institutions in Democratic Brazil*. Baltimore: Johns Hopkins University Press.

Bächtiger, A., S. Niemeyer, M. Neblo, R. M. Steenbergen, and J. Steiner. 2010. "Disentangling Diversity in Deliberative Democracy: Competing Theories, Their Blind Spots and Complementarities." *The Journal of Political Philosophy* 18 (1): 32-63. doi:10.1111/j.1467-9760.2009.00342.x.

Bohman, J. 2012. "Representation in the Deliberative System." In *Deliberative Systems – Deliberative Democracy at the Large Scale*, edited by J. Parkinson and J. Mansbridge, 72–94. Cambridge: Cambridge University Press.

Boswell, J. 2015. "Toxic Narratives in the Deliberative System: How the Ghost of Nanny Stalks the Obesity Debate." *Policy Studies* 36 (3): 314–328. doi:10.1080/01442872.2015.1065966.

Chambers, S. 2003. "Deliberative Democratic Theory." *Annual Review of Political Science* 6: 307–326. doi:10.1146/annurev.polisci.6.121901.085538.

Chambers, S. 2009. "Rhetoric and the Public Sphere: Has Deliberative Democracy Abandoned Mass Democracy?" *Political Theory* 37 (3): 323–350. doi:10.1177/0090591709332336.

Chambers, S. 2012. "Deliberation and Mass Democracy." In *Deliberative Systems – Deliberative Democracy at the Large Scale*, edited by J. Parkinson and J. Mansbridge, 52–71. Cambridge: Cambridge University Press.

Cohen, J. 1989. "Deliberation and Democratic Legitimacy." In *The Good Polity: Normative Analysis of the State*, edited by A. Hamlin and P. Pettit, 17–35. Oxford: Basil Blackwell.

Cohen, J. 2007. "Deliberative Democracy." In *Deliberation, Participation and Democracy: Can the People Govern?* edited by S. W. Rosenberg, 219–236. Basingstoke: Palgrave Macmillan.

Dean, J. 2009. "Who's Afraid of Third Wave Feminism?" *International Feminist Journal of Politics* 11 (3): 334–352. doi:10.1080/14616740903017711.

Deveaux, M. 2003. "A Deliberative Approach to Conflicts of Culture." *Political Theory* 31 (6): 780–807. doi:10.1177/0090591703256685.

Dodge, J. 2009. "Environmental Justice and Deliberative Democracy: How Social Change Organizations Respond to Power in the Deliberative System." *Policy & Society* 28 (3): 225–239. doi:10.1016/j.polsoc.2009.08.005.

Dryzek, J. 2010a. "Rhetoric in Democracy: A Systemic Appreciation." *Political Theory* 38 (3): 319–339. doi:10.1177/0090591709359596.

Dryzek, J. 2010b. *Foundations and Frontiers of Deliberative Governance.* Oxford: Oxford University Press.
Dryzek, J. S. 1990. *Discursive Democracy: Politics, Policy, and Political Science.* Oakleigh, NY: Cambridge University Press.
Dryzek, J. S. 2000. *Deliberative Democracy and Beyond: Liberals, Critics, Contestations.* New York, NY: OUP.
Dryzek, J. S. 2009. "Democratization as Deliberative Capacity Building." *Comparative Political Studies* 42 (11): 1379–1402. doi:10.1177/0010414009332129.
Dryzek, J. S. 2011. "Global Democratization: Soup, Society, or System?" *Ethics & International Affairs* 25 (2): 211–234. doi:10.1017/S0892679411000074.
Elstub, S. 2010. "The Third Generation of Deliberative Democracy." *Political Studies Review* 8 (3): 291–307.
Elstub, S. 2014. "Mini-Publics: Issues and Cases." In *Deliberative Democracy: Issues and Cases*, edited by S. Elstub and P. McLaverty, 166–188. Edinburgh: Edinburgh University Press.
Elstub, S., and P. McLaverty. 2013. "Ten Issues for a Deliberative System." In *Paper Prepared for Delivery at the 2013 APSA Annual Meeting.* Chicago. August 29–September 1.
Ercan, S. A., and J. S. Dryzek. 2015. "The Reach of Deliberative Democracy." *Policy Studies* 36 (3): 241–248. doi:10.1080/01442872.2015.1065969.
Ercan, S. A., C. M. Hendriks, and J. Boswell. 2015. "Studying Public Deliberation after the Systemic Turn: The Crucial Role of Interpretive Research." *Policy and Politics.* doi:10.1332/030557315X14502713105886.
Fishkin, J. S. 1995. *The Voice of the People: Public Opinion and Democracy.* New Haven: Yale University Press.
Fung, A. 2003. "Survey Article: Recipes for Public Spheres: Eight Institutional Design Choices and Their Consequences." *Journal of Political Philosophy* 11 (3): 338–367. doi:10.1111/1467-9760.00181.
Fung, A., and E. O. Wright. 2003. *Deepening Democracy – Institutional Innovations in Empowered Participatory Governance.* London – New York, NY: Verso.
Gastil, J., and P. Levine, eds. 2005. *The Deliberative Democracy Handbook: Strategies for Effective Civic Engagement in the Twenty-First Century.* San Francisco: Jossey-Bass.
Goodin, R. 2008. *Innovating Democracy.* Cambridge: Cambridge University Press.
Goodin, R. E. 2005. "Sequencing Deliberative Moments." *Acta Politica* 40 (2): 182–196. doi:10.1057/palgrave.ap.5500098.
Grönlund, K., A. Bächtiger, and M. Setälä, eds. 2014. *Deliberative Mini-Publics. Involving Citizens in the Democratic Process.* Colchester: ECPR Press.
Gutmann, A., and D. Thompson. 2004. *Why Deliberative Democracy?* Princeton: Princeton University Press.
Habermas, J. 1996. *Between Facts and Norms.* Cambridge: Polity Press.
Habermas, J. 2005. "Concluding Comments on Empirical Approaches to Deliberative Politics." *Acta Politica* 40 (3): 384–392. doi:10.1057/palgrave.ap.5500119.
Hendriks, C. M. 2004. "Public Deliberation and Interest Organisations: A Study of Responses." PhD dissertation. Research School of Social Sciences, Australian National University, Canberra.
Hendriks, C. M. 2011. *The Politics of Public Deliberation: Citizen Engagement and Public Advocacy.* New York, NY: Palgrave Macmillan.
Mansbridge, J. 1999. "Everyday Talk in Deliberative Systems." In *Deliberative Politics: Essays on Democracy and Disagreement*, edited by S. Macedo, 211–239. New York, NY: Oxford University Press.
Mansbridge, J., J. Bohman, S. Chambers, T. Christiano, A. Fung, J. Parkinson, D. Thompson, and M. E. Warren. 2012. "A Systemic Approach to Deliberative Democracy." In *Deliberative Systems – Deliberative Democracy at the Large Scale*, edited by J. Parkinson and J. Mansbridge, 1–26. Cambridge: Cambridge University Press.
Mendonça, R. F. 2008. "Representation and Deliberation in Civil Society." *Brazilian Political Science Review* 2 (2): 117–137.

Mendonça, R. F., and E. S. Cunha. 2014. "Can the Claim to Foster Broad Participation Hinder Deliberation?" *Critical Policy Studies* 8 (1): 78–100. doi:10.1080/19460171.2013.843468.

Neblo, M. 2005. "Thinking through Democracy: Between the Theory and Practice of Deliberative Politics." *Acta Politica* 40: 169–181. doi:10.1057/palgrave.ap.5500102.

Neblo, M. 2007. "Family Disputes: Diversity in Defining and Measuring Deliberation." *Swiss Political Science Review* 13 (4): 527–557. doi:10.1002/spsr.2007.13.issue-4.

Niemeyer, S. 2014. "Scaling Up Deliberation to Mass Publics: Harnessing Mini-Publics in a Deliberative System." In *Deliberative Mini-Publics: Involving Citizens in the Democratic Process*, edited by K. Grönlund, A. Bächtiger, and M. Setälä, 177–202. Colchester: ECPR Press.

O'Flynn, I., and N. Curato. 2015. "Deliberative Democratization: A Framework for Systemic Analysis." *Policy Studies* 36 (3): 298–313. doi:10.1080/01442872.2015.1065965.

Owen, D., and G. Smith. 2015. "Survey Article: Deliberation, Democracy, and the Systemic Turn." *Journal of Political Philosophy* 23 (2): 213–234. doi:10.1111/jopp.2015.23.issue-2.

Parkinson, J. 2006. *Deliberating in the Real World: Problems of Legitimacy in Deliberative Democracy*. Oxford: OUP.

Parkinson, J. 2012. "Democratizing Deliberative Systems." In *Deliberative Systems – Deliberative Democracy at the Large Scale*, edited by J. Parkinson and J. Mansbridge, 151–172. Cambridge: Cambridge University Press.

Parkinson, J., and J. Mansbridge, eds. 2012. *Deliberative Systems – Deliberative Democracy at the Large Scale*. Cambridge: Cambridge University Press.

Sulkin, T., and A. F. Simon. 2001. "Habermas in the Lab: A Study of Deliberation in an Experimental Setting." *Political Psychology* 22 (4): 809–826. doi:10.1111/pops.2001.22.issue-4.

Thompson, D. 2008. "Deliberative Democratic Theory and Empirical Political Science." *Annual Review of Political Science* 11: 497–520. doi:10.1146/annurev.polisci.11.081306.070555.

Warren, M. 2007. "Institutionalizing Deliberative Democracy." In *Deliberation, Participation and Democracy: Can the People Govern?* edited by S. W. Rosenberg, 272–288. Basingstoke: Palgrave Macmillan.

Young, I. M. 1996. "Communication and the Other: Beyond Deliberative Democracy." In *Democracy and Difference: Contesting the Boundaries of the Political*, edited by S. Bebhabib, 120–135. Princeton: Princeton University Press.

The boundaries of a deliberative system: the case of disruptive protest

William Smith

ABSTRACT
The idea of a deliberative system has been employed to demonstrate that deliberative democracy should not be limited to the give-and-take of reasons, but can also incorporate a range of apparently non-deliberative actions. Despite the appeal of this move, the inclusive spirit of the systemic turn is indicative of a general problem with its theoretical framework. The problem is that the boundaries of a deliberative system have not been drawn with sufficient precision, such that it is not possible to reach a clear determination about what is internal and what is external to the system. The article resolves this problem through suggesting that a deliberative system should only include modes of action that embody substantive norms of deliberative action. This suggests a more nuanced approach to the relationship between deliberative systems and non-deliberative action than is typically found in the existing literature, which is illustrated here through considering the case of disruptive protest.

Introduction

The idea of a *deliberative system* has been introduced by a number of scholars to orientate conceptual and empirical analysis of deliberation at the societal level. An influential chapter by Mansbridge et al. defines a deliberative system as 'a set of distinguishable, differentiated, but to some degree interdependent parts, often with distributed functions and a division of labour, connected in such a way as to form a complex whole' (Mansbridge et al. 2012, 4). The systemic turn is notable for its willingness to embrace certain *non-deliberative* forms of action, such as rhetoric, partisan campaigns, and self-interest. These modes of conduct are defended as a resource that can increase 'deliberative capacity', which is associated with the degree of epistemic-reflective, inclusive, and consequential deliberation across the system as a whole (Dryzek 2010, 10). So, for example, partisan campaigning might fail to embody deliberative norms, but might nonetheless function as a means of combating unequal access to or influence over the public sphere and the policymaking process. This type of partisanship is said to be highly useful from a systemic perspective, provided that over time other elements of the system can counter-balance any shortfall brought about in terms of epistemic subtlety (Mansbridge et al. 2012, 6–7).

The systemic turn is a promising development for deliberative theory, but an important ambiguity in the concept of a deliberative system must be resolved before it can make good on its normative and empirical ambitions. The problem is that the *boundaries* of a deliberative system must be drawn with greater precision than has hitherto been the case, in order that a clearer determination can be made about what is internal and external to the system. The treatment of non-deliberative action by systems theorists exacerbates this problem, as it not clear whether such behavior should be conceptualized as a constitutive element of the system or as an external variable that can nonetheless increase its capacity. There is, it should be stressed, more at stake here than a matter of conceptual clarity. The broader deliberative turn in democratic theory is associated with the normative claim that policymaking and public debate should, as far as possible, approximate an ideal of informed and inclusive dialogue (Cohen 1989). There is, to be sure, no shortage of critics willing to castigate this claim as naïve or idealistic, but it is central to both the moral appeal and the critical purchase of the deliberative paradigm. The embrace of non-deliberative action by systems theorists not only blurs the boundaries of a deliberative system, but also appears to dilute the commitment to dialogue that is – for many – the major attraction of deliberative democracy (Owen and Smith 2015).

The argument of this article is that the conceptual coherence and normative integrity of the systemic turn can be preserved, but only if the boundaries of a deliberative system are drawn in a clear and compelling fashion. The approach that is favored here is to fix the boundaries through reference to an account of *deliberative action*, which requires elements of a deliberative system to embody paradigmatic features of deliberative conduct to an appropriate degree. This approach has the general advantage of sharpening the distinction between deliberative and non-deliberative action, which is often applied by systems theorists in a manner that is inattentive to the nuances and diversity of dialogic conduct. The argument is elaborated across three sections.

The first section takes a closer look at the boundary problem, by suggesting that prominent attempts to address this issue within the systems-theory literature are subject to serious objections. The second section begins the task of overcoming these objections through introducing the concept of deliberative action, which categorizes behavior as deliberative if it is suitably reflective, respectful, and dialogic. The third section applies this concept to the boundary problem, through presenting the deliberative system as a regulative ideal that is constituted by deliberative action. The implications of this approach for political practices are illustrated through reconsidering the case of non-deliberative action, focusing in particular on the relationship between deliberative systems and disruptive protest. The analysis differentiates dialogic and non-dialogic forms of protest, treating the former as an element of a deliberative system and the latter as an external element that might nonetheless be appropriate in certain systemic contexts. This approach thus enables us to draw the boundaries of a deliberative system in a way that retains the normative presumption in favor of dialogic conduct and addresses the practical issue of the real-world circumstances that allow this presumption to be overridden.

The boundary problem

The focus on non-deliberative action on the part of systems theorists can be interpreted as part of a broader trend within deliberative democratic theory. There has been considerable criticism of deliberative democracy insofar as it marginalizes or delegitimizes modes of political conduct that depart from calm, orderly, and reflective dialogue (Young 2000). There has, in response, been an effort to show how deliberative democracy can accommodate much greater diversity, including humor, narrative, negotiation, rhetoric, and protest. The systemic turn is, in many ways, a culmination of this trend, as it affirms the importance of non-deliberative modes of action to deliberative democracy (Mansbridge et al. 2012). This has prompted some deliberative democrats to wonder how far this inclusive spirit can be taken before the distinctive emphasis of deliberative democracy on reason and reflection is lost (Bächtiger et al. 2010). This concern can be explored here in relation to the *boundaries* of a deliberative system.

The boundaries of a deliberative system should enable us to distinguish what is internal and what is external to it. These boundaries might be conceptualized solely in spatial terms, such that we think of a deliberative system as a distinct set of sites and linkages between them. This approach appears to be suggested in John Dryzek's influential formulation, according to which a deliberative system is comprised of 'public spaces' – informal arenas within which agents engage in everyday talk about issues of shared concern – and 'empowered spaces' – the more formal arenas within which agents interact in their capacity as decision-makers and policymakers (Dryzek 2010, 11). The literature on deliberative systems, in fact, appears to suggest that the boundaries of the system should be understood in a rather different way. This alternative approach defines a system not merely through reference to particular spaces, but also through reference to modes of conduct and, in particular, communication.

This broader conception is implied by Dryzek (2010, 66–84) when he discusses the role of certain types of rhetoric within a deliberative system and by Mansbridge et al. (2012, 6–9) when they discuss the roles of partisanship or everyday talk in the system. The attraction of this broader conceptualization is that it captures the intuition that the deliberative system should not merely be described as a kind of structure, architecture, or scaffolding. It is, as Mansbridge et al. note, a dynamic network, which is comprised of complex patterns of *action* carried out by a plurality of agents (Mansbridge et al. 2012, 5). This more action-orientated way of thinking about boundaries allows us to retain the idea that spaces or forums are a component part of a deliberative system, but those spaces are seen as sites for a certain type of action. This can be illustrated most clearly in the case of 'mini-publics' that are designed by agents to facilitate a particularly rigorous type of deliberation, but might also be illustrated through the more informal arenas, ad hoc forums, or online spaces within which ordinary citizens, members of social movements, and civil society actors can engage in discussion and debate (Fung 2003). The boundaries of a deliberative system, then, can be conceptualized as conterminous with relationships and spaces that facilitate a certain type of interaction on the part of relevant agents.

This action-orientated approach helps to fix ideas about the variable that is relevant to conceptualizing the boundaries of a deliberative system, but it is not yet clear how those boundaries should be drawn. The challenge here is to identify the type of action that is constitutive of a deliberative system, such that it becomes possible to delineate the concept. The literature on deliberative systems suggests two possible accounts of how the boundaries of a deliberative system can be drawn, but neither is particularly compelling.

The first account focuses our attention on action that is orientated toward reaching *collective decisions*. The boundaries of the deliberative system, on this account, should be drawn around action of citizens that contributes to or influences a particular decision-making process. This is inclusive of decision-making within empowered *and* public space, as Mansbridge et al. emphasize in their discussion of 'societal decisions' (Mansbridge et al. 2012, 8). The approach to decision-making adopted here is somewhat broad, such that 'our criteria for inclusion in a deliberative system are that the discussions in question involve matters of common concern and have a practical orientation' (Mansbridge et al. 2012, 9). This has the intuitive appeal of reminding us that deliberative democracy is intended to be a practical framework geared toward enabling publics to solve problems and reach decisions (Cohen 1989).

The problem is that orientation toward decision-making cannot by itself function as a means of defining the boundaries of a deliberative system. First, decision-making is at best a necessary rather than a sufficient condition for action to be included within a deliberative system. This is because collective decisions can be an outcome of actions that have no connection at all to the dialogic or communicative focus of deliberative theory, such as drawing lots, coin tosses, or aggregative mechanisms such as voting. This is implicitly recognized by Mansbridge et al., as it becomes clear that their candidates for inclusion in a deliberative system should embody a 'talk-based approach to political conflict and problem-solving – through arguing, expressing and persuading' (Mansbridge et al. 2012, 2–3). Second, even if we seek to draw the boundaries of a deliberative system around action that has a communicative or discursive dimension, this would still fail to capture intuitions about the nature and complexion of deliberative problem solving. This is because it would sanction the inclusion of any and all forms of communication irrespective of whether and to what extent that action could be characterized as deliberative. There is, on this account, nothing to prevent a decision-making system being described as deliberative even if *none* of its component parts embody deliberative norms to any degree (Parkinson 2006, 7). This appears to be deeply counter-intuitive.

The second approach adopts a more *functionalist* perspective, through suggesting that the boundaries of a deliberative system should be drawn around action that contributes to realizing its deliberative capacity. The idea of deliberative capacity, to recall, is associated with the extent of epistemic-reflective, inclusive, and consequential deliberation across the system as a whole. As noted in the introduction, systems theorists are open to the possibility that deliberation can be a practice that is distributed across different elements of a complex matrix (Owen and Smith 2015, 218–219). This idea is implicit in accounts that identify deliberative systems as expansive networks of interrelated parts, each of which perform a useful function in sustaining the system as a whole. Those actions that, all things considered, enhance the epistemic, inclusive, or consequential credentials of the system might be categorized as internal to it, while those actions that likewise frustrate these functions might be categorized as external to the system.

There are, though, two difficulties with this kind of approach. First, it is difficult to avoid what Mansbridge et al. refer to as the 'blind spot' of old style functionalism, which is that 'everything can be seen as, in one way or another, contributing to the system' (Mansbridge et al. 2012, 19). This is not a fatal problem, as it may be possible to undertake empirical investigations that would place us in a better position to distinguish between function-enabling and function-disabling action. It would, though, be preferable if a more straightforward means of fixing the concept of a deliberative system could be found, for the simple reason that doing so would help to provide a focal point for the research that is necessary to ascertain the impacts of different types of actions on systemic functionality. Second, as in our discussion of decision-making, the functionalist approach is vulnerable to the charge that it generates counter-intuitive conclusions about the content of deliberative systems. The problem is not merely that we might be left with an account allowing for deliberative systems with no component parts that embody deliberative norms. It is also that the functionalist approach might actually recommend *excluding* component parts that embody deliberative norms to a high degree. This is because it is quite possible that the deliberative capacity of a system as a whole would be poorly served, all things considered, by the introduction of a highly deliberative element. This can be illustrated through considering the case of a microcosmic deliberative forum. The forum might be crafted in such a way that it facilitates a high standard of deliberation among participants, but nonetheless have the intended or unintended effect of delegitimizing or marginalizing socially beneficial campaigns of advocacy organizations that operate outside of the forum (Mansbridge et al. 2012, 6). Although such a forum might have a deleterious impact on deliberative capacity, it would be strange to take that as a basis for denying that the forum is a 'part' of the system. It is, after all, highly deliberative in its design, such that it can be comfortably reconciled with our intuitions about what a deliberative system might contain. The functional approach appears to make the mistake of conflating the optimum functioning of a system with our account of what the system *is*.

These reflections might be vulnerable to concerns about their broader relevance to the systemic turn. The thought here is that it might not really matter if we do not have a clear account of how to identify the boundaries of a deliberative system. There is, of course, room for a certain degree of indeterminacy, as is suggested by the affirmation of Mansbridge et al. that we should not 'require a system to have clearly identifiable boundaries' (Mansbridge et al. 2012, 5). There is, though, a limit to the level of indeterminacy that we should regard as tolerable in delineating the concept of a deliberative system. The empirical and normative aspirations of the systemic turn would be poorly served by a core concept that is too fuzzy around the edges.

The empirical purchase of the concept is dependent on its capacity to chart a system with a distinctive set of component parts and relationships. If the concept of a deliberative system is too fuzzy, it may be difficult and perhaps even impossible to apply it in social scientific analysis of interaction within societal, governmental, transnational, or other contexts. This is because researchers will lack a clear idea about the constitutive elements of a deliberative system, thus making it difficult to get a clear fix on their subject matter.

Of rather more concern is that the normative appeal of the concept would be undercut if we lack a clear idea about the boundaries of the concept. This is because, picking up again on a recurring theme of the preceding discussion, a system should only be described as *deliberative* if it can be shown to possess constitutive features that warrant the application of that label. The normative appeal of deliberative democracy, for better or for worse, is intimately connected to a belief in the value of deliberation as a means for agents to resolve collective problems and negotiate political conflicts. This commitment to deliberation as an activity carried out through interpersonal relationships, rather than a practice that is dispersed across an impersonal system, is offered a robust defense by Owen and Smith (2015, 219). First, interpersonal deliberation is said to realize the significant ethical good of cultivating our capacities to reason, reflect, and adopt a generalized perspective. Second, interpersonal deliberation realizes the significant cognitive good of helping us to forge new perspectives through participation in reason-giving with others. It is, of course, appropriate and sometimes necessary to resort to non-deliberative activity if deliberation cannot get off the ground or breaks down in some way. The problem is that many critics of deliberative democracy might wonder whether a system comprised almost entirely of non-deliberative elements could or should qualify *as* deliberative. This intuition resonates with concerns about the implications of broadening the deliberative framework to include modes of action, such as self-interest or disruptive protest, that have been seen as the polar opposite of the modes of conduct traditionally favored by the paradigm. As Parkinson puts it, 'I, and I suspect many other deliberative democrats, feel somewhat uncomfortable about making such a recommendation, because at the end of the day the deliberative movement, if we can call it that, is in large part about replacing power plays and political tantrums with the mild voice of reason' (Parkinson 2012, 158).

Deliberative action

These concerns can be addressed in a number of ways, but the rest of this article sketches one possible direction for the future elaboration of the systemic turn. The guiding idea is that we should reclaim the distinctive commitment of deliberative democracy to dialogue, but without abandoning the system-theoretic focus on the macro-level and on non-conventional forms of political action. This idea is pursued by employing a conception of *deliberative action* in order to draw the boundaries of a deliberative system. Deliberation is sometimes contrasted with action, as is the case when we speak about, say, activists engaging in deliberation prior to instigating their campaigns and protests. There is nothing objectionable about this tendency, provided that it does not obscure the sense in which deliberation itself is a form of action. It is a form of action in that it is purposive and intentional behavior, which actors attach subjective meaning to. Deliberative action, as it is understood here, refers to a mode of behavior that embodies a certain kind of normative value, though this value can be realized to a greater or lesser degree in practice. There are three paradigmatic features of deliberation.

The first feature of deliberative action is that it is a *reflective* mode of being in the world. The practice of deliberation entails the engagement of our capacities for practical judgment in the course of reaching considered conclusions about a particular course of action. The reflexivity of deliberation presupposes that participants have access to the information that is relevant to the decision that has to be reached. It also presupposes that participants have the ability and willingness to weigh and balance the relevant considerations that bear on a particular issue. The idea of reflexivity thus captures the cognitive, or epistemic, dimension that must be present in deliberation but may be absent in other modes of expression or conversation.

This may create the impression that deliberative action is limited to the impartial and impersonal give and take of reasons. Although reason-giving can be an embodiment of the deliberative ideal, it is not the only means of engaging in deliberation. This point is illustrated by recent discussions that distinguish between deliberative and non-deliberative types of rhetoric. Simone Chambers has argued that 'deliberative rhetoric makes people think, it makes people see things in new ways, it conveys information and knowledge, and it makes people more reflective' (Chambers 2009, 335). This is contrasted with non-deliberative, or 'plebiscitary' rhetoric, which she defines as 'speech that is concerned first and foremost with gaining support for a proposition and only secondarily with the merits of the arguments or persuasion' (Chambers 2009, 337). The key difference between deliberative and non-deliberative rhetoric, on this account, is that the former is committed to triggering thought and reflection on the part of an audience, whereas the latter has no such ambition. The case of rhetoric demonstrates that there is more to deliberation than impartial and impersonal reason-giving.

The second feature of deliberative action is that it is *respectful* of others. It is respectful in the sense that it adopts an appropriate attitude toward the rational agency of our interlocutors. There is an intimate connection between the reflective and respectful dimensions of deliberation, because modes of interaction that engage the practical faculties of participants presuppose a conception of those participants as beings capable of self-authorship. This insight is expressed by Mansbridge et al. (2012, 11):

> To deliberate with another is to understand the other as a self-authoring source of reasons and claims. To fail to grant to another the moral status of authorship is, in effect, to remove oneself from the possibility of deliberative influence. By the same token, being open to being moved by the words of another is to respect the other as a source of reasons, claims, and perspectives.

The link between reflection and respect can be illustrated through returning to Chambers' distinction between deliberative and plebiscitary rhetoric. Deliberative rhetoric embodies respect for listeners because it engages their capacity for autonomous choice, whereas plebiscitary rhetoric disrespects its listeners through treating them merely as a means to power or influence (Chambers 2009, 337). The link between reflection and respect is also exemplified in the deliberative aversion to force or pressure as a mode of interaction. The achievement of goals through threats, force, or sanctions, rather than through reason or argument, is difficult to reconcile with an appropriate respect for persons as agents. There is, though, scope for considerable debate about the range of acts that might be described as compatible with an appropriate attitude of respect for others. A mode of communication that appears disruptive or offensive might, for example, be redeemed as respectful if it has the goal of activating our faculties for judgment or understanding. The action might be condemned as disrespectful, by contrast, if it drowns out the appeal to our faculties or treats us merely as a means to the achievement of some goal or aim (Brownlee 2012, 20–21).

The third feature of deliberative action is that it is *dialogic*. It is dialogic in the sense that it involves agents elaborating and exchanging opinions that are relevant to reaching collective decisions (Bohman 1996, 57–66). The importance of dialogue is that it is a mechanism through which various perspectives are articulated and subjected to critical scrutiny. The dialogic feature of deliberation thus contributes to its reflective dimension, in the sense that it enables participants to engage with perspectives that differ from their own. The dialogic feature also contributes to its respectful dimension, in the sense that listening to the perspectives of others and revising our opinions in the face of compelling counterarguments can be an important expression of respect for our discursive interlocutors.

The dialogic dimension of deliberative action can be realized through what Robert Goodin describes as both its 'external-collective' aspect, understood as the discursive interactions that occur between actors in public or empowered space, and its 'internal-reflective' aspect, understood as the mental processes through which individuals reflect upon competing perspectives (Goodin 2000). The dialogic dimension can also be realized through verbal and nonverbal modes of expression.[1] This suggestion might strike some readers as implausible, but it follows naturally from an appreciation of dialogue as a practice. There are many contexts where a nonverbal mode of expression, such as a facial expression, a bodily movement, an image, or an action, can be a means of not merely initiating but of participating in dialogic interaction (Brownlee 2012, 43–44). It is, in fact, a significant mistake to disregard the layers of meaning that can be conveyed through nonverbal modes of behavior, which can embody deliberative features to a greater degree than non-reflective, disrespectful, or non-dialogic speech. The failure to recognize the diverse ways in which agents can contribute to dialogue contributes to an impoverished and inaccurate picture of deliberative practice.

The features of deliberative interaction discussed above can be realized to a greater or lesser extent, such that our conduct must embody these features to an appropriate degree to qualify as deliberative. There is scope for considerable debate about what constitutes an 'appropriate degree' in this context.[2] Both theoretical reflection and empirical analysis can play a role in fixing our ideas about forms of action that realize the features of deliberation to an appropriate degree. The role of theory is to define paradigm cases of deliberative action, such that we have a clear idea about unproblematic instances of this form of conduct. There is scope for the use of hypothetical examples to illustrate the complexion of deliberative action, as shall be seen later in the discussion of disruptive protest. The role of empirical analysis, by contrast, is to ascertain whether and to what extent this form of action is realized in practice. There is scope for the use of case studies, provided that these exhibit features that can be interpreted as illustrative of deliberative action. Hypothetical examples and case studies can also play a role in illustrating how certain forms of action fail to embody the features of deliberative action to an appropriate degree.

This theoretical and empirical analysis can be guided by two further considerations. The first is that all three features of deliberative action must be present for any particular action to be categorized as deliberative. This means that an action could not be described as deliberative if, for instance, it is suitably reflective and respectful, but not dialogic. The account of deliberative action developed here insists on the realization of all three paradigmatic features of deliberative action, because of the intimate connection that has been charted between them. It is, in fact, difficult to envisage how deliberative action could fail to embody less than the full set, because of the close relationship between reflection, respect, and dialogue.

The second is that the paradigmatic features of deliberation require agents to adopt a certain attitude toward their conduct. The agents should, in other words, understand their behavior as a contribution to an ongoing process of internal or external deliberation. Their conduct must be a genuine effort to instigate reflection, which displays the appropriate kind of respect toward their dialogic interlocutors. This is significant because the extent to which a mode of action appropriately realizes the features of deliberation is likely to depend upon its relation to an observable and broader pattern of behavior by the relevant actor. This can be illustrated through reference to the dialogic dimension of deliberation.

The requirements of dialogue can be quite demanding, such that demonstrating a genuine commitment to dialogue entails more than simply communicating our views to others. It also requires more than a willingness to defend our positions to others through salient reasons or considerations. A genuine commitment to dialogue requires us to listen to the counter-arguments of our discursive interlocutors and to appraise the merits of these arguments. An actor engaged in authentic dialogue is, as Robert Talisse puts it, 'able and willing to offer justifications for her views and actions, *but is also* prepared to consider alternate views, respond to criticism, answer objections, and, if necessary, revise or abandon her views' (Talisse 2005, 427–428). This entails that an actor's conduct cannot be categorized as deliberative if he or she refuses to listen to the arguments of opponents or to respond to criticism of his or her behavior. The point is that the extent to which actors are committed to dialogue can be ascertained through observing their conduct toward discursive interlocutors, or their apparent willingness to subject their beliefs to challenge through debate. The determination of whether the paradigmatic features of deliberation are realized to an appropriate degree in any given instance can, then, be ascertained through careful analysis of the conduct and context of the relevant action.

Disruption in the deliberative system

This account of deliberative action can be employed to define the boundaries of a deliberative system. The system is conceptualized as a complex network of spaces and relationships that facilitate deliberation among a plurality of actors. It is a political ideal that reflects the normative value of deliberation and as such establishes a presumption in favor of modes of problem solving and conflict resolution that approximate the features of deliberative action. This might be seen as an unfortunate retreat from one of the more notable features of the systemic turn, which is the willingness to welcome into the deliberative fold modes of action that tend to be treated as non-deliberative. The argument developed here adopts a more nuanced perspective, which holds that (a) actions are often mistakenly characterized as non-deliberative and (b) non-deliberative actions can sometimes be regarded as legitimate departures from deliberative norms. This position is illustrated here through reference to the case of disruptive protest.

The ideal of a deliberative system

The ideal of a deliberative system requires societal and political actors to take steps that enable and embed deliberative action at multiple sites. The action that constitutes a deliberative system is, moreover, characterized by its orientation toward influencing or shaping collective decisions. The deliberation that is constitutive of such systems has, as Chambers notes, 'a practical orientation and involves giving, assessing, and evaluating reasons for and against courses of action' (Chambers 2012, 58). This type of deliberation, in line with the positions defended by Dryzek and Mansbridge et al., can take place in public and empowered spaces, such that a system is inclusive of societal decisions that emerge gradually by accretion and political decisions reached through various governance and policymaking mechanisms (Mansbridge et al. 2012, 7–10). And the elements of the system should embody the broadly democratic values associated with deliberative capacity, namely reflection, inclusivity, and impact (Dryzek 2010).

The interpretation of the systemic turn favored here is distinct from that of Mansbridge et al. Their approach conceptualizes the deliberative system in a loose and inclusive sense, such that it lacks clear boundaries and incorporates a plurality of elements. This account, by contrast, conceptualizes the system in a tighter and somewhat more exclusionary sense, such that it possesses clearer boundaries and is inclusive only of action that can be characterized as deliberative. It would be a mistake, though, to assume that all parts of the system must achieve a high standard of deliberation. The extent to which the features of deliberative action are realized is a matter of degree, such that it is likely that some components of the system will more perfectly or completely realize those features than others.

The system can thus include the kind of microcosmic forums that are designed to realize deliberative norms to a high degree, but also forums or patterns of behavior in which the quality of deliberation may be lower. The type of deliberation that takes place in a microcosmic forum might be higher in the sense that it is informed by the widest possible range of perspectives, or subject to forms of moderation that promote high levels of mutual respect (Smith 2009). The deliberation that takes place in empowered spaces, such as legislative assemblies, or public spaces, such as online forums, is perhaps unlikely to reach this level, but it could still be included within the system if the three dimensions of deliberative action are appropriately realized. This would be the case if, for instance, empirical study of the space in question supports a plausible interpretation of it as reflective, respectful, and dialogic (Steiner et al. 2004). A similar approach can be adopted to the transmission mechanisms that link various sites of the system, such that different linkages might approximate deliberative norms to a greater or lesser extent.

The deliberative system is an ideal that has a range of implications for the design and decisions of public institutions and regulatory regimes, as well as actors operating within more informal public spaces. This can be illustrated through briefly considering policymaking at local, national, or regional levels. The case for introducing deliberative action within policymaking processes has been advanced by a number of scholars, with particular focus given to the epistemic and ethical advantages it enjoys as a mode of problem detection and problem solving when compared with bargaining or aggregation (Cohen and Sabel 1997). The basic argument is stated with considerable force by Yannis Papadopoulos (2012, 127):

Being a remedy for uncertainty on the causes of public problems and solutions to them, it is expected that deliberation involving a wide range of participants will contribute to more competent policymaking and that it is, in that respect, a necessary ingredient for the technical improvement of policy outputs. Deliberation is also expected to help take account of others' needs and interests, to enhance respect, recognition, tolerance, and empathy.

This argument for deliberation is premised on both the incorporation of a sufficiently wide range of perspectives and the dialogic processes through which shared knowledge is produced. The systemic perspective insists that policymaking processes must not only be deliberative in their design, but also related in appropriate ways to affected publics. There are, as Papadopoulos argues, a range of emergent policymaking techniques that embody deliberative norms to a certain extent, but which fail to be sufficiently inclusive of or accountable to affected publics. The rise of cooperative governance through policy networks, for instance, embraces stakeholder participation in policymaking, but often culminates in elite-driven processes that operate without the participation or even awareness of the population at large. This might be counteracted through seeding microcosmic forms that are more representative of the broader population within cooperative governance schemes, along with measures such as greater transparency and oversight by elected representatives. The general idea is to open up deliberative policymaking, by ensuring that it is one element of a broader set of interrelated practices inclusive of the public that is regulated by the policymaking body (Papadopoulos 2012, 149).

The practical relevance of the systemic ideal can also be considered through returning to the issue of non-deliberative action in political life. The systemic approach adopts a critical approach to non-deliberative action, but this does not mean that it envisages no legitimate role for it. First, the account of deliberative action can be employed to interrogate assumptions about the boundary between deliberative and non-deliberative action. This approach is anticipated by the distinction between deliberative and non-deliberative rhetoric (Chambers 2009). On the one hand, this distinction illustrates that deliberative action is a more capacious and inclusive concept than has sometimes been supposed. It thus challenges the tendency to treat rhetoric as a mode of communication that is necessarily distinct from deliberation, while also opening up opportunities to study the deliberative pedigree of public debate at the macro, or societal, level. On the other hand, the distinction opens up the concept of deliberation in a way that avoids an 'anything goes' approach. It, therefore, challenges the tendency to stretch the concept of deliberation too much, such that any and all forms of communication are seen as deliberative. The fact that certain types of rhetoric fail to embody the features of deliberative action means that the deliberative paradigm retains its critical dimension, in that it can diagnose some rhetorical contributions to macro-level debate as non-deliberative. This approach to rhetoric illustrates how an account of deliberative action can be utilized to challenge settled intuitions about the non-deliberative status of certain actions, without necessarily diluting the concept of deliberation.

Second, the creation or maintenance of a deliberative system might confront certain obstacles or obstructions that render non-deliberative action a suitable response. It is, for instance, possible to envisage scenarios where the use of non-deliberative rhetoric might play a legitimate role in public debate. This might be the case if it is used to combat a populist political movement that has introduced non-deliberative rhetoric into a deliberative system in order to transmit a message of hate or discrimination. Of course, it does not follow from such cases that the presumption in favor of deliberative action should be treated as a norm that can be easily overridden. The resort to non-deliberative action must be defended in the strongest possible terms, such that a reasonable case for preferring it over deliberative action is presented.

The systemic turn has, as Owen and Smith contend, often failed to acknowledge this, by downplaying the harms and costs associated with non-deliberative action (Owen and Smith 2015, 223). The use of non-deliberative rhetoric, even as a response to a movement that threatens the normative goods associated with a deliberative system, imposes a genuine cost in terms of its lack of concern with appealing to the rational capacities of its addresses. And even if the use of such rhetoric is legitimate, it should not be treated as a component of the system but as an external variable that might have positive or negative impacts on its deliberative capacity. The alternative is to treat deliberative systems in a somewhat totalizing fashion, in the sense that the system would assimilate any and all political phenomena that impacts upon its functioning. The approach favored here retains the conceptual coherence and normative integrity of the deliberative system as an ideal that favors dialogic over non-dialogic modes of action.[3]

Civil disobedience as deliberative disruption

This dual-pronged systemic approach to non-deliberative action can be illustrated through considering the case of disruptive protest. There is a tendency in the systems literature to treat all forms of protest as a departure from deliberative norms, which might nonetheless be legitimate in certain circumstances (Mansbridge et al. 2012, 17–19). This tendency can be faulted for showing insufficient sensitivity to the diversity of actions that are included within the repertoire of contemporary protest movements. Kimberley Brownlee's theory of civil disobedience is highly relevant in this context, because it shows how certain forms of peaceful protest can be conducted in a way that approximates the features of deliberative action to a surprising degree. This theory thus points toward an approach to disruptive protest that is analogous to the theory of rhetoric advanced by Chambers. It allows us, in other words, to distinguish between deliberative and non-deliberative forms of disruption.

Civil disobedience is described by Brownlee as 'a deliberate breach of law taken on the basis of steadfast personal commitment in order to communicate our condemnation of a law or policy to a relevantly placed audience' (Brownlee 2012, 18). This characterization presents civil disobedience as a *reflective* mode of action that involves the expression of our conscientious convictions. It is, furthermore, a *respectful* action that recognizes the agency of an audience that is to be rationally persuaded rather than forced or compelled into accepting those convictions. It is, finally, a *dialogic* action in the sense that it is a means 'to communicate our convictions to others in an effort to engage them in reasoned deliberation about its merits' (Brownlee 2012, 42). The key insight here is that communication through disruption is not in and of itself incompatible with the features of deliberative action:

> Suppose I hold a peaceful sit-in in a government building to protest against our military's activities in another country, and by doing so, I prevent you temporarily from carrying out your job as a civil servant. I have used you as a means to highlight my cause, but the impact on you is modest and my usage does not deny your status as an end. (Brownlee 2012, 21)

The plausibility of categorizing civil disobedience as deliberative disruption depends upon whether the conduct of protesters embodies each of the paradigmatic features of deliberative action. The case described by Brownlee, for instance, might be regarded as incompatible with respect for rational agency if the sit-ins become a daily occurrence, such that civil servants and citizens experience ongoing and significant restrictions on their day-to-day routines (Moraro 2014). This does not detract from Brownlee's fundamental point that suitably conducted protests can be reflective, respectful, and dialogic. The merit of Brownlee's position is that it is sensitive to the complex ways in which agents can initiate and conduct a deliberative exchange, even if their tactics are far removed from the calm and structured interactions that take place in a minipublic or committee. As she puts it, 'thwarting and sabotage can be civilly disobedient since appeals to reason can be long-term, nuanced, and indirect' (Brownlee 2012, 20).[4]

This account of civil disobedience shows that certain forms of disruptive protest can be treated as constitutive features of a system that is restricted in its content to forms of action that embody deliberative norms. These instances of deliberative disruption can be further evaluated in terms of their contribution to the capacity of the system. Civil disobedience can, for instance, increase the degree of epistemic-reflective deliberation throughout the system. The disruption of routines and spaces is an oft-discussed method of triggering reflection, which accounts for the potential superiority of a well-crafted protest over conventional advocacy as a means of reaching out to an audience.

Pollyanna Ruiz illustrates this point through a protest carried out in a Starbucks in Brighton (UK), to draw attention to the fact that the company sold coffee to military personnel stationed in Guantanamo. The occupations involved two activists dressed in the familiar orange-overalls and black hoods of Guantanamo inmates, either kneeling or standing in silence while other activists read statements that invited customers to reflect upon Starbucks' policy, the imprisonment and treatment of internees, and general issues surrounding Guantanamo. This protest functions on at least two levels. First, it works as a more-or-less straightforward means of communicating a thematically linked range of issues to customers and the anonymous publics that follow the action through online and local media. Second, it operates on a more sophisticated level by temporarily disrupting an enclosed space normally taken to be free from politics and teasing out unexpected associations between this space and the treatment and incarceration of terrorist suspects. The protest thus triggers cognitive processes of learning and reflection, as it 'jolts spectators out of their usual state of distraction and encourages them to re-evaluate the discourses which surround them' (Ruiz 2014, 136). These processes could be triggered through less confrontational means of communication, but disruptive protest has the advantage of unsettling expectations and creating striking images for dissemination and consumption through alternative and mass media.

Civil disobedience can also establish connections between different elements of the system, by transmitting opinion and information from one site to another. This can be illustrated by a campaign carried out by Greenpeace, which aimed to highlight linkages between the trade in palm oil and the destruction of Indonesian rainforests. The campaign included eye-catching acts of civil disobedience, such as occupations of Unilever premises by activists dressed as orangutans, to draw attention to a species that is seriously affected by rainforest destruction. These acts might appear to be straightforward instances of non-dialogic pressure, but they assume a different complexion when viewed in their proper context.

Greenpeace had an ongoing relationship with Unilever and other industry actors as a result of their shared membership of the Roundtable for Sustainable Palm Oil (RSPO), a nongovernmental forum in which industry and civil society stakeholders agree upon standards for the global trade in palm oil (Brassett, Richardson, and Smith 2012). Their shared membership in this forum means that Greenpeace and Unilever participate in discussions about appropriate industry practices, such as constraining profit-making activity in line with the shared goal of sustainable production and trade. These acts of civil disobedience are thus an adjunct to a broader dialogic engagement, carried out to punctuate the urgency of preserving the rainforests and to remind Unilever of its global responsibilities as an RSPO member.

The protest action is also intended to communicate the impacts of deforestation to a much broader public, which is why the use of orangutan costumes is significant. The symbolic meaning of such a protest is quickly conveyed to anonymous audiences through photographic images, video footage, and news commentary in the public sphere. These simple but effective communicative dynamics play an important role in enhancing the epistemic quality of society-wide deliberation, by promoting awareness and understanding of salient issues. The invitation to dialogue implicit in such acts is particularly important given that, as noted, complex regulatory networks such as RSPO tend to operate without the participation or knowledge of such broader publics. The use of attention-grabbing protest can thus be a useful means of opening up these transnational regulatory spaces to the scrutiny of dispersed publics.

Direct action as non-deliberative disruption

The preceding argument does not hold that all forms of disruptive protest embody the paradigmatic features of deliberative disruption. The case of *direct action* is relevant here, defined as a disruptive activity carried out with the aim of deterring or obstructing practices that are opposed by activists. This form of disruptive action is 'direct' because it is an attempt to stop a perceived wrong from occurring, rather than an attempt to communicate opposition to that wrong (Shaw 2013, 185). Direct action can – and often does – have the effect of drawing attention to a perceived wrong, but the primary rationale is not to publicize but to disrupt wrongdoing and/or wrongdoers (Milligan 2013, 28–31). This form of protest thus differs from civil disobedience, as it is not conducted as a reflective, respectful, or dialogic engagement with an audience. Although direct action cannot be treated as a component part of a deliberative system, its use might be defensible if certain features of the systemic context suggest that deliberative action would be inappropriate or ineffectual. It is beyond the scope of this discussion to identify all the factors relevant to a defense of direct action, but there are at least two considerations that might contribute to its legitimacy.

The first relevant context is a deliberative system that has coalesced around the view that a contentious activity is wrongful and has taken action to reflect this fact. This would be the case if a plurality of actors had, after reflective dialogue within and across multiple sites, passed and enacted authoritative resolutions in relation to the activity, such that it is now regulated, restricted, or prohibited. It may be the case that recalcitrant parties refuse to accept the outcome of this process, or exploit loopholes in violation of the spirit of the outcome, because they believe that they are morally entitled and/or politically able to ignore or subvert its authority. A credible defense of direct action against this recalcitrant wrongdoing may be forthcoming, insofar as activists invoke the authority of the resolutions passed to regulate, restrict, or prohibit the activity. Activists may contend that direct action is preferable to deliberative action in such cases, as a deliberative process has already run its course and the immediate priority is not to instigate further deliberation but to ensure that the resolution is enforced.

There are difficulties in matching this scenario to real-world contexts, as questions might be raised about the adequacy of the deliberative process that generated the resolution, the extent to which apparently recalcitrant behavior is against the spirit or letter of the resolution, and the implied superiority of direct action to deliberative or communicative action as a means of enforcing the resolution. A real-world case that approximates this scenario to some degree is the use of direct action tactics by activists at sea to disrupt or prevent whaling. The relevant context is the imposition of a moratorium on whaling by the International Whaling Commission, with exceptions that allowed Norway, Iceland, and Japan to engage in 'scientific' whaling. The claim of anti-whaling activists, and others, is that 'scientific whaling is actually a cover for a continued (but sharply reduced) commercial catch; the whale products are still used as before, and precious little science comes from the dead whales' (Dryzek 2000, 126). The anti-whaling activists thus frame their direct action not as a communicative protest, but as an informal attempt to police the moratorium. As Milligan puts it, 'defence of whales is not claimed as civil disobedience precisely because such a claim might detract from the illegality of hunting' (Milligan 2013, 124).

The second relevant context is the presence of pathologies that prevent the emergence of system-level deliberation about contentious practices. This might be due to a familiar range of dynamics, such as failure to include relevant societal perspectives, inequalities that enhance the influence of certain perspectives at the expense of others, and entrenched discourses that lead to deliberative inertia.[5] These dynamics might be contested through deliberative disruption, such as suitably conducted civil disobedience campaigns that correct for the pathologies that block system-level deliberation (Markovits 2005). If these resources have been attempted without apparent success, or there is compelling reason to think that such attempts would be ineffective, this may strengthen the case for direct action. According to Archon Fung, activists have reason to favor such tactics in circumstances where 'obstacles are so high – perhaps because systems of decision making in that arena are highly entrenched and bureaucratized or because the inequality of power is so great – that there is no feasible path to advance deliberation' (Fung 2005, 411).

There is no hard-and-fast test to determine when activists should give up on deliberative strategies, but the ability and willingness of perceived wrongdoers to reciprocate an invitation to dialogue is obviously an important consideration. The case of the anti-globalization movement, according to Fung, illustrates the limits of deliberative strategies and the scope for militant confrontation. As he puts it, 'the governance arrangements that set the terms of world trade and international finance among states are not now, nor will they become in the foreseeable future, fair and inclusive deliberations' (Fung 2005, 412). This resonates with the experiences of those anti-globalization activists who suspended their protests to attend meetings with representatives of global governance bodies, only to find a preset agenda that mostly consisted of listening to prepared speeches by officials. The perception of some activists was that their willingness to participate in discussion was being exploited by discursive opponents as a means of co-opting and dampening their opposition (Young 2001, 680–681). These experiences suggest that activists enjoy greater moral leeway to engage in forms of direct action that disrupt and raise the costs of 'business as usual' for these institutions. The decision to engage in forms of direct action is strategic to a significant degree; activists must decide whether and to what extent their actions can make a genuine contribution to disrupting perceived wrongdoing.

These circumstances give some practical guidance to agents contemplating departures from deliberative norms, but it is important to remain cautious about the prospects for non-deliberative acts as a means of enhancing system-level deliberation (Stevenson and Dryzek 2014, 145–146). There is, for example, sobering evidence about the limitations of direct action as a trigger for society-wide deliberation about contentious practices. Neil Gavin analyses the media coverage of a direct action carried out by environmental activists at a UK airport. The coverage was mostly 'episodic', in that it provided superficial reporting of the event, rather than 'thematic', in that it did not explore the underlying issues and motivations of protesters. The reports were, furthermore, generally negative across a broad spectrum of papers, with journalists tending to emphasize the canceled flights and inconvenience to passengers (Gavin 2010, 462). The findings lead Gavin to suggest that such direct actions are counter-productive for environmentalism as they draw attention away from moderate groups and provide ammunition for critics to discredit the movement as a whole (Gavin 2010, 471).

These objections may be less compelling in relation to deliberative disruption because, as Brownlee notes, civil disobedience has greater reason to disavow forceful or radical tactics that may drown out their message or compromise their moral appeal (Brownlee 2012, 20). The comparative disadvantages of direct action thus offer further support for the intuition that it is best treated not as a potential element of a deliberative system but an external variable. The case for direct action may, as in the case of the anti-globalization movement, be at its strongest in those contexts where a deliberative system is least likely to emerge or function as it should. This underscores the sense in which non-deliberative action might best be seen not as a supplement to a deliberative system, but as a potentially legitimate alternative in contexts that are unconducive to the deliberative resolution of conflicts or problems.

Conclusion

This article has argued that the systemic turn in deliberative theory is a promising evolution of the paradigm, but that the core concept of a deliberative system must be drawn with greater precision than has hitherto been the case. The constructive suggestion that deliberative action can be a means of clarifying the concept of a deliberative system might not, however, be universally welcomed by systems theorists. The reason is that at least some of these theorists may want to move the paradigm away from a focus on deliberation as an embedded practice, in favor of a methodological conceptualization of deliberation as a dispersed and depersonalized process. The concept of deliberative action, from this perspective, could be seen as something of a backward step, which tethers deliberative systems to a mode of political interaction that may appear idealistic and toothless in the face of contemporary political realities.

The article has tried to offset this impression, at least to some degree, through drawing out the range and diversity of deliberative action without diluting its central normative commitments. It has also drawn attention to the problematic implications of conceptualizing deliberative systems in the overly inclusive way that is favored by some of the leading proponents of the systemic turn. There are, to be sure, alternative ways of refining the systemic turn, which may ultimately prove to be superior to the proposals that have been offered here. The fundamental message of this article, though, is that the boundaries of the deliberative system must be clarified if the systemic turn is to deliver theoretical and empirical advances on previous iterations of the deliberative ideal.

Notes

1. The idea of 'verbal exchange' is used here as a catch-all term to incorporate modes of communicative interaction that convey meaning through speech, writing, or signing.
2. The term 'appropriate degree' is taken from Brownlee (2004), in which it is suggested that certain conduct-related constraints must be realized to an appropriate degree in order for our action to qualify as civil disobedience. In her account, 'the standards for what constitutes an appropriate degree may be provided by common sense' (Brownlee 2004, 339ff).
3. This might prompt the objection that non-deliberative elements can only have the kind of impacts envisaged here if connected in some way to the system, which would by definition make them a part of the system. This is not a conclusion I accept, because a system does not need to be conceptualized in such a way that anything that impacts upon it is, by definition, a part of the system. It is conceptually coherent to speak of a system that can be influenced by factors that are external to it, as is illustrated by Habermas' well-known claim that democratic legislation can 'steer' bureaucratic systems or market systems in particular directions (Habermas 1996). Thanks to Stephen Elstub for pressing this objection.
4. The difficulty of reconciling protest and dialogue is perhaps not given sufficient attention by Brownlee in her otherwise impressive analysis of civil disobedience. The dialogic credentials of civil disobedience require not merely the adoption of peaceful and non-coercive tactics, but also an appropriate orientation to our discursive opponents. This might entail, for instance, a disavowal of certain type of stigmatizing rhetoric, or a willingness to take up opportunities to debate with our opponents.
5. For discussion of these dynamics, see Brownlee (2012, 174–178), Dryzek (2000, 81–114), Smith (2011), and Young (2001).

Acknowledgements

A version of this paper was presented at a workshop on 'Deliberative Systems: A Critical Engagement', at the University of Westminster. Thanks to audience members and also to Stephen Elstub and two anonymous reviewers for their helpful comments. This paper was supported by a grant from the Research Grants Council of the Hong Kong Special Administrative Region, China (Project No. CU14409814).

Disclosure statement

No potential conflict of interest was reported by the author.

Funding

This paper was supported by a grant from the Research Grants Council of the Hong Kong Special Administrative Region, China [Project No. CU14409814].

References

Bächtiger, A., S. Niemeyer, M. Neblo, M. R. Steenbergen, and J. Steiner. 2010. "Disentangling Diversity in Deliberative Democracy: Competing Theories, Their Blind Spots and Complementarities." *The Journal of Political Philosophy* 18 (1): 32–63. doi:10.1111/j.1467-9760.2009.00342.x.

Bohman, J. 1996. *Public Deliberation: Pluralism, Complexity, and Democracy*. Cambridge, MA: MIT Press.

Brassett, J., B. Richardson, and W. Smith. 2012. "Private Experiments in Global Governance: Primary Commodity Roundtables and the Politics of Deliberation." *International Theory* 4 (3): 367–399. doi:10.1017/S1752971912000188.

Brownlee, K. 2004. "Features of a Paradigm Case of Civil Disobedience." *Res Publica* 10 (4): 337–351. doi:10.1007/s11158-004-2326-6.

Brownlee, K. 2012. *Conscience and Conviction: The Case for Civil Disobedience*. Oxford: Oxford University Press.

Chambers, S. 2009. "Rhetoric and the Public Sphere: Has Deliberative Democracy Abandoned Mass Democracy?" *Political Theory* 37 (3): 323–350. doi:10.1177/0090591709332336.

Chambers, S. 2012. "Deliberation and Mass Democracy." In *Deliberative Systems: Deliberative Democracy at the Large Scale*, edited by J. Parkinson and J. Mansbridge, 52–71. Cambridge: Cambridge University Press.

Cohen, J. 1989. "Deliberation and Democratic Legitimacy." In *The Good Polity*, edited by A. Hamlin and P. Pettit, 17–34. Blackwell: Oxford.

Cohen, J., and C. Sabel. 1997. "Directly Deliberative Polyarchy." *European Law Journal* 3 (4): 313–342. doi:10.1111/1468-0386.00034.

Dryzek, J. S. 2000. *Deliberative Democracy and Beyond: Liberals Critics Contestations*. Oxford: Oxford University Press.

Dryzek, J. S. 2010. *Foundations and Frontiers of Deliberative Governance*. Oxford: Oxford University Press.

Fung, A. 2003. "Survey Article: Recipes for Public Spheres: Eight Institutional Design Choices and Their Consequences." *The Journal of Political Philosophy* 11 (3): 338–367. doi:10.1111/1467-9760.00181.

Fung, A. 2005. "Deliberation Before the Revolution: Toward an Ethics of Deliberative Democracy in an Unjust World." *Political Theory* 33 (3): 397–419. doi:10.1177/0090591704271990.

Gavin, N. T. 2010. "Pressure Group Direct Action on Climate Change: The Role of the Media and the Web in Britain – A Case Study." *The British Journal of Politics & International Relations* 12 (3): 459–475. doi:10.1111/j.1467-856X.2010.00411.x.

Goodin, R. E. 2000. "Democratic Deliberation Within." *Philosophy & Public Affairs* 29 (1): 81–109. doi:10.1111/j.1088-4963.2000.00081.x.

Habermas, J. 1996. *Between Facts and Norms: Contributions to a Discourse Theory of Law and Democracy*. Translated by W. Rehg. Cambridge: Polity.

Mansbridge, J., J. Bohman, S. Chambers, T. Christiano, A. Fung, J. Parkinson, D. Thompson, and M. Warren. 2012. "A Systemic Approach to Deliberative Democracy." In *Deliberative Systems: Deliberative Democracy at the Large Scale*, edited by J. Parkinson and J. Mansbridge, 1–26. Cambridge: Cambridge University Press.

Markovits, D. 2005. "Democratic Disobedience." *The Yale Law Journal* 114: 1897–1952.

Milligan, T. 2013. *Civil Disobedience: Protest, Justification, and the Law*. London: Bloomsbury.

Moraro, P. 2014. "Respecting Autonomy Through the Use of Force: The Case of Civil Disobedience." *Journal of Applied Philosophy* 31 (1): 63–76. doi:10.1111/japp.12034.

Owen, D., and G. Smith. 2015. "Survey Article: Deliberation, Democracy and the Systemic Turn." *The Journal of Political Philosophy* 23 (2): 213–234. doi:10.1111/jopp.12054.

Papadopoulos, Y. 2012. "On the Embeddedness of Deliberative Systems: Why Elitist Innovations Matter More." In *Deliberative Systems: Deliberative Democracy at the Large Scale*, edited by J. Parkinson and J. Mansbridge, 125–150. Cambridge: Cambridge University Press.

Parkinson, J. 2006. *Deliberating in the Real World: Problems of Legitimacy in Deliberative Democracy*. Oxford: Oxford University Press.

Parkinson, J. 2012. "Democratizing Deliberative Systems." In *Deliberative Systems: Deliberative Democracy at the Large Scale*, edited by J. Parkinson and J. Mansbridge, 151–172. Cambridge: Cambridge University Press.

Ruiz, P. 2014. *Articulating Dissent: Protest and the Public Sphere*. London: Pluto Press.

Shaw, R. 2013. *The Activist's Handbook*. 2nd ed. Berkeley: University of California Press.

Smith, G. 2009. *Democratic Innovations: Designing Institutions for Citizen Participation*. Cambridge: Cambridge University Press.

Smith, W. 2011. "Civil Disobedience and the Public Sphere." *The Journal of Political Philosophy* 19 (2): 145–166. doi:10.1111/j.1467-9760.2010.00365.x.

Steiner, J., A. Bächtiger, M. Spörndli, and M. R. Steenbergen. 2004. *Deliberative Politics in Action: Analysing Parliamentary Discourse*. Cambridge: Cambridge University Press.

Stevenson, H., and J. S. Dryzek. 2014. *Democratizing Global Climate Governance*. Cambridge: Cambridge University Press.

Talisse, R. 2005. "Deliberativist Responses to Activist Challenges: A Continuation of Young's Dialectic." *Philosophy & Social Criticism* 31 (4): 423–444. doi:10.1177/0191453705052978.

Young, I. M. 2000. *Inclusion and Democracy*. Oxford: Oxford University Press.

Young, I. M. 2001. "Activist Challenges to Deliberative Democracy." *Political Theory* 29 (5): 670–690. doi:10.1177/0090591701029005004.

Mitigating systemic dangers: the role of connectivity inducers in a deliberative system

Ricardo Fabrino Mendonça

ABSTRACT
This article seeks to critically discuss the notion of deliberative systems, attempting to contribute to the strengthening of the concept through a less laudatory perspective. Initially, it challenges the current use of deliberative systems as a panacea against any critique of deliberation. It argues that the concept in itself opens new dilemmas to deliberative theorists and practitioners. The article argues that the idea of deliberative systems may (1) create political asymmetries; (2) increase decision makers' discretionary powers; and (3) neglect the incompatibility of very different discursive dynamics. The article, then, argues that these criticisms may be partially remedied through the strengthening of connections between discursive arenas, and discusses the role that three types of actors may play to induce connectivity in deliberative processes: (1) bureaucrats; (2) the media; (3) activists.

The concept of *deliberative systems* has recently gained increasing attention among deliberative democrats. To put it briefly, the notion seeks to explain how deliberation may be possible in complex societies, where a fully encompassing assembly of citizens does not seem possible. Deliberative systems, it is argued, would emerge from the connection of different discursive spheres and deliberative moments (Mansbridge et al. 2012).

Emphatically welcomed by the most prominent scholars of the field, the concept still lacks, nevertheless, deeper theoretical confrontation. Although some recent criticisms have started to test this model, the theoretical scrutiny of deliberative systems needs to be advanced. This article engages with three practical and theoretical problems related to the notion of deliberative systems, namely: (1) the creation of political asymmetries; (2) the expansion of decision makers' discretionary powers; (3) the incompatibility of drastically different discursive dynamics.

The article argues, then, that these criticisms may be mitigated through the strengthening of connections between discursive arenas. However, and despite the broad acknowledgment that connectivity across arenas is essential, few scholars have discussed potential *inducers of connectivity* that link different processes and arenas of communication. I argue that three types of actors may work as potential inducers of connectivity: (1) bureaucrats; (2) the media; and (3) activists who act as representatives in multiple venues.

The article is structured in three sections. The first provides an overview of the literature on deliberative systems. The second develops the above-mentioned dangers nourished by the use of the concept. Lastly, the third section proposes the notion of *inducer of connectivity* and claims that each inducer discussed may help mitigate some of the dangers linked to the systemic turn.

It is important to clarify that the article does not aim at providing an exhaustive list of inducers and it does not advance the argument that different inducers may foster different types of connection, although both tasks seem to be important for future steps in this research agenda. It neither fully develops all the possible relations between the inducers of connectivity discussed and deliberative theory. More modest, the article's argument seeks: (1) to offer theoretical friction to a concept broadly advocated; and (2) to propose how inducers of connectivity are important to challenge some of the political dangers nurtured by the systemic approach.

The systemic turn on deliberative theory

The notion of *Deliberative Systems* was initially proposed by Jane Mansbridge at the end of the 1990s. According to her, deliberation should not be reduced to a one-to-one dialogue, but understood in terms of a wide process that traverses different arenas, where discourses are made public. Although systematically formulated by Mansbridge, the idea of an interrelation of parts for the constitution of a deliberative process is not entirely new. It can be traced back to Habermas' (1996) two-track model, to Benhabib's (1996) *anonymous public conversations*, to Dryzek's (1990, 2000) un-individualistic conception of a public *contestation of discourses*, and to Young's (2000) *de-centered politics*.

Conceptually elaborated and systematized by Jane Mansbridge (1999), the concept was promptly embraced by deliberative scholars as a way to respond to the major criticisms raised against deliberative democrats. The idea was, first of all, helpful in challenging the charge that deliberation was an unfeasible utopia. After all, democracy does not need a face-to-face simultaneous assembly in order to have public debate. Broad deliberation is feasible if the clash of discourses can happen through intersecting asynchronous processes.

Second, the systemic approach fostered the investigation, through deliberative lenses, of phenomena not usually seen as deliberative, making the theory more useful and applicable. Contentious discursive exchanges (such as political campaigns) and superficial or aggressive expressions of position (such as comments in news websites) can play a role in deliberative politics. As Chambers (2009) convincingly argues, deliberative scholars must focus on broader political issues, besides minipublics, in order to make their approach central to democratic advancement.

Third, deliberative scholars could build a more nuanced comprehension of the roles played by different arenas and actors in different moments. John Parkinson (2006a) showed how a number of discursive environments and political actors could offer different contributions at different phases of a policy process. And Robert Goodin (2005, 2008) argued for a *sequencing of deliberative moments*, distributing the task of deliberation.

Fourth, the systemic approach was helpful in addressing the criticisms regarding the legitimacy of minipublics. The possibility of linking these discursive processes to broader public debates was a way to make them accountable, grounding political legitimacy beyond political authorization (Parkinson 2006a; Dryzek and Niemeyer 2008; Mendonça 2008; Bohman 2012). The institutional design of these initiatives should aim at strengthening the connections between informal conversations and decision-making arenas (Warren 2007).

Fifth, the concept of deliberative systems allowed deliberative democrats to deal with the criticism that most conversations tend to happen within groups, whose individuals share similar perspectives. Like-minded conversations, intra-public discussions, and everyday talk are important for democracy, because they may strengthen the positions of weaker political actors and foster the reinterpretation of public clashes of discourses (Neblo 2005; Conover and Searing 2005; Polletta and Lee 2006; Mansbridge 1999).

If the notion of deliberative systems propelled new research agendas and offered responses to recurrent criticisms against deliberative theory, it initially lacked theoretical and empirical friction capable of pointing out to some of its limits. An exception in these earlier works was Carolyn Hendriks' (2006) seminal piece proposing an *integrated model of deliberation*. Hendriks notes that Mansbridge framed the system as a *continuum*, failing to 'acknowledge the possible incompatibility between deliberative spaces' (2006, 26). In addition, she argued that Mansbridge did not emphasize the connections across arenas.

The recent book edited by Mansbridge and Parkinson (2012) on deliberative systems also points out to some problems related to the notion. The book's introductory chapter claims that the tight coupling of arenas, the decoupling of discursive spheres, and the domination of the system can be problematic in real-world systems. Simone Chambers (2012) deepens her previous note of caution that public deliberation should be made more inclusive and massive if it is to be democratic. Papadopoulos (2012) adopts a more skeptical view about *deliberative systems*, arguing that the strengthening of deliberative theory must be thought of in the context of broader transformations that are leading to technocratic and elitist processes and decisions.

In the concluding chapter of the book, Parkinson (2012) sharply raises four caveats. The first one is that contributions dispersed in the broad system may receive unequal treatment, as some are labeled as more reliable than others. The second caveat is the absence of empowered referees to control the game, which can affect the inclusivity of the system. Third, Parkinson notes that the channels of communication between citizens and representatives should be deeply investigated to be promoted. The fourth caveat is the danger of undermining the epistemic function of deliberation once one broadens its conception.

These caveats are important for the development of the arguments I would like to advance in this article. In the next section, I suggest how the idea of deliberative systems may fuel undemocratic practices. If the concept of deliberative systems was important to expand deliberative theory and turn it into a more feasible and inclusive perspective, it can also have exclusionary effects.

Systemic dangers: can the systems approach nurture undemocratic practices?

It is exactly because the systemic approach is necessary for deliberative democracy that it must be critically discussed. It is only through an encompassing cartography of its dilemmas that the approach may be strengthened and made fruitful both for academic research and for the deepening of democratic practices.

This section aims at discussing some of the problems that can emerge from the adoption of a systemic approach to deliberation. More specifically, I argue that the advocacy of deliberative systems may lead (1) to the creation of political asymmetries; (2) to the expansion of decision makers' discretionary powers; and (3) to a neglect of the incompatibility of drastically differing discursive dynamics.

The advocacy of a systemic approach may nurture political asymmetries

The first danger worth highlighting is related to the creation, or strengthening, of political asymmetries. Parkinson (2012) acknowledges this possibility in the first caveat he discusses. According to him, there is a risk that 'not every contribution to the pool of perspectives is treated equally' within a deliberative system (Parkinson 2012, 155). Selen Ercan (2013) claims that there are some actors usually perceived as more legitimate by society, having their views more seriously considered. I agree with these arguments and believe that they should be further developed.

The case may be that some contributions are not treated equally not solely because some actors are seen as more credible than others, but simply because the deliberative system may increase the costs of making a perspective visible. This may sound contradictory, because the systemic approach claims to lower the costs of publicity by broadening the scope of arenas considered relevant. In this situation, actors who have no access to formal arenas can throw their perspectives into the pool of discourses with the expectation that other actors will select these discourses and move them forward (Mansbridge 1999, 220). Nevertheless, the very act of broadening the scope of the arenas considered may destabilize relatively weak actors, as they do not have the resources to make their positions present in many arenas. Some actors are not strong enough to push their discourses across the various levels of the system and they end up becoming invisible. Other actors may strategically interpret this type of invisibility not as proof of the weakness of the actors, but of the positions they advocate.

An interesting case illustrates this possibility. Locatelli (2011) analyzed the discursive processes around the construction of hydroelectric dams in Brazil. He investigated the communicative strategies adopted by the different actors related to the *Foz do Chapecó Power Plant*, including environmental movements, homeowners' associations, state agencies, and the companies responsible for the construction. By following their actions in different contexts, Locatelli illustrated how the extensive resources of the builders enabled the presence of their discourses in many arenas across the system. Moreover, the builders constructed their own micro-systems by organizing hundreds of local meetings. By dividing and spreading potentially critical actors across the 'system,' these companies were successful in making their positions invisible.

This case is insightful and highlights the risk of disempowering weak actors through a systemic approach. A lack in financial and human resources can lock up some actors and, more importantly, their perspectives in specific discursive arenas, while maintaining their consideration as full participants in the system. By following this path, the system warrants and nurtures a vicious cycle of political exclusion, while claiming to maintain the appearance of inclusion. If unequal resources already hindered the participation of certain groups and individuals in specific arenas (such as minipublics), this problem becomes more acute once deliberation is spread through multiple venues, simply because it is more costly to make ones' voice present in many arenas and moments.

Another illustrative case from Brazil is worth mentioning. The Minas Gerais State Legislature (Brazil) implemented several participatory institutions since the 1990s. One of these institutions is the *Legislative Seminar*, involving several meetings throughout the state, before a final meeting where proposals were actually discussed and voted (Mendonça and Cunha 2014). In this final meeting, wealthier institutions and institutions from the capital city were often over-represented, and this affected the decisions taken. Weaker actors could not afford the advancement of their ideas throughout the system. In spite of that, their presence in a very specific (limited) moment of the system was used to legitimate the process.

Similar to the case of the hydroelectric dams, the distribution of the tasks of deliberation did not foster actual inclusivity. Instead, this distribution legitimized a process of decision-making that was pervaded by embedded asymmetries. The system resulted in reinforcing obstacles for the development of some arguments. It hindered deliberation, while claiming to promote it.

The expansion of decision makers' discretionary powers

The second danger to be addressed is related to a concept at the heart of democratic theory, namely *legitimacy*. The foundation of the deliberative approach is that democratic legitimacy is not anchored on the aggregation of individual opinions. Legitimate democratic decisions should involve a public exchange of reasons, through which different alternatives are tested. The systemic approach to deliberative democracy argues that these exchanges should not be located in specific moments or venues; legitimacy is something produced across arenas (Mansbridge et al. 2012, 2).

The danger of this perspective is that the process may become so disperse and loose, that anything can be claimed to have derived from it. There are so many discourses occurring, in so many arenas, at different moments, that fragments can sometimes be extracted from the process in order to warrant certain decisions. Legitimacy may be claimed on the basis of resonance with some specific arenas or fragments and not on the basis of a resonance to the *constellation of discourses* to use Dryzek's (2001) notion. In a broad process in which discourses ignore or neglect each other, specific discourses (or fragments of this constellation) may be mobilized as if they were the result of a proper deliberative process of opinion formation. Discursive fragments can, hence, be taken as representative of the public opinion and not as *isolated stars* within the *constellation*.

This dispersion strengthens decision makers' discretionary powers. It becomes difficult to hold them accountable simply because they can mobilize different portions of the constellation of discourses to justify whatever they wish to. It can be claimed that when this happens, the system no longer exists and that this strategy implies the corruption of the concept of deliberative systems in itself. I agree with this argument, but the problem here does not seem to be exclusively the result of personal strategies to usurp the power from the people. The dispersion of the debate tends to generate fragmentation, and it becomes harder for decision makers – even if it is their desire – to recompose this public discussion.

In this sense, and if deliberative democracy first appeared as a heterodox theory aimed at democratizing existing democratic practices, the systemic approach may reverse this inclination and justify the established procedures of decision-making. The systemic approach, built to radicalize the critical dimension of deliberation, can be easily mobilized to warrant the existent liberal democracies. After all, public debates that cut across informal and formal arenas usually exist, and decision makers are potentially influenced by some of these voices in various ways. Democratic institutions do guarantee some form of revisability of decisions. At certain moments, public opinion does affect decision makers to incorporate citizens' contributions. So what does the systemic approach provide that is different from what already exists?

A statement made by a senior public servant in Brazil serves to illustrate this issue.[1] When questioned about his reasons for supporting a broad systemic deliberative design for a particular right-wing regional government, despite the presence of financial problems, he simply stated: 'It is not *despite* the financial problems, but *because* of them.' He explained that the time required to generate a decision – partially inflated by the dispersion of discourses around a certain topic – would allow that particular government to gain time.

The main point worth highlighting is that the conceptual openness of the idea of deliberative systems may lead polities in different directions. On the one hand, advocates of radical and participatory forms of democracy may use the systems' approach in order to foster inclusiveness, advocating that more individuals could have a say and that more discourses could be represented if more arenas were considered. On the other hand, conservatives seeking to sustain politics as usual may also employ the systemic approach in order to strengthen those already in power. This dangerous convergence can approximate actors who have entirely different goals.

Incompatible discursive dynamics

In order to understand the third danger to be discussed here, it is important to remind that the systems approach requires the idea that different discursive arenas may offer different contributions to a deliberative process. Such view is entirely compatible with the developments in linguistics that draw attention to the inextricable relationship between discourses and the context in which they are expressed (Charaudeau 2006; Fairclough 2003). These developments point out how human expression is always grounded on tacit rules and expectations that create the conditions under which discourses are formulated. From this perspective, discourses are always a combination of text and context that cannot be reduced to the substance of what is being expressed or to the intentions of the actors expressing them (Charaudeau 2006; Fairclough 2003).

It is in this sense, that the assumption made by the advocates of deliberative systems – according to which different contexts are necessary for the division of deliberative labor – makes perfect sense. Arenas are not simply channels where preferences and arguments are expressed, but ambiences that allow (or hinder) the expression of certain discourses. They play a constitutive role in the elaboration of discourses and the differences among them may push the deliberative system forward.

The acknowledgment of the centrality of context in discursive formulation and expression, however, also points out to the possibility of deep-rooted incompatibilities between discursive arenas. Incompatibility may emerge simply because debates took entirely different routes in specific moments or arenas. It may also emerge, nonetheless, because the logics, dynamics, and nature of given arenas may push debates in contrasting directions that cannot be combined. Even if content may flow across arenas and the substance of a speech may be translated, discourse cannot be reduced to its 'content'. Discourse is not simply a parcel that can be removed from its context and moved to other places. It is embedded in the arenas where it was formulated.

This incompatibility of communicative dynamics can contribute to keeping certain feelings and worldviews invisible, due to a lack of translatability. If the advantage of the systemic approach is that it acknowledges different types of communicative arenas and different modes of communication, the process still depends on an assumption that experiences can be easily translated. Nonetheless, there are processes that occur in diverse arenas that simply cannot be transposed to other types of arenas.

A tricky aspect of this argument is that one of the pathologies pointed out by Mansbridge et al. (2012), namely the decoupling of arenas, may now appear as intrinsic to systems. The literature on deliberative systems has pointed to the fruitfulness of adding the virtues of different moments and venues, but it has not properly discussed the risks for conflicts and contradictions that may affect the system. Without a better understanding of these risks, the systemic approach may strengthen processes that do not foster coherent and informative discussions. Rather, this practice may nurture fragmented processes that simply cannot deliver the epistemic gains and legitimate solutions that are expected. More worryingly, not considering these risks may justify results that are contrary to deliberative goals.

Inducers of connectivity and the mitigation of systemic dangers

So far, I have discussed three problems related to the notion of deliberative systems. I have argued that, in the name of a systemic approach to deliberation, power asymmetries may be reinforced, dispersion may foster the discretionary power of decision makers and incompatibilities between discursive arenas may be neglected. There is no easy solution for these problems and a theoretical dilemma becomes evident: the notion of deliberative systems – advocated exactly as a way to make deliberative democracy more feasible, inclusive, and emancipatory – may be nurturing the accommodation of democracy to existent asymmetrical power relationships.

If these problems have multiple causes and implications that cannot be addressed in a simple fashion, they can, at least, be mitigated through the strengthening of connectivity between discursive spheres. A systems approach to deliberation should, first and above all, insist on the interactions between the many communicative arenas composing the process.

A deliberative system depends on the connection of different discursive spheres. Connection across the system can happen through multiple forms of relationships between different arenas and moments of a public debate. The variety of these forms of relationship is an interesting research agenda, which deserves proper development in another article.[2] The key point to be made here, however, is that, from a systemic perspective, diverse discursive arenas and moments of a deliberative process cannot remain isolated from each other. The actors discussing in a particular point in time and space ought to be affected by, whilst also affecting, discussions happening in other points in time and space, if a system is to be a system. The multiple arenas across a deliberative system cannot ignore each other or become impermeable to the discourses expressed in other venues.

Despite the centrality of the idea connectivity for the systemic approach to deliberation, there are important gaps concerning the comprehension of such connections in the existing literature. There has not been much work devoted to discuss possible strategies and actions to enhance the integration of arenas into an encompassing process. There is a lack of concrete proposals regarding the ways to connect different deliberative moments or settings.

I here propose the notion of *inducers of connectivity*, claiming that more work must be done to reveal potential inducers and the mechanisms through which they act. Inducers of connectivity are factors that can contribute to promote an actual system, in which the parts do not ignore each other or operate independently. Such inducers may promote not only an awareness of what has been said in other arenas, but the consideration of discourses throughout the system. Deliberative systems do not exist naturally, and they cannot be assumed as being already or always there. The porosity between discursive arenas must be built and supported, requiring inducers that contribute to stitching the parts together.

Many factors may be thought of as potential inducers of connectivity. Technologies, rules, institutional design, and political culture, for instance, can operate in ways that may enhance connectivity across a system. In this article, however, I would like to draw attention to the importance of three actors as potential inducers of connectivity. In the following sections, I will present how bureaucrats, the media, and activists may foster connectivity between discursive arenas, and, in this way, help address the aforementioned problems of deliberative systems.

It must be very clear that I am not claiming that only actors may be inducers of connectivity. In addition, I do not aim at offering an exhaustive list of actors. My effort is to provide a focused argument that contributes to a broader program of mapping potential inducers of connectivity. By saying potential, I hope to have clarified that these actors do not always behave as inducers. Under certain conditions, they may generate opaqueness instead of porosity, and disconnection. This is another interesting research topic that requires further development.

The argument advanced here should not be read, nonetheless, as a vague statement according to which anything may, or may not, induce connectivity. My purpose is to claim that more attention should be paid to these specific potential inducers in order to create the conditions for a deliberative system to work. I want to argue that bureaucrats, the media, and activists are essential in fostering systemic connectivity. I further claim that when these actors play their potential role as inducers of connectivity, they contribute to the mitigation of the three systemic dangers developed in the previous section. It is for these reason that topics often neglected by deliberative scholars – such as the actual role of bureaucrats and media regulation – deserve more attention within the deliberative literature.

Bureaucrats

Bureaucrats are key actors in politics. This point has been widely acknowledged since the work of Max Weber. Literature about the role of bureaucrats in the course of policy-making is abundant and attempts to address the different functions these groups of non-elected officials have in the diverse phases of a policy cycle (Aberback, Putnam, and Rockman 1981; Evans, Rueschemeyer, and Skocpol 1985; Fisher and Sirianni 1994; Peters 2009; Durant 2010).

In spite of the centrality of the work of bureaucracies on political processes, deliberative democrats have seldom mentioned their structures, activities, roles, and modus operandi. There are, of course, broad statements about administrative power in the work of Habermas (1996), for instance. There are also several studies concerned with the dilemmas raised by the role of technical experts on contemporary complex democracies (Christiano 2012; Bohman 2000, 1996; Fisher 2000), as well as references to the implications of the instrumental rationality of bureaucrats (Dryzek 2000).

However, deliberative theories seem to 'underplay the extent to which bureaucracies make policy' (Mackenzie and Warren 2012, 103). The day-to-day work of bureaucrats and their role in designing, implementing, and evaluating policies is often neglected. Many deliberative democrats seem to restrict state decision-making to the formal approval of bills by legislatures or to the implementation of policies by the Executive branch, thus focusing on elected representatives and their relationship with civil society. Bureaucrats, if mentioned, are either considered to be consultants or transparent delegates of the representatives' decisions. Even John Parkinson (2006a), who explicitly acknowledges the role of bureaucracy, tends to place bureaucrats tangentially in the political process, claiming they help and subsidize decision makers and implement policies. Bureaucrats do not seem very autonomous in this approach.

A full theorization of bureaucracy's role in deliberative democracy would be beyond the scope of this article. My aim is simply to shed light on the importance of bureaucrats in connecting discursive spheres within a deliberative system. In order to advance this argument, I will present an empirical illustration from Brazil.[3]

As already mentioned, the Minas Gerais State Legislature (Brazil) has promoted, since the early 1990s, a series of institutional innovations, which include several participatory experiments. Traditionally, these experiments were thought of as isolated forums. In 2011, however, the legislature sought a more systemic approach: the topic of poverty was broadly discussed throughout the year in different settings and at varying moments, including a *Cycle of Debates* (with experts), a *Legislative Seminar* (with hundreds of civil society representatives), and 12 *regional meetings* with citizens from diverse municipalities. These events nurtured a process that happened at the end of the year involving the discussion of the state's budgetary laws.

The process was very complex and involved diverse actors. Bureaucrats were essential for linking the different moments of the system. To begin with, public servants from this state legislature were actively engaged in the organization of the participatory events, interacting with civil associations in the planning of these forums. In the process, they also systematized the results of one forum, in order to nourish the following ones. Such systematizations involved filtering, gathering, and contextualizing proposals, so as to strengthen them. Issue consultants from the Legislature followed specific themes under discussion. Their work was particularly significant in the above-mentioned systematizations and included attempts to link proposals to pending bills and constitutional requirements. In addition, public servants offered a course on budgetary laws to enable interested citizens to comprehend the process they were engaged with. Finally, public servants from the legislature conducted formal meetings with public servants from the state's Executive branch, in order to assure the inclusion of the citizens' proposals in the agenda of projects to be implemented.

In this particular case, bureaucrats played a very significant role in fostering connections across different arenas and thus facilitating a systemic approach to deliberation. Skeptics may argue that they had too much power and that their filters and systematizations intervened in the process. I agree with this assertion, although one could defend bureaucrats by saying that their interventions were open to public scrutiny and were actually submitted to assessments in the following phases of the system. Even though weaker actors face more challenges in exerting such scrutiny, it is easier to scrutinize and follow the process once it is systematized and organized (and when there is someone that can be addressed) than in situations in which the dispersion runs across many venues and moments.

The point is that in this case, the unavoidable role of bureaucrats was assumed as such. In doing this, the design of the experience consciously sought to incorporate the potential of bureaucrats as inducers of connectivity. It is this role that I claim as being relevant to deliberative systems.

But how can bureaucrats help address the three problems discussed in the first part of this article? In inducing connectivity across the system, they may, first of all, push forward the reasons of weaker actors that cannot make themselves present throughout the system. They can assure that relatively isolated discourses make it through the system and survive the fragmentation that could nurture political asymmetries.

Second, bureaucrats may constrain the expansion of decision makers' discretionary powers, by refining and rearticulating discourses that would not have survived otherwise. The case of the Minas Gerais State Legislature is paradigmatic in this sense, in assuring that citizens understood a complex process and in working for the proper elaboration and qualification of their positions, bureaucrats made voices that would have been easily bypassed present throughout the system. They fostered not only the consideration of a constellation of discourses, but the strengthening of the different discourses that compose this constellation.

I do not think that the connectivity fostered by bureaucrats may mitigate the problem related to the incompatibility of very different discursive dynamic. As a matter of fact, I believe this is a somehow insurmountable problem related to the logics of discourse. In the following sections, however, I will argue that other inducers of connectivity can at least expose some of these incompatibilities.

Media

A second potential inducer of connectivity to be discussed is the media, whose role has been recently highlighted by some advocates of the deliberative system. Chambers (2009), most notably, has argued that deliberative theory must comprehend the media if it is to be inclusive and democratic in contemporary complex societies. She notes that 'the media, while being massively studied in some academic circles, is not a central topic within deliberative theory' (Chambers 2009, 342). Habermas (2006) has also re-assessed his interpretation of the media, claiming that mediated communication remains essential for the public sphere. Scholars such as Gastil (2008), Wessler (2008) and Ettema (2007) agree that the press must be considered as a very significant ambiance and/or actor for public reason-giving. And Parkinson (2012, 164) argues that one of the caveats for the literature on deliberative systems is to comprehend the channels of communication that crisscross the system, including the mass media and online social networks.

There are, however, severe doubts about the deliberative potential of the media. Gutmann and Thompson (2004, 36), for example, argue that the media is market-oriented and unfriendly to deliberation, while Bohman (2007) criticizes the power mass media has in setting the public agenda and in framing political issues. Robert Goodin (2000) claims that the publicization of perspectives is not a synonym of deliberation. And Parkinson (2006a, 2006b) has argued that the modus operandi of the media circumvents the presentation of issues in all of their complexities, focusing on what is non-ordinary, dramatic, polarized, and personal.

These criticisms are relevant to understand the media critically. I agree that the media is mainly driven by the motive of profit and not by interest in critical debate. I also concur with the idea that the routines of *newsmaking* may constrain the give-and-take of reasons. I am aware that certain frameworks can induce sensationalism or cynicism against political institutions. I further acknowledge that the media cannot assure social actors will take the views of one another into account. I am not, therefore, arguing that the media is essentially deliberative or that it always works inducing connectivity across the system. It may actually hinder deliberation in many ways.

However, a systemic approach to deliberation demands going beyond this broad criticism. Despite all these problems, the media is not inimical to public exchanges of reasons (Simon and Xenos 2000; Ferree et al. 2002; James 2004; Wessler 2008; Peters, Tanjev, and Wimmel 2010; Maia et al. 2012). Even if the media frames issues, 'Framing itself cannot be the problem. All information, even face-to-face information, is framed.' (Chambers 2009, 341). The problem is that some scholars seem to expect that mediated deliberation should have the same features as face-to-face deliberative exchanges or simply reproduce them.

Such a view emerges, for instance, in the criticisms Parkinson (2006a, 2006b) directs toward the television coverage of Fishkin's deliberative polls. Parkinson complains that the television devoted a higher percentage of time to the plenary as opposed to what the section actually represented. He also criticizes the fact that the journalist who presented the process spoke during 37% of the coverage. He concludes: 'Television does not show an audience "what went on": it shows just one of many possible new things constructed from the pieces of what went on' (Parkinson 2006a, 112).

This analysis seems to require a coverage that is simply inadequate for the media grammars. The argument ends up condemning the media for not reproducing the same patterns of interaction observed in the face-to-face conversations of the deliberative poll[4] If his analysis discloses the filters and procedures of news making, his normative expectation still reveals the hope for a transparent transmission. He seems to believe the role of the media is simply to report 'what went on'.

This view has been severely challenged in the field of communication studies (Hall 1973; Silverstone 1999). The role of the media is not to mirror the world as it is. The media underpins the establishment of different types of social relations, and in doing so it is actively implicated in the process of constructing reality. In order to understand the media as a potential inducer of connectivity in deliberative systems, this aspect must be made clear. The media should not transmit deliberations happening elsewhere. The media pervades other arenas of social interaction, thus affecting the structure of other venues and the actions therein performed (Silverstone 1999).

A brief example helps clarifying my argument. Brazil has recently experienced a lively debate around the impacts and social consequences of a *mega-sports-events*, such as the FIFA World Cup. This debate has mainly happened throughout mediated forms of communication, including social networks, television interviews, and articles to cite a few examples. The media did not report 'what went on' in a debate that is external to it. It functioned as a field of symbolic battles and its grammars affected the way other actors produced their discourses. Some activists organized demonstrations paying attention to newsworthiness criteria in order to foster the visibility of their claims. Other actors felt compelled to say something in this debate because of the media visibility it had acquired.

At this point in my argument, it is important to highlight the need to consider the media in the plural. Not only are there many media systems (Hallin and Mancini 2004) and institutions of mass media, but also there are different types of media including community, personal, commercial, public, and educational. Moreover, many diverse 'things' are usually covered by the use of the term 'media'. Mediated communication can refer to the press, soap operas, experiences of infotainment, and live televised debates, just to mention a few possibilities. In addition, each of these discursive experiences is pervaded by very different elements. As pointed out by Peters, Tanjev, and Wimmel (2010), for instance, in a newspaper, editorials, articles, interviews, commentaries, and reportages are very different and play diverse roles.

It is, therefore, overly simplistic to restrain deliberative potentials to one of those discursive elements or to define one standard of deliberation against which these (drastically!) different 'things' should be tested. These different ambiences provide different contexts of communication, offering various contributions (and dangers) to a deliberative process.

These different contexts of communication, I argue, are essential for the setting of the discursive infrastructure, without which a broad deliberative system cannot exist. By infrastructure, I am not implying mere technical channels through which meanings are transported. As claimed by Boullier (2004), the media structures (disputed) shared terrains that pervade conversations in different venues. Such terrains are essential for the translation of issues into ordinary language, thus allowing their circulation through society. They are also important in putting actors and discourses in touch with other actors and discourses. Moreover, these shared terrains impose constraints on what can and cannot be said. It is thus through the generation of socially shared grounds that the media, in all their variety, may act as potential inducers of connectivity in deliberative systems.

In acknowledging this potential, I must emphasize again that I do not mean that the media inevitably produces connectivity. There are (many) circumstances in which the mainstream media ignores significant parts of potential systems. What I do claim is that a deliberative system cannot operate democratically without the media. Exactly for this reason, issues such as media regulation, accountability of media institutions, and the pluralization of the media system (Porto 2012; Waisbord 2009; Curran 2000; Thompson 1998) should occupy a more central role in the agenda of deliberative scholars. These elements are important to assure the vocalization of different discourses in the public sphere, as well as the existence of a public scrutiny over a central source of symbolic power in contemporary world.

Having claimed that the media has a key role for public deliberation in general and for the connectivity across deliberative systems, more specifically, it is important to turn, once again, to the three dangers diagnosed in the first part of this article. First, the media may constrain the possibility of new political asymmetries when galvanizing attention to discourses that could have remained isolated in invisible pockets within complex discursive processes. Even if some political actors cannot afford making their voices heard through many arenas, the media can keep these discourses alive and compel other actors to consider them. Public embarrassment is a powerful weapon, and the media (or actors that acquire media visibility) may play with it in order to constrain power asymmetries.

Second, and for the same reason, media discourses may raise some limits to decision makers' discretionary powers. When fostering connectivity across systems, the media increases the need to justify one's position and to consider the consequences of this justification from the lenses of an expanded visibility. Such a wide visibility retroacts over actors, shaping their discourses and making it very costly to simply ignore relevant arguments. This does not solve the problem of dispersion I have discussed in the first part of this article, but it makes decisions and arguments more susceptible to public scrutiny. If decisions can, at a certain moment, be based on fragments of the broader discursive constellation, the media may offer effective possibilities (through its symbolic stocks, its broad visibility, and its capacity of intersecting other arenas) to challenge decisions and temporary stabilizations.

Third, the media cannot overcome the incompatibility of discursive arenas. I have argued this is intrinsic to the dynamic of language use. It, nonetheless, can expose some of these incompatibilities. In continuously attempting to translate discourses in order to make them available to broader audiences, the media continuously faces the limits of these translations and is challenged by social actors who do not agree with the way their discourses have been represented. These debates over media content may bring to the surface the existence of opacities and insurmountable incompatibilities between spheres. This can have positive effects in systemic terms, because a deliberative system should acknowledge its own internal limits in order to remain skeptical about its results.

Activists

A third potential inducer of connectivity in deliberative systems is the circulation of activists that are considered to exert some type of representativeness. There are persons deeply engaged with certain issues and they end up taking part in multiple conversations that occur across multiple arenas and moments of a deliberative system. Although this mode of articulation may seem relatively simple, it appears to be very important: certain individuals do operate as connectors crisscrossing informal and formal settings of discussion on a topic.

Despite the existence of a significant body of literature about activists and deliberative democracy,[5] little attention has been given to their potential as inducers of connectivity across broad discursive processes. By this, I do not claim activists necessarily induce connectivity across systems. In many circumstances, they may deliberately work to isolate certain actors and discursive arenas, thus weakening some positions. Activists may (and often do) undermine deliberative processes in many ways. The point, however, is to acknowledge that they may also connect different venues and moments of a system in some contexts and circumstances.

In order to discuss this potential, the role of activists as political representatives must be considered. A growing number of scholars have emphasized the need to pluralize the concept and the contexts of representation, beyond authorization through electoral procedures.[6] Representation must be thought of as a relationship that may assume different formats, mechanisms of authorization, and instruments of accountability. Such pluralization becomes particularly relevant in contemporary contexts, marked by the need of transnational governance and by the spread of empowered participatory experiments. Civil associations, experts, and citizens may act as representatives of interests, perspectives, and discourses as long as they feed the circularity between state and society (Urbinati 2006). The legitimacy of these representatives may emerge through their affinity with specific causes (Avritzer 2007), expertise, and experience (Almeida and Cunha 2012), discursive accountability (Mendonça 2008), and the mechanisms applied for their selection, which may vary from elections to random sampling (Dryzek and Niemeyer 2008; Sintomer 2010).

Ideally speaking, a deliberative system should be populated by different types of representatives, acting in different contexts. The whole idea of the deliberative system is based on the premise that different modes of discourse and interaction are required at different moments, in order to enrich the features of deliberative processes. Representatives must emphasize the interests, perspectives, or discourses shared by portions of that specific political community at different moments and venues of communicative exchange. This requires the use of diverse modalities of discourse.

Interestingly, few individuals may exert this variety of representative relationships. Within *policy communities*, very often, certain activists become highly engaged. They participate in several informal and formal arenas and they end up becoming inducers of connectivity themselves. Almeida and Cunha (2012) make this point when discussing empirical data about Health Councils and Social Assistance Councils in Brazil. They found that the integration of deliberative systems around these participatory institutions was promoted by the circulation of certain activists, who were engaged in micro and macro processes of deliberation. Some persons may acquire an expertise (on technical issues or on the participatory process in itself) that almost automatically qualifies them for other levels and instances of representation. Some individuals thus become regular actors in different contexts.

These regular representatives may cut across the system, linking the diverse moments of a broad deliberative process. Their presence works as a potential inducer of connectivity, fomenting the coherence of the system or, at least, some kind of continuity. These actors tend to become well known (in a positive or negative way) within policy communities, and are usually regarded as individuals whose positions cannot be ignored. Some of these representatives go one step further and act across issues, occupying seats in forums related to different concerns and themes. My claim asserts that these highly engaged representatives play an important role in bringing parts of the system closer to each other. In making this claim, I do not advocate that their participation is more complex or is in itself systemic. I also do not allege that all the arenas of a system should have the same participants. I am simply arguing that there are higher chances of connections between arenas if some actors are present in different arenas.

In playing this role of inducing connectivity across the system, activists may help address the three systemic dangers discussed in this article. First, when activists represent traditionally invisible voices and discourses in multiple arenas, they challenge the political asymmetries that emerge when some voices are confined to one arena. In representing perspectives, interests, and discourses, they are strengthening views that could remain forgotten in the neglected corners of the system. Representation, in itself, is a form to challenge these asymmetries, vocalizing positions and arguments across the system.

Second, the scrutiny exerted by activists throughout the system may restrain decision makers' discretionary powers. Activists may challenge the technocratic reduction of politics throughout the system and re-state the centrality of the participation of those affected by an issue. When they are able to do this in several arenas, they contribute not only through the direct consideration of the arguments they advocate, but also through the strengthening of a public culture that values enduring civic participation.

Third, and for the same reason discussed in the previous section, activists can contribute to the exposure of incompatibilities between different discursive dynamics. Activists must connect everyday experiences of suffering, cultural interpretive frameworks, and formal processes of decision-making in their struggles. In actually engaging with discourses in their different contexts, they can experience the multiple dimensions of what is being said and its contextual significance. By this, I am not saying activists have a power to translate what I had said may be untranslatable. But the permanent laborious attempt of producing translations may evince incompatibilities and opaqueness throughout the system. This awareness, as already argued, may have positive effects, as a deliberative system, in perceiving its restrictions, may foster its own self-reflexivity.

Concluding remarks

This article sought to address important gaps in the literature about *deliberative systems*. After presenting an overview of key studies focusing on the concept, the article has outlined three dangers related to deliberative systems: (1) the creation of political asymmetries; (2) the expansion of decision makers' discretionary powers; and (3) the negligence to incompatible discursive dynamics. Through these three dangers, the idea of deliberative systems might lend legitimacy to processes that fall far short of the normative expectations raised by the concept.

The article, then, argued that these dangers can be mitigated through the strengthening of the connectivity across the system. Such connectivity is not an a priori, but must be politically promoted through many factors. The article focused on three types of actors that may work as potential inducers of connectivity, namely: (1) bureaucrats; (2) the media; and (3) activists. When fostering connectivity across the system, each of these actors have a contribution for the mitigation of the aforementioned dangers.

It would be important, however, to advance this research agenda in order to show, when and how these actors may induce connectivity across the system and when and how they can hinder connectivity. In advocating that these specific actors are essential for the structuring of broader societal deliberative systems, the article points to the urgent need for a research agenda that pays close attention to the actual operation of these actors through deliberative lenses. Deliberative scholars must comprehend the conditions, factors, limitations, and contexts that foster the accomplishment of this role of inducing connectivity.

It must be, therefore, very clear that my aim throughout the article has not been to argue that the concept of deliberative systems should be discarded. On the contrary, I believe that it is essential if deliberative democracy is to be feasible. However, the concept must be submitted to more critical theoretical and empirical tests. Deliberative systems cannot simply be a tool mobilized by scholars whenever they find criticisms against the normative ideals of deliberative democracy. If the concept is used carelessly, it may easily lose its critical potential and heuristic fruitfulness. Moreover, the idea of deliberative systems may end up paradoxically feeding both the radical critics of deliberation and the conservative liberals in their crusade against deliberative democracy. Thinking deliberative systems critically is a way to make it a more consistent concept, capable of actually advancing democracy.

Notes

1. The interviewee has not authorized his identification. For this reason the example is reported with some vagueness.
2. This point was suggested by John Parkinson in a personal conversation (held in Belo Horizonte, November 2015). I am thankful to his suggestion, and I intend to further develop this idea through a typology of forms of connectivity that may act for the establishment of a system. This development would be, nonetheless, beyond the scope of this article.
3. This case has been the subject of a broader analysis in another article (Mendonça and Cunha 2014).
4. Curiously, Parkinson becomes prey to a problem he would present six years later: Deliberative democrats tend to treat the media as perfect transmission mechanisms (Parkinson 2012, 165).
5. For a few examples see: della Porta (2005, 2013); Dryzek et al. (2003); Young (2003); Medearis (2005); Levine and Nierras (2007); Mendonça and Ercan (2014).

6. For some examples, see: Young (2000); Mansbridge (2003); Castiglione and Warren (2005); Urbinati (2006); Parkinson (2006a); Dryzek and Niemeyer (2008); Saward (2009); Urbinati and Warren (2008); Mendonça (2008); Bohman (2012); Avritzer (2012).

Acknowledgments

A previous version of this article was presented at the 2013 APSA Annual Conference. I am grateful to John Dryzek, Selen Ercan, Stephen Elstub and Frank Fischer for their comments on this initial version. This work was supported by the Fapemig [grant number CSA - PPM-00211-13]; the Pró-reitoria de Pesquisa da UFMG [grant number Edital PRPq 12/2011]; and the CNPq [grant number 305117/2014-9/445955/2014-7].

Disclosure statement

No potential conflict of interest was reported by the author.

Funding

This work was supported by the Fapemig [grant number CSA - PPM-00211-13]; the Pró-reitoria de Pesquisa da UFMG [grant number Edital PRPq 12/2011]; and the CNPq [grants number 305117/2014-9/445955/2014-7].

References

Aberback, J., R. Putnam, and B. Rockman. 1981. *Bureaucrats and Politicians in Western Democracies*. Cambridge: Harvard University Press.
Almeida, D., and E. Cunha, 2012. "As dinâmicas da representação: a complexidade da interação institucional nas cidades brasileiras." Paper prepared for delivery at the 2012 Congress of the Latin American Studies Association, San Francisco, CA, May 23–26.
Avritzer, L. 2007. "Sociedade civil, instituições participativas e representação: da autorização à legitimidade da ação." *Dados, Rio de Janeiro* 50 (3): 443–464.
Avritzer, L. 2012. "Democracy beyond Aggregation: The Participatory Dimension of Public Deliberation." *Journal of Public Deliberation* 8: 2.
Benhabib, S. 1996. *Democracy and Difference: Contesting the Boundaries of the Political*. Princeton: Princeton University Press.
Bohman, J. 1996. *Public Deliberation: Pluralism, Complexity and Democracy*. Cambridge: MIT.
Bohman, J. 2000. "The Division of Labour in Democratic Discourse: Media, Experts and Deliberative Democracy." In *Deliberation, Democracy and the Media*, edited by S. Chambers and A. Costain, 47–64. New York: Rowman & Littlefield Publishers.

Bohman, J. 2007. "Political Communication and the Epistemic Value of Diversity: Deliberation and Legitimation in Media Societies." *Communication Theory* 17 (4): 348–355. doi:10.1111/comt.2007.17.issue-4.

Bohman, J. 2012. "Representation in the Deliberative System." In *Deliberative Systems – Deliberative Democracy at the Large Scale*, edited by J. Parkinson and J. Mansbridge, 72–94. Cambridge: Cambridge University Press.

Boullier, D. 2004. "La fabrique de l'opinion publique dans les conversations télé." In *Figures du publique*, edited by D. Mehl and D. Pasquier, 59–87. Paris: Lavoisier.

Castiglione, D., and M. Warren, 2005. "Rethinking Representation: Seven Theoretical Issues." Midwest Political Science Association Annual Conference, Chicago, April 6–10, 2005.

Chambers, S. 2009. "Rhetoric and the Public Sphere: Has Deliberative Democracy Abandoned Mass Democracy?" *Political Theory* 37 (3): 323–350. doi:10.1177/0090591709332336.

Chambers, S. 2012. "Deliberation and Mass Democracy." In *Deliberative Systems – Deliberative Democracy at the Large Scale*, edited by J. Parkinson and J. Mansbridge, 52–71. Cambridge: Cambridge University Press.

Charaudeau, P. 2006. *Discurso das mídias*. São Paulo: Contexto.

Christiano, T. 2012. "Rational Deliberation among Experts and Citizens." In *Deliberative Systems – Deliberative Democracy at the Large Scale*, edited by J. Parkinson and J. Mansbridge, 27–51. Cambridge: Cambridge University Press.

Conover, P. J., and D. D. Searing. 2005. "Studying 'Everyday Political Talk' in the Deliberative System." *Acta Politica* 40 (3): 269–283. doi:10.1057/palgrave.ap.5500113.

Curran, J. 2000. "Rethinking Media and Democracy." In *Mass Media and Society*, edited by J. Curran and M. Gurevitch, 120–154. London: Arnold.

Della Porta, D. 2005. "Deliberation in Movement: Why and How to Study Deliberative Democracy and Social Movements." *Acta Politica* 40 (3): 336–350. doi:10.1057/palgrave.ap.5500116.

Della Porta, D. 2013. *Can Democracy Be Saved*. Cambridge: Polity.

Dryzek, J. 2001. "Legitimacy and Economy in Deliberative Democracy." *Political Theory* 29 (5): 651–669. doi:10.1177/0090591701029005003.

Dryzek, J., D. Downes, C. Hunold, D. Schlosberg, and H. K. Hernes. 2003. *Green States and Social Movements*. New York: Oxford University Press.

Dryzek, J. S. 1990. *Discursive Democracy: Politics, Policy, and Political Science*. New York: Cambridge University Press.

Dryzek, J. S. 2000. *Deliberative Democracy and Beyond: Liberals, Critics, Contestations*. New York: OUP.

Dryzek, J. S., and S. Niemeyer. 2008. "Discursive Representation." *Apsr* 102 (4): 481–483.

Durant, R. 2010. *Oxford Handbooks of American Politics*. Oxford: Oxford University Press.

Ercan, S. A. 2013. "A Deliberative Systems Approach to Conflicts of Culture." Paper prepared for the American Political Science Association Conference, Chicago, August 29–September 1.

Ettema, J. S. 2007. "Journalism as Reason-Giving: Deliberative Democracy, Institutional Accountability, and the News Media's Mission." *Political Communication* 24 (2): 143–160. doi:10.1080/10584600701312860.

Evans, P., D. Rueschemeyer, and T. Skocpol. 1985. *Bringing the State Back In*. New York: Cambridge University Press.

Fairclough, N. 2003. *Analysing Discourse: Textual Analysis for Social Research*. London: Routledge.

Ferree, M. M., W. A. Gamson, J. Gerhards, and D. Rucht. 2002. *Shaping Abortion Discourse: Democracy and the Public Sphere in Germany and the United States*. Cambridge: Cambridge University Press.

Fisher, F. 2000. *Citizens, Experts, and the Environment: The Politics of Local Knowledge*. Durham, NC: Duke University Press.

Fisher, F., and C. Sirianni. 1994. *Critical Studies in Organization and Bureaucracy*. Philadelphia: Temple University Press.

Gastil, J. 2008. *Political Communication and Deliberation*. Thousand Oaks, CA: Sage.

Goodin, R. 2008. *Innovating Democracy*. Cambridge: Cambridge University Press.
Goodin, R. E. 2000. "Democratic Deliberation Within." *Philosophy & Public Affairs* 29 (1): 81–109. doi:10.1111/j.1088-4963.2000.00081.x.
Goodin, R. E. 2005. "Sequencing Deliberative Moments." *Acta Politica* 40 (2): 182–196. doi:10.1057/palgrave.ap.5500098.
Gutmann, A., and D. Thompson. 2004. *Why Deliberative Democracy?* Princeton: Princeton University Press.
Habermas, J. 1996. *Between Facts and Norms: Contributions to a Discourse Theory of Law and Democracy*. Cambridge, MA: MIT Press.
Habermas, J. 2006. "Political Communication in Media Society: Does Democracy Still Enjoy an Epistemic Dimension? The Impact of Normative Theory on Empirical Research." *Communication Theory* 16 (4): 411–426. doi:10.1111/comt.2006.16.issue-4.
Hall, S. 1973. *Encoding and Decoding in the Television Discourse*. Birmingham: Centre for Contemporary Cultural Studies.
Hallin, D., and P. Mancini. 2004. *Comparing Media Systems: Three Models of Media and Politics*. New York: Cambridge University Press.
Hendriks, C. M. 2006. "Integrated Deliberation: Reconciling Civil Society's Dual Role in Deliberative Democracy." *Political Studies* 54 (3): 486–508. doi:10.1111/j.1467-9248.2006.00612.x.
James, M. R. 2004. *Deliberative Democracy and the Plural Polity*. Lawrence: University Press of Kansas.
Levine, P., and R. M. Nierras. 2007. "Activists' View of Deliberation." *Journal of Public Deliberation* 3 (1): 1–14.
Locatelli, C., 2011. "Comunicação e barragens: o poder da comunicação das organizações e da mídia na implantação da Usina Hidrelétrica Foz do Chapecó (Brasil)." Thesis (PhD), Federal University of Rio Grande do Sul.
Mackenzie, M. K., and M. Warren. 2012. "Two Trust-Based Usesof Minipublics in Democratic Systems." In *Deliberative Systems – Deliberative Democracy at the Large Scale*, edited by J. Parkinson and J. Mansbridge, 95–124. Cambridge: Cambridge University Press.
Maia, R. (with A. Marques, D. Cal, and R. Mendonça). 2012. *Deliberation, the Media and Political Talk*. New York: Haptom Press.
Mansbridge, J. 1999. "Everyday Talk in Deliberative System." In *Deliberative Politics: Essays on Democracy and Disagreement*, edited by S. Macedo, 211–239. New York: OUP.
Mansbridge, J. 2003. "Rethinking Representation." *The American Political Science Review* 97 (4): 515–528. doi:10.1017/S0003055403000856.
Mansbridge, J., J. Bohman, S. Chambers, T. Christiano, A. Fung, J. Parkinson, D. Thompson, and M. E. Warren. 2012. "A Systemic Approach to Deliberative Democracy." In *Deliberative Systems – Deliberative Democracy at the Large Scale*, edited by J. Parkinson and J. Mansbridge, 1–26. Cambridge: Cambridge University Press.
Medearis, J. 2005. "Social Movements and Deliberative Democratic Theory." *British Journal of Political Science* 35: 53–75. doi:10.1017/S0007123405000037.
Mendonça, R. F. 2008. "Representation and Deliberation in Civil Society." *Brazilian Political Science Review* 2 (2): 117–137.
Mendonça, R. F., and E. Cunha. 2014. "Can the Claim to Foster Broad Participation Hinder Deliberation?" *Critical Policy Studies* 8 (1): 78–100. doi:10.1080/19460171.2013.843468.
Mendonça, R. F., and S. A. Ercan, 2014. "Deliberation and Protest – Still Strange Bedfellows? Revealing the Deliberative Potential of Recent Protests in Brazil and Turkey." Paper prepared for the American Political Science Association Conference, Washington, DC, August 28-31.
Neblo, M. 2005. "Thinking through Democracy: Between the Theory and Practice of Deliberative Politics." *Acta Politica* 40: 169–181. doi:10.1057/palgrave.ap.5500102.
Papadopoulos, Y. 2012. "On the Embeddedness of Deliberative Systems: Why Elitist Innovations Matter More." In *Deliberative Systems – Deliberative Democracy at the Large Scale*, edited by J. Parkinson and J. Mansbridge, 125–150. Cambridge: Cambridge University Press.

Parkinson, J. 2006a. *Deliberating in the Real World: Problems of Legitimacy in Deliberative Democracy.* Oxford: OUP.

Parkinson, J. 2006b. "Rickety Bridges? Using the Media in Deliberative Democracy." *British Journal of Political Science* 36 (1): 175–183. doi:10.1017/S0007123406000093.

Parkinson, J. 2012. "Democratizing Deliberative Systems." In *Deliberative Systems – Deliberative Democracy at the Large Scale*, edited by J. Parkinson and J. Mansbridge, 151–172. Cambridge: Cambridge University Press.

Peters, B., S. Tanjev, and A. Wimmel. 2010. "Contemporary Journalism and Its Contributions to a Discursive Sphere." In *Public Deliberation and Public Culture the writings of Bernhard Peters, 1993 - 2005*, edited by H. Wessler, 134–159. New York: Palgrave Macmillan.

Peters, G. 2009. *The Politics of Bureaucracy – An Introduction to Comparative Public Administration.* London: Routledge.

Polletta, F., and J. Lee. 2006. "Is Telling Stories Good for Democracy? Rhetoric in Public Deliberation after 9/11." *American Sociological Review* 71 (5): 699–721. doi:10.1177/000312240607100501.

Porto, M. 2012. *Media Power and Democratization in Brazil: TV Globo and the Dilemmas of Political Accountability.* London: Routledge.

Saward, M. 2009. "Authorisation and Authenticity: Representation and the Unelected." *The Journal of Political Philosophy* 17 (1): 1–22. doi:10.1111/jopp.2008.17.issue-1.

Silverstone, R. 1999. *Why Study the Media?* London: Sage.

Simon, A., and M. Xenos. 2000. "Media Framing and Effective Public Deliberation." *Political Communication* 17 (4): 363–376. doi:10.1080/10584600050178979.

Sintomer, Y. 2010. *O poder ao povo – Júris de cidadãos, sorteio e democracia participativa.* Belo Horizonte: Editora UFMG.

Thompson, J. B. 1998. *A mídia e a modernidade: uma teoria social da mídia.* Petrópolis: Vozes.

Urbinati, N. 2006. *Representative Democracy: Principles and Genealogy.* Chicago: The University of Chicago Press.

Urbinati, N., and M. E. Warren. 2008. "The Concept of Representation in Contemporary Democratic Theory." *Annual Review of Political Science* 11: 387–412. doi:10.1146/annurev.polisci.11.053006.190533.

Waisbord, S. 2009. "Bridging the Press-Civic Society Divide: Civic Media Advocacy in Latin America." *Nordicom Review* 30: 105–116.

Warren, M. 2007. "Institutionalizing Deliberative Democracy." In *Deliberation, Participation and Democracy: Can the People Govern?*, edited by S. Rosenberg, 272–288. New York: Palgrave MacMillan.

Wessler, H. 2008. "Investigating Deliberativeness Comparatively." *Political Communication* 25 (1): 1–22. doi:10.1080/10584600701807752.

Young, I. 2000. *Inclusion and Democracy.* Oxford: Oxford University Press.

Young, I. 2003. "Activist Challenges to Deliberative Democracy." In *Debating Deliberative Democracy*, edited by J. Fishkin and P. Laslett, 102–120. Malden: Blackwell.

Deliberative elitism? Distributed deliberation and the organization of epistemic inequality

Alfred Moore

ABSTRACT
In the systemic turn, deliberative theory seems to have come full circle. After a phase of empirically engaged research on practices of deliberation in various 'natural' settings, and experiments in the production of considered public opinions in 'minipublics' and other citizen panels, deliberative theory is returning to problems of locating deliberation within democratic systems. This paper explores the question of how expert authority might be integrated into a deliberative democracy, thereby addressing an important tension between the principle of democratic equality and the inequalities implied by expert knowledge. The problem of locating expertise within deliberative politics, I argue, is just a special case of a general problem in deliberative systems: How to locate the different deliberative 'moments' with respect to each other and to observing publics. In answering this question I emphasize the importance of 'metadeliberation' on the value and functions of divisions of deliberative labor. I describe deliberation among experts, contestation in the critical public sphere and deliberation in minipublics from the point of view of their capacity to support a wider context of public judgment of expertise. And I conclude with a discussion of the problem of 'deliberative elitism'.

In this essay, I consider the problem of locating expertise in deliberative politics. Given its importance in processes of opinion formation among policymakers and wider publics on issues such as climate change, expert deliberation is a significant topic in its own right. However, I also suggest that the problem of locating expertise within deliberative politics is just a special case of a more general problem in deliberative systems: How to locate different deliberative 'moments' with respect to each other and to observing publics. One aspect of this problem involves the need to take on trust the outcomes of deliberations in other parts of the system, which raises a problem of authority: it involves not making one's acceptance of a command or proposition conditional on an independent examination of the grounds of the command or proposition. This problem arises with respect to public acceptance of the claims issuing from expert deliberation, but it also arises with respect to the outcomes of minipublics that have themselves sometimes been conceived as a response to the problem of bringing public judgment to bear on expertise.[1] It is in part in response to this problem that some critics have described minipublics as a form of 'deliberative elitism' (Lafont 2014; Urbinati 2010), displacing rather than supplementing public judgment. Far from being a democratic remedy for potentially exclusive and elitist expert deliberation, minipublics are thus thought to themselves represent a form of elitism. In this essay, I attempt to locate the problem of 'deliberative elitism' in a broader discussion of the problem of expertise within a democratic system, and the more general question of the grounds on which one might accept the outcomes of a deliberation in which one was not a participant. In answering this question, I emphasize the importance of providing conditions that support public judgment at the level of 'metadeliberation' on the value and functions of divisions of deliberative labor itself.

I begin the essay with a discussion of the idea of a deliberative system, with particular reference to the problem of expertise. I then consider deliberation *among* experts, that is, exemplified by expert committees and commissions, where, on the one hand, participation is exclusive and members are selected for competence, and on the other there is a strong orientation to reason-giving and equality among participants. However, internal means of securing deliberative ideals only go so far. In the third section, I describe three ways in which societal practices of contestation and critique contribute to the conditions of possibility of public judgment of expert claims and practices: the articulation of new issues and identities; oversight and scrutiny of expert practices; and the exercise of powers of prevention. In the fourth section, I consider the role of minipublics and citizen panels in relation to the problem of generating the conditions of possibility for public judgments of expertise. And I conclude with a discussion of the danger of 'deliberative elitism'.

1. The problem of expertise in a deliberative system

The idea that people ought to have an equal opportunity to contribute to deliberation on matters that affect them seems to be short-circuited by the inequalities in knowledge that are necessary for the effective analysis, regulation and management of complex social and technological problems. This generates serious difficulties for the ideal of government by discussion that is at the heart of deliberative democratic theory. As Dennis Thompson recently noted, democratic theorists have failed to show 'how to incorporate the need for expertise and technical administration in a deliberative democracy' (Thompson 2008, 515). However, these difficulties become more tractable if we think in terms of a deliberative *system*. On the systems view, deliberation is functionally differentiated or distributed, such that 'different segments or components contribute in different ways to weighing matters that the public ought to discuss, through, e.g., public forums, interest groups, enclaves, everyday talk, and individual contemplation' (Mansbridge 2010, 41). Empirical studies of deliberative democratic practice have tended (understandably) to focus on particular sites, modes and moments of deliberation, from established institutions such as parliaments (Steiner et al. 2004) and committees (Nullmeier and Pritzlaff 2010) to recent innovations such as minipublics (Fung 2003), citizens' assemblies (Warren and Pearse 2008) and deliberative polls (Fishkin and Luskin 2005). However, the systems approach, while building on this work, shifts the focus from the 'best possible single deliberative forum' (Mansbridge et al. 2012, 2) to the approximation of deliberative ideals in the interactions between different modes, institutional locations and temporal moments of deliberation.

The deliberative system comprises many sites and venues, including parliaments, expert committees, courtrooms, everyday talk and civil associations or social movements. These sites can have different deliberative functions and different styles of reasoning and norms of argument. Further, 'each element in such a system may not be perfectly deliberative or democratic in its own right, but may still perform a useful function in the system as a whole' (Parkinson 2006, 7; see also; Mansbridge 1999, 224). Indeed, deliberative values may conflict (Thompson 2008, 511), and it is possible that deliberative values at the system level can in fact be better served by departing from deliberative ideals in particular instances. The deliberative value of a particular part of the system depends not only on its internal structure and conduct but on its context and its relations to other moments.

We can usefully distinguish three ways of thinking about the value of deliberative parts in their relations to one another. The first is aggregation, where one part of the system adds a bit of deliberative value to the aggregate whole. Here the deliberative moments are treated as plug-ins or pieces of a puzzle. The deliberative value of the system is equal to the sum of the deliberative value of its parts. The second is sequencing, where deliberative moments have value in virtue of being 'in the right combinations and the right order' (Goodin 2005, 193). Third is iteration, in which the value of the system depends on opportunities for reopening, revising and contesting particular decisions, settlements and routine decision processes (Thompson 2008, 515). Iterative processes can engage different institutions, harness different deliberative capacities and go through many phases. In contrast to the formality of an ordered sequence of deliberative moments, the 'iteration' model emphasizes the reversibility and revisability of decisions and decision-processes.

While deliberation may be distributed across different moments and institutional locations, the broad regulative ideal remains that 'power in the sense of coercive power is absent in a deliberative system' (Mansbridge et al. 2010, 41). Yet the systems view must also, as Ferejohn argues, recognize the 'inevitability of a political division of labour and deference within deliberative processes' (Ferejohn 2008, 203). This gives us a sharper view of a problem that looms large when considering a democratic theory of expertise: How might we have relations of power and deference within a deliberative system and yet imagine that it could approach the regulative ideal of the absence of coercive power? A common response to this question is that divisions of labor and inequalities of influence must themselves be capable of being justified through democratic deliberation. We might say that Thompson's (1999, 185) democratic justification of secrecy, that 'first order secrecy' must be justified through a process based on 'second-order publicity', extends to many less extreme forms of asymmetry. Minimally, policies and processes must be public in order to be potential objects of consent. A crucial feature of the systems approach, then, is that at the 'meta-deliberative' level, the 'place of deliberation in the larger process should be open to deliberative challenge itself' (Thompson 2008, 515).[2] Bohman makes a similar point: Democratic change 'relies on the reflexivity of the democratic order', and this means that not only must citizens in a democracy 'be able to deliberate about matters of common concern', but they must also 'be able to deliberate about the procedures by which they deliberate, the reasons they accept as public reasons, their practices of self-government and so on' (Bohman 2005, 1). A central claim of the deliberative systems approach, then, is that the relations between parts or moments in the deliberative system – the division of deliberative labor – must itself be subject to deliberative justification (Mansbridge et al. 2010). How is this 'meta-deliberation' supposed to take place? How are we to think of the relations between deliberative moments as themselves being subject to deliberation?

One part of the problem is that distributed deliberation requires those 'outside the room', so to speak, to exercise judgment with regard to deliberations 'inside the room', whose content and experience they do not share. How can those 'outside the room' have grounds to trust the outcome of deliberations at which they were not present? This difficulty is especially acute where expert deliberations are concerned. To consider this problem, we can distinguish between 'internal' and 'external' legitimacy.[3] Internal legitimacy derives from the acceptance by the participants of the outcome of a deliberation within a particular institution or body, who 'could see that all views were fully and civilly considered, and that their groups and in the plenary sessions they had opportunities to shape and influence the course of the deliberation, even if they perhaps did not agree with its outcome' (Bohman 2005, 10; see also; Ferejohn 2008, 209). External legitimacy, on the other hand, derives from acceptance by institutions or publics outside of the deliberative forum. The idea is that there can be good reasons to accept the outcomes of a deliberation at which one was not present, and these reasons may be different to the ones that establish internal legitimacy for those in the room. The distinction between internal and external legitimacy emphasizes (i) the separation between those who are in the room and those who are not and (ii) that the reasons shared by those in the room will not be necessarily be the same as the reasons that convince those not in the room to accept the outcomes of their deliberation. The problem is that those outside the room share neither the substantive matter of the deliberations, nor the experience that the deliberation was fairly conducted and so on. It is for this reason that Ferejohn describes the situation of those outside the room as one of 'trust without reason-giving' (2008, 208).

This problem can be framed in terms of the sharpness of the boundary between internal and external reasons. If the boundary is impermeable, then what is left to those outside the room is only acclamation or rejection. Such a strict division of labor would, as Chambers points out, 'exclude citizens from substantive deliberation about the issues altogether' (2004, 397). This in turn raises three concerns. It could protect elite deliberation from substantive scrutiny and challenge. It could effectively hand democratic ratification over to a fully 'plebiscitory' (and nondeliberative) process (Chambers 2004, 397). And, as Bohman (2005) argues, to restrict public judgment to the approval or rejection of the initiatives of others could preclude public influence over agenda setting. Chambers, usefully, speaks of whether secluded deliberations are 'porous'. 'Ideally what we want', she suggests, 'is a public sphere not entirely dominated by plebiscitory reason and closed sessions not entirely dominated by private reason' (Chambers 2004, 398). The 'porousness' of secluded deliberations is particularly important when considering expertise. The problem here concerns the extent to which substantive deliberation can be undertaken by those outside the room as well as those in the room. Another way to put this issue is the extent to which 'internal' or substantive judgments are required or involved in the trust judgment. This gives important democratic shape to the extensive discussions in sociology of science and social epistemology of the capacity of lay people to exercise judgments with respect to expert claims.

There are two senses in which contestation is crucial to maintaining the division of deliberative labor associated with expertise. One is that secluded deliberation requires a degree of active scrutiny, interaction and even contestation in order to prevent such seclusion from amounting to the insulation of expert deliberation from substantive scrutiny and challenge. The idea that deliberation is to unfold under the 'force of the better argument' means principally the exclusion of influence deriving from inequalities in wealth and power. However, as Knight and Johnson rightly observe, deliberative equality does not involve equal participation or equal distribution of decision power in the form of votes. Rather, 'the procedures that govern the deliberative phase of democratic decision-making protect equality by ensuring that all claims and counter-claims are subject to critical public scrutiny and that, when challenged, any participant must defend her proposal or back her objection with reasons' (Knight and Johnson 1997, 288). Deliberative equality requires not equal participation, but a context of active public scrutiny. Part of the value of such scrutiny and contestation is that it has the potential to influence the behavior of those who are being scrutinized. What is at stake is not merely the communication of reasons and justifications, such that the norm of public deliberation is honored merely by the fact that reasons are given by officials for public actions and approved by those subject to their effects, but the influence of the democratic public on expert deliberation.

Another crucial reason for emphasizing active challenge has to do with tacit consent. A key feature of tacit consent is that consent only becomes evident by the conspicuous absence of objection over time, and it can only be assumed where there is the live possibility of refusing it. Only where there is the realistic possibility of protesting or refusing to go along with policies and processes can we assume consent from the fact that a policy or process is largely uncontested. Though he does not frame his argument in terms of tacit consent, Warren (1996) makes the possibility of challenge from a 'critical public sphere' central to the generation of authority in a deliberative democracy. His key point, which applies also to expertise, is that authority relations are warranted to the extent that they could be publicly scrutinized and challenged and that the authorities thus have to give justifications in terms of the goods served by such authority. And this in turn requires that such relations, from time to time, actually are brought into question. In the case of a recent vaccine controversy in the UK (see Moore and Stilgoe 2009), although the challenge of vaccine-critical activists brought no substantive policy change, it did raise questions about existing practices, and it did bring to light justifications for those practices in terms of the basic goods the authorities in question were supposed to serve. The point here is twofold. First, the effect of such challenges is not simply to 'erode' authority, but rather to bring to the surface the basic justifications of such practices and present them to a wider public audience. If such practices are indeed successfully justified, then we could be said to have moved from a technocratic to a critical mode of expert authority. Second, by demonstrating the possibility of such challenge and successfully meeting it (if they successfully meet it), the assumption of public consent to those policies and practices that are not contested acquires plausibility. The demonstration of the live possibility of scrutiny and contestation serves to actualize tacit consent. While the regulative ideal of the absence of coercion is highly demanding and often points to the need for secluded deliberation, the presence of criticism at least gives some grounds for the assumption that when authority relations and divisions of labor are not questioned, the absence of criticism indicates tacit consent rather than latent or suppressed dissent.

2. Deliberation *among* experts

Expert deliberation differs from the broader public deliberation that has been the principal concern of many deliberative theorists in that it typically does not address moral norms or the common good in any direct way, but rather aims at more narrowly technical judgments.[4] It is governed not by a principle of maximal inclusion, but rather selection of participants according to their competence. However, expert deliberation epitomizes the priority of the quality of argument that is insisted upon by many deliberative democrats. For this reason, small group deliberation among specialists has been treated as exemplary by some political theorists. Chambers, for instance, emphasizes the high deliberative quality that can be achieved 'behind closed doors' (2004). Rawls describes the Supreme Court as the archetype of public deliberation. And Philippe Urfalino (2006, 2012) describes 'Areopagos'[5] deliberations, that is, institutions of committees of the wise, as approximating the conditions in which the force of the better argument and the epistemic quality of deliberation and decision is given the highest priority. I do not regard such expert deliberations as either the archetype or the most important site of deliberation in a democracy. But I think that in making sense of the place of expertise in a democratic system, we must attend closely to expert deliberation. In my discussion in this section, I will examine what goes on behind closed doors, and in particular the relation between deliberation and decision, and I will address the problem of how those outside the room can critically relate to a deliberation whose substance they cannot easily access and whose experience they did not share.

Why would citizens lend authority to the views of a group of experts? There are many reasons, but perhaps the most common, and the one I will consider in the rest of this section, is that their deliberations have concluded with consensus. In discussions of the relation between expert knowledge and public deliberation, expert consensus is often thought of as a precondition for informed public deliberation (see Christiano 2012, 52). Yet while it is common to talk of expert consensus, there are two quite different sorts of consensus that can result from expert deliberation. The first is consensus in the sense of uniformity of belief and evaluation. This is what Turner (2003) calls a 'scientific consensus', and it involves a judgment about the status of a putative scientific fact that is not time-constrained or tailored to the demands of a particular situation. Consensus represents the point at which debate within a scientific community comes naturally to rest. This sort of consensus cannot be forced; it is rather the by-product of deliberators arguing over claims and evidence with no time limit and no external demand to close the debate (Rescher 1993, 17).[6] This image of consensus has had considerable influence on theories of democratic deliberation, in which the ideal of political deliberation has sometimes been framed in terms of a community of impartial inquirers commonly seeking solutions to the various moral and practical problems of living together.

The second is consensus as mode of collective decision across difference. This sort of consensus can be described as decision by 'apparent consensus' (Urfalino 2006) or 'decision by interpretation' (Steiner and Dorff 1980), in which the decision is signaled by the absence of opposition to a proposed consensus statement. Consensus as a mode of collective decision turns on the willing suspension of disagreement, but – in contrast to consensus as uniformity of belief – it does not necessarily involve the *disappearance* of disagreement. Expert committees and commissions often involve this sort of expert decision, and it also characterizes some of the collective statements issued by bodies such as the Intergovernmental Panel on Climate Change. Yet despite its ubiquity, this sense of expert consensus has been far less well explored.

Beatty and Moore frame such active consensus among experts in terms of 'deliberative acceptance', a model of expert deliberation that highlights the normative potentials of a form of agreement that combines unity with disagreement, unity at the procedural level and disagreement at the level of substance. Deliberative acceptance is an adaptation of Margaret Gilbert's (1987) notion of 'joint acceptance', designed to make explicit the deliberative potentials of this form of collective decision. They propose that

> [a] group deliberatively accepts p if and only if the individual members, *based on the quality of their deliberation*, have openly agreed to let p stand as the position of the group.

Deliberative acceptance involves the willing suspension of disagreement *based on the quality of their deliberation*. Deliberative acceptance emphasizes the demand that the absence of opposition follows a free and full discussion in which the participants themselves agreed that their views were given a fair hearing. One crucial condition for deliberative acceptance is that all participants have an *equal* opportunity to influence the outcome of the process. This does not mean granting equal weight to opinions in the way that we grant equal weight to votes ahead of the process of tallying them. The weight that attaches to arguments must itself be determined within the deliberative process (problematic as this may be). Equality here means participants have an equal opportunity to persuade one another relying only on the 'force of the better argument'. As Knight and Johnson (1997, 288) rightly observe, the opportunity of equality of influence in deliberative processes does not involve giving equal weight to all opinions, but rather seeks to exclude the influence of inequalities that are arbitrary from the point of view of making arguments oriented to the common good. Deliberative acceptance, then, ideally involves people having an equal opportunity to influence the deliberative process, but if they have pressed their argument yet failed to convince their peers of its value, they may feel compelled to stop opposing a consensus proposal.

Deliberative acceptance also requires that diverse arguments were fully developed and contested. The quality of deliberation has in large part to do with the development and vigorous confrontation of diverse arguments. Without the multiplication, clarification and contestation of argumentative positions, participants may go along with a position without fully considering alternatives and without sufficiently exploring the grounds for the position. Deliberative acceptance aims not for full uniformity of belief, but rather at developing disagreement to an extent that those who find themselves in the minority are willing to concede that their arguments were given a fair hearing even if they did not prove persuasive (Beatty and Moore 2010, 209). Deliberative acceptance is in this respect different from Bohman and Richardson's notion of 'deep compromise' – in which agents disagree but their mutual concern and respect leads 'one or both [to] adjust[] his or her ends or goals on the basis of that concern or respect' (Bohman and Richardson 2009, 271; see also; Richardson 2002, 147), for deliberative acceptance does not require that agents actually adjust their ends or goals. Deliberative acceptance is also importantly different from Sunstein's 'incompletely theorized agreement', which involves participants 'accept[ing] an outcome ... without understanding or converging on an ultimate ground for that acceptance' (Sunstein 1999, 125). Rather than avoiding or remaining silent on areas of disagreement, deliberative acceptance requires their thorough exploration.

The development of diverse arguments in a context of deliberative equality is consistent with joint acceptance behind closed doors. In order to give confidence to those outside, however, it is necessary to *show* that strong alternatives were considered, that the minority was heard and that they all agreed to let that position stand. It is for this reason that 'deliberative acceptance... involve[s] a vote, which is appropriate for deliberators who count each other as equals' (Beatty and Moore 2010, 210). The vote contributes to the transparency of the proceedings, as well as showing that the position was favored by a majority of deliberative equals (Beatty and Moore 2010, 210). '[T]here is more to deliberative acceptance than a vote', they write, '[b]ut, in this case, the count of votes matters' (Beatty and Moore 2010, 210). Does deliberative acceptance simply collapse into majority rule? Is a decision by deliberative acceptance just a decision by majority rule in disguise? I think not, for there are two important theoretical differences. First, under majority rule each person's opinion is at the very outset granted equal weight in the final decision, whereas in deliberative acceptance the strength of each person's view is indexed on its persuasiveness to others during the course of the deliberation. In contexts such as an expert committee, as Urfalino emphasizes, a participant cannot assert her opinion as one will of equal weight to the others – it is her 'good reason to choose X', and not her 'preference' for it, that has value (Urfalino 2006, 19). Second, majority rule presumes a *prior* unanimous agreement to be bound by the outcome of a vote, whereas in deliberative acceptance, 'even the minority agreed to let the position in question stand as the group's' (Beatty and Moore 2010, 209). This concession is achieved *in situ*, in a context where the minority had the live possibility of refusing it. 'What is conceded to the minority is acknowledgement of their persistent concerns, as deliberative equals. But deliberative agreement still extracts from the minority a significant concession, the acknowledgement that they were heard, but had not proven persuasive' (Beatty and Moore 2010, 209). Thus, for deliberative acceptance you have to not only secure a majority but also secure from the minority an agreement that their concerns were heard where they had the live possibility of preventing agreement altogether.

From the point of view of those outside the room, an expert agreement worth deferring to would be one in which (i) there was a minority that forcefully argued its case and (ii) the minority willingly suspended its dissent and signed on to a group position in virtue of the quality of the deliberation. That is, we would want to see an agreement among experts in which it is evident that a minority went along with the group judgment because of the 'exhaustion of acceptable objections'. This sort of agreement should give people more confidence in the collective judgment of the experts; it would signal and partially reveal the 'internal' quality of deliberation.

3. The value of public scrutiny

It is certainly important that experts present the results of their 'internal' deliberations as decisions, that is, that they do not give the impression that nature is speaking through them. Yet it is not enough that expert deliberations signal in their conclusions *that* a process of decision was taking place. There also needs to be a context of active public scrutiny and contestation. Societal practices of contestation and critique are conditions of possibility of the exercise of citizen judgment with regard to complex, expert-mediated issues, and are thus in fact vital to the generation of the democratic authority of expertise. In general terms, social movements and protest groups play a key role in generating the 'context of public criticism' that Warren finds crucial to warranted trust in authority (1996, 56). A number of critical science studies scholars have highlighted the epistemically generative role of 'lay' citizens, who lack formal accreditation but possess experiential knowledge in particular contexts (see Fischer 2000; Wynne 1989). I emphasize here a related role, viewing it not as an alternative expertise but as part of a dynamic process of critical scrutiny of expert authority. There are at least three ways in which such practices of contestation contribute to the conditions of possibility of public judgment of expert claims and practices: the articulation of new issues and identities; oversight and scrutiny of expert practices; and the exercise of powers of prevention.

One important effect of societal practices of contestation and critique is the articulation of issues. Social studies of science have identified in the realm of science and expertise Nancy Fraser's 'subaltern counter-publics', whose value is to 'invent and circulate counter-discourses' and 'formulate oppositional interpretations of their identities, interests and needs' (Fraser 1990, 57). For example, new knowledge suggesting a link between a certain gene and an increased risk of developing breast cancer makes carriers of that gene into concerned parties, without a firm identity as such, nor a clear set of interests, yet with a claim to inclusion as affected parties, and an entitlement to contribute to their self-definition (Callon, Lascoumes, and Barthe 2009, 30). Stephen Epstein's study of AIDS activism, for instance, focuses on the 'interventions of lay people in the proclamation and evaluation of scientific claims' (1996, 3). Systemically, such activities can contribute to the 'iteration' of deliberation through the introduction of new actors, arguments and problem framings into decision processes.

The second contribution is through oversight and scrutiny. The ability of citizens to scrutinize elite power is a longstanding democratic concern, and is particularly pressing in the face of the danger of expert domination. As Jasanoff rightly observes, 'growing awareness that policy framings not only solve problems but allocate power ... has led commentators on the politics of science and technology to recommend greater democratic scrutiny of framing processes' (Jasanoff 2005, 194–195). I want to emphasize two important general points about oversight. First, it requires a measure of substantive engagement and deliberative capacity. Second, and related, oversight is active, not passive. It requires the generation of new information and alternative interpretations of existing information. This in turn often calls for the deployment or acquisition of expertise – Epstein's AIDS activists put in a great deal of work to be able to interact with experts and articulate their concerns. This is hardly a passive 'watching' in the manner of the parent at the pool keeping half an eye on the kids (Schudson 1999). It requires resource-intensive gathering and processing of information on the part of particular actors. Social movements and 'knowledge associations' (Turner 2003, 77) are often able to take up opportunities to scrutinize the substantive content of expert deliberation in a way that individual citizens are not. Turner (2003, 78) highlights this function of what he calls 'knowledge associations', and Richardson, in a similar vein, emphasizes the importance of 'intermediary advocates' such as the Clean Air Coalition for realizing the 'possibility of contesting or appealing any specially authorized expert determinations' (Richardson 2012, 92).

Empowerment to resist is one further dimension of practices of contestation and critique, which can have the effect of calling forth communicative justifications. The focus on the exercise of powers of prevention draws our attention to the power of social movements and knowledge associations to oppose policies through direct action, boycotts, protests and the withdrawal of cooperation. Such refusal and powers of prevention were vividly exemplified in the case of AIDS activists, whose plausible threat of disruption through both protest and noncooperation in clinical trials was an important condition for their inclusion in the research collective. The threat of exit gave them the opportunity to exercise voice. Such confrontation does not in itself answer any of the substantive questions about what decisions are to be taken in particular cases. The democratic effect comes from forcing putative authorities into communicative justifications of their practices, as Bohman notes in his discussion of this case, including 'even epistemic norms of validity, reliability, and evidence' (Bohman 1999, 590). This point does not rest on any claims that the groups involved are themselves experts in some sense or possess lay knowledge, even though some emblematic cases have involved both. Rather, it makes the limited claim that such practices of contestation and confrontation open up internal expert deliberation to scrutiny and questioning.

4. Minipublics as a mode of scrutiny

Another mode of enabling and supporting considered judgments in the deliberative system with regard to expertise comes from organized minipublics and other deliberative and participatory democratic innovations. These have been the focus of much attention as aspects of the democratization of expertise (see Fischer 2000; Brown 2009, 251–255; Hamlett 2003). One way to frame their role in a deliberative system is in terms of their ability to support meta-deliberation. This in turn can be analyzed in terms of informing the deliberation of wider publics. Yet informing public deliberation here does not mean reproducing among a wider public the level of debate found in the deliberative forum or providing citizens with substantive information on the issue at hand so that they can judge for themselves. Rather, it involves giving good grounds for taking up the judgments of others.

Why would citizens lend authority to the views of a randomly selected group of their peers? One sort of answer has to do with representativeness (see MacKenzie and Warren 2012, 105–107). As Goodin and Dryzek (2006, 221) put it, the minipublic should represent 'the diversity of social characteristics and plurality of initial points of view in the larger society'. Fishkin speaks of the sample of citizens in his minipublics as a 'mirror' of the broader public. Yet to talk of minipublics 'reflecting' the wider population would be to miss an important wrinkle: they resemble the public *minus the partisans*. They construct a 'pure' public (Braun and Schultz 2010) using random selection (or stratified random sampling for smaller groups) and excluding 'partisans', citizens who already have strong commitments on the issue at hand, as well as any citizens with direct financial, familial or professional conflicts of interest. The representativeness of the mini public thus involves not strict resemblance. Nor is it representation in the sense of being authorized, accountable or responsive to constituents. Rather, the representativeness takes the form of generality, an absence of organized particular interests. One reason for preferring 'pure' publics is that they can promote inclusion of 'interests and perspectives that are unorganized, inarticulate, and latent in proportion to their presence in the larger public' (MacKenzie and Warren 2012, 106). Further, those already engaged in a particular issue have a discursive advantage in any deliberative context, and their inclusion thus introduces a discursive inequality (Kadlec et al. 2007, 10). Nor must it be the case that 'pure' publics are pliable publics. Kleinman, Delborne, and Anderson (2011) show, for instance, that the exclusion of organized interests does not mean that citizen participants are mere 'blank slates'.

Another broad set of reasons for granting special weight to the judgments of minipublics has to do with the claim that they are 'better informed on the issues and had the opportunity and motivation to examine those issues seriously' (Fishkin 1997, 162). MacKenzie and Warren have described this sort of deference in terms of trust in minipublics as 'information proxies'. By 'information proxy' they mean that citizens who did not share the information and argument, or the experience of the deliberation, may nonetheless choose to defer to the judgment of the minipublic if they think it was competent and representative of the broader public. The value of the minipublic is to provide 'information shortcuts' to an inattentive broader public (MacKenzie and Warren 2012, 103). Yet it would seem that this role for minipublics involves not so much *informing* public deliberation, as *displacing* it. The minipublic would do the job of weighing a wide range of information and arguments, balancing conflicting interests and reaching a considered collective judgment. The wider public, on the 'information proxy' account, would treat the collective judgment of the minipublic as a signal about how they ought to vote. Trusting the judgment of the minipublic in this case is an alternative to informing oneself of all the substantive arguments. When MacKenzie and Warren talk of trust in general terms they seem to invoke the idea of blind deference: 'When an individual makes a decision to trust, he is entrusting a good in which he has an interest to another agent – to an individual, a group, or an institution. In deciding to trust, he is also deciding *to forgo any direct judgment about the use or protection of a good. All problems of knowing about the good – how to maintain, protect, further, or develop it – are off-loaded onto the trustee*' (MacKenzie and Warren 2012, 99; my emphasis). Trust in this sense is consistent with total ignorance on the substance of the matter in question. It also means foregoing any 'monitoring or other forms of active engagement' (MacKenzie and Warren 2012, 99). Monitoring would signal an absence of trust altogether. However, while citizens may be ignorant on the substance of the issue, the 'trust decision' depends principally, they suggest, on judgments about the motivation and the competence of those who would be deferred to. MacKenzie and Warren recognize that the 'shortcut' citizens are looking for is one that tells them about the quality of the deliberation in the room, that is, their decision to defer depends on a judgment as to whether the 'information cues emanating from minipublics might be considered trustworthy *because* these recommendation have been tried, tested, and accepted by informed participants in a discursive arena' (MacKenzie and Warren 2012, 113).

This has led Lafont to claim that the 'information proxy' function relies on 'blind deference' (Lafont 2014, 11). This is not entirely fair, since there is clearly an active judgment taking place (at least ideally), and this judgment is related to suppositions about the quality of the deliberation. The confusion, I think, comes from MacKenzie and Warren's framing of the information proxy function in terms of passivity. The ambiguity is that passivity could be taken to apply either to the dimension of participation or to the dimension of judgment. Thus, when they emphasize that citizens make 'active choices to remain passive' (MacKenzie and Warren 2012, 99), they mean that citizens are making an active *judgment* to remain passive in the dimension of *participation*. To be passive in the dimension of judgment would indeed be to blindly defer. It is possible, of course, that blind deference could be construed as improving deliberative quality at the system level by enriching the environment in which citizens more or less unreflectively take their informational cues – the deliberative equivalent of adding fluoride to the water supply rather than relying on citizens to remember to brush their own teeth. But this is not what they argue. Rather, they emphasize the value of providing the means for citizens to make active judgments about when and where to direct their critical attention and participatory energies. Thus, when they talk of 'good' passivity, they mean nonparticipation informed by an active judgment. They are arguing not for blind (or passive) deference, but for active deference to the judgments of a minipublic. The active judgment here does not bear on the substantive arguments and information. It bears rather on second-order or external reasons. Without actually sharing the information, arguments and experience of deliberation, those outside the room can, nonetheless, have good reasons of a different sort to trust the judgments of those in the room. This is neither a straightforward matter of informing or displacing public judgment, but providing opportunities for citizens to use their judgment to allocate their attention and participation in a more fruitful way.

The idea of deferring to the judgments of a minipublic involves entrusting to them the job of weighing conflicting interests and making judgments. Yet if we are to trust the political judgment of a group, both the strength of opinion in the group and the quality of argument are crucial considerations. Here we encounter a variant of the problem discussed above in the context of expert deliberation. MacKenzie and Warren (2012) point to the need for 'consensus' in the room, arguing that unanimity or near unanimity among the deliberators is more likely to command deference than a bare majority. A bare majority would signal a clearly divided group. This would alert us to pay closer attention to the substance of the dispute and make it harder choose a side. However, while unanimity or near unanimity can be a mark of genuine convergence on a common answer, it can also mean that the deliberation was pushed to premature consensus or that the participants had a hidden bias. Does this mean we should look for somewhere between bare majority and unanimity? Lafont, picking up on this point, incredulously asks what degree of consensus should 'trigger trust' (2014, 18). 65%? 55%? 95%? She then rejects the 'quantitative' approach to trust altogether (2014, 17), declaring that the decision whether to 'endorse a specific recommendation... cannot be a matter of degree' (Lafont 2014, 17). Yet it seems to me that instead of asking what degree of agreement within the room would command authority outside the room (55%? 65%? 95%), the key is what outsiders can infer about the quality of deliberation in the room from the character of the agreement. In particular, we should separate the question of the degree of substantive agreement on the issue, and the agreement to endorse the collective outcome based on the quality of the deliberative procedure. In the terms I have been using, the participants may be near unanimous in their acceptance of an outcome which is only positively endorsed by a smaller majority – we thus might frame the combination of strength of opinion and quality of argument in terms of 'deliberative acceptance'. Recall that after the British Columbia Citizens' Assembly had decided on two electoral systems that most closely maximized the values they thought an electoral system should realize, they voted between these two options, with STV winning 123–31. They next voted 142–11 against recommending retaining the current system. And then finally they voted 146–7 to recommend a version of STV to the citizens of British Columbia in a referendum. We might expect the first and third votes to be the same. Why would someone who favored MMP over STV then vote to recommend STV to the wider electorate? It seems plausible to say they still *believe* that MMP would be better than STV. But the latter result addresses precisely the question involved in deliberative acceptance: whether you endorse this as the opinion of the group. This latter vote, we might then say, is an indicator of the participants' assessment of the quality of deliberation, a claim that 'epistemic justice was done', as Beatty and Moore (2010, 209) put it, that their arguments were heard but that they did not win out. It is this kind of agreement, I think, that best justifies MacKenzie and Warren's intuition about the value of near unanimity as a signal for outsiders who might take up the conclusions of a minipublic.

5. Deliberative elitism?

On one level, there is a similarity between the ways in which small group public deliberations and expert deliberations can reach a conclusion. MacKenzie and Warren's account of voting and consensus in the production of a collective judgment at the end of the BC Citizens' Assembly strongly resembles 'deliberative acceptance'. In both cases, it remains to be explored how the different ways of concluding deliberation open up or foreclose opportunities for those outside the room to exercise judgment in taking up (or rejecting) the results of those deliberations. Thus, recent research on the relation between deliberative quality and the mode of collective decision has explored the possibilities of various forms of decision-making such as 'apparent consensus' (Urfalino 2006), 'deliberative acceptance' (Beatty and Moore 2010), 'meta-consensus' (Dryzek and Niemeyer 2006) and even 'deliberative voting' (Moore and O'Doherty 2014). This contributes to a small but growing body of work on the ways of reaching 'non-coercive communicative agreement[s]' that involve neither full unanimity nor mere modus vivendi, but which conclude with 'a kind of consensus' in the sense of a 'genuine agreement that the outcomes are right or fair' (Mansbridge et al. 2010, 70).

However, at the systemic level, one of the important functions of minipublics is as a means of enacting public scrutiny, yet in a way that does not fall prey to the characteristic biases of contestation by movements in the public sphere. The scrutiny function that can potentially be provided by minipublics, then, is distinct from, and complementary to, the sort of scrutiny embodied in the movements and advocacy groups of the critical public sphere. This raises an important systemic danger, which is that minipublics and other innovations of 'invited' participation could diminish or even displace the more informal processes of social movement contestation and protest (Mansbridge et al. 2012, 17). On this basis, it has even been argued that minipublics represent 'a peculiar variety of *elite* rather than *deliberative* democracy' (Lafont 2014, 9). They imply a form of *elite* democracy in that citizens are asked to 'blindly defer to the deliberations of a few selected citizens' (Lafont 2014, 9), but it is *peculiar* because those few selected citizens are neither experts nor a consolidated political elite, but a randomly selected group of ordinary citizens. Both Urbinati (2010, 73–75) and Lafont argue that, while mini publics may not *formally* substitute for public debate and democratic decision, the logic implicit in the claim that mini publics should be authoritative in public debates points to an alarming endgame in which mini publics would crowd out both deliberation in the public sphere and undercut the collective decisions issuing from electoral-representative institutions. They would thus contract rather than enrich democracy (Urbinati 2010, 74) and 'diminish rather than increase the legitimacy of the deliberative system as a whole (Lafont 2014, 2). The deeper concern, then, is not just that minipublics might in practice be captured by elite interests, but that they are *essentially* elitist, that the *better* they work, the more they undermine democracy.

Lafont's argument involves an all-or-nothing account of citizen deliberation: either they fully own the arguments for themselves (the long march, we might say), or they 'blindly defer' to others (the 'short cut'). Lafont seems to deny the possibility of citizen judgment in deciding whether or not to take up the results of the deliberations of others. She does not consider the possibility of second-order or external reasons for choosing to rely on the judgments of others in particular contexts. She insists that any 'recommending force' must amount to 'blind deference' – she cannot imagine citizens having good reasons to take up the outcomes of the deliberations of others that are not the same as the reasons shared in the room. This is particularly odd in view of a comment she makes in passing to the effect that she thinks citizens *could* have such reasons to defer to *real* expert deliberations. Lafont appears to accept that a perfectly good option for passive citizens would be to rely 'on the recommendations of groups whose political views they share or on experts whose judgments they trust. However imperfect, this type of deference is still less blind than deference to the majority of a randomly selected group of citizens' (Lafont 2014, 18). Elsewhere she asks, 'why should their judgments have any more recommending force than those of other experts *that may be substantively superior on their merits*?' (Lafont 2014, 11; my italic). The problem with minipublics, it seems, is that they are too informed to descriptively represent a broader public, but not quite well-informed enough to be worthy of the deference owed to *real* experts. She mentions the comparison to expert deliberation only in passing, and does not explain why choosing to rely on a minipublic you believe to be representative and competent would be any more 'blind' than relying on experts you believe to be competent and without conflicts of interest.

Both Lafont and Urbinati argue that at the systemic level, minipublics displace rather than supplement the activities of the critical public sphere. Whether this sort of crowding out is evident in practice is an empirical question. Yet the theoretical danger is that it mistakes the democratic potentials of minipublics by treating them as a microcosm of a deliberative democracy that would displace, and not simply supplement, contestatory discourse in the public sphere and collective decision in electoral-representative institutions. Because Lafont's criticisms effectively test the value of a deliberative mini public against the standards of a complete theory of democratic legitimacy, they miss the more limited potentials of minipublics as supplementary institutions that have the potential to enhance in particular and limited ways the conditions for the formation of collective judgments in the public sphere and the alignment of policy with legitimately constructed democratic decisions. Rather than viewing minipublics as the thin end of a wedge that threatens to weaken both civil society contestation and electoral-representative legitimacy, we might frame them as having democratic potentials as a way of informing wider citizen deliberation and scrutinizing, monitoring and judging expert government. That they do so in a context of social movements and critical associations (which will orient more confrontationally) is important; but that they have functions that are distinct from those of confrontation is also important. These potentials fall well short of participatory ideals, but they need not simply amount to a new form of elitism.

6. Conclusion

In this essay, I have framed the systemic role of expertise in democracy in terms of a dynamic tension between the need for expert deliberations to remain both distinct from and responsive to wider public concerns. This means, on the one hand, that deliberations among experts need to be conducted in ways that remain porous or open to the possibility of judgment by those outside the room. I suggested that 'deliberative acceptance' is one useful way of conceptualizing the need both for consensus among experts and for ways of signaling that such consensus amounts to a decision, a collective judgment of experts, which is to be deferred to, if at all, on the basis of judgments of the deliberative conditions under which it was reached. On the other hand, public judgment requires that there is an active context of scrutiny and critique. This is produced by the social movements and activists who populate the critical public sphere, and who direct critical attention to the claims made by experts and the conditions under which they produced them (critics of the climate science consensus produced by the IPCC, for instance, would fall under this heading). Yet minipublics may find a place as a complementary mode of scrutiny of expert practices. Thus, the integration of expert authority in a democratic system must take into account not only expert deliberative moments themselves but also the wider context of scrutiny and contestation in civil society, and the potential for minipublics in mediating and moderating this scrutiny function.

Notes

1. It was in the context of his discussion of the difficulties of bringing competent citizen judgment to bear on delegation to experts in government (seeking delegation without alienation) that Robert Dahl first developed the idea of a 'minipopulus' (Dahl 1985, 76).
2. The systems approach, as I understand it here, is consistent with post-positivism in the sense that it sets expert knowledge within a framework of popular judgment, that is, it locates claims to expertise within a broader interpretive perspective.
3. This is legitimacy in a local and situated sense rather than at the level of the political system as a whole, though it nonetheless involves some deliberative norms.
4. This observation does not apply to ethics councils, which are a kind of expert deliberative forum which aims specifically at ideas of justice and the common good (see Moore 2010).
5. The Aeropagos was the court of appeal for civil and criminal cases in ancient Athens.
6. On the idea of consensus as essentially a by-product see also Fuerstein (2014).

Disclosure statement

No potential conflict of interest was reported by the author.

Funding

This research was funded by the European Community's Seventh Framework Programme (FP7/2007-2013) under grant agreement n° 237230.

References

Beatty, J., and A. Moore. 2010. "Should We Aim for Consensus?" *Episteme: A Journal of Social Epistemology* 7 (3): 198–214. doi:10.3366/epi.2010.0203.
Bohman, J. 1999. "Democracy as Inquiry, Inquiry as Democratic: Pragmatism, Social Science, and the Cognitive Division of Labor." *American Journal of Political Science* 43 (2): 590–607. doi:10.2307/2991808.
Bohman, J. 2005. "Legitimate Institutions for Democratic Renewal: Constitutional, Democratic, and Deliberative." Paper presented to the Citizen-Designed Democratic Processes Workshop, Peter Wall Institute, University of British Columbia, Vancouver, BC, June 10–11.
Bohman, J., and H. S. Richardson. 2009. "Liberalism, Deliberative Democracy, and 'Reasons that All Can Accept.'." *Journal of Political Philosophy* 17 (3): 253–274. doi:10.1111/jopp.2009.17.issue-3.
Braun, K., and S. Schultz. 2010. "'…a Certain Amount of Engineering Involved': Constructing the Public in Participatory Governance Arrangements." *Public Understanding of Science* 19 (4): 403–419. doi:10.1177/0963662509347814.
Brown, M. 2009. *Science in Democracy: Expertise, Institutions and Representation*. Cambridge, MA: MIT Press.
Callon, M., P. Lascoumes, and Y. Barthe. 2009. *Acting in an Uncertain World: An Essay on Technical Democracy*. Cambridge, MA: MIT Press.

Chambers, S. 2004. "Behind Closed Doors: Publicity, Secrecy and the Quality of Deliberation." *The Journal of Political Philosophy* 12 (4): 389–410. doi:10.1111/j.1467-9760.2004.00206.x.

Christiano, T. 2012. "Rational Deliberation Among Experts and Citizens." In *Deliberative Systems: Deliberation at the Large Scale*. Vol. 2012, edited by J. Parkinson and J. Mansbridge, 27–51. Cambridge: Cambridge University Press.

Dahl, R. 1985. *Controlling Nuclear Weapons: Democracy versus Guardianship*. Syracuse, NY: Syracuse University Press.

Dryzek, J. S., and S. Niemeyer. 2006. "Reconciling Pluralism and Consensus as Political Ideals." *American Journal of Political Science* 50 (3): 634–649. doi:10.1111/ajps.2006.50.issue-3.

Epstein, S. 1996. *Impure Science: AIDS, Activism and the Politics of Knowledge*. Berkeley, CA: University of California Press.

Ferejohn, J., 2008. "Conclusion: The Citizens' Assembly Model." In *Designing Deliberative Democracy: The British Columbia Citizen's Assembly*, edited by H. Pearse and M. E. Warren, 192–213. Cambridge: Cambridge University Press.

Fischer, F. 2000. *Citizens, Experts and the Environment: The Politics of Local Knowledge*. Durham and London: Duke University Press.

Fishkin, J. 1997 [1995]. *The Voice of the People. Public Opinion and Democracy*. New Haven: Yale University Press.

Fishkin, J., and R. Luskin. 2005. "Experimenting with a Democratic Ideal: Deliberative Polling and Public Opinion." *Acta Politica* 40 (3): 284–298. doi:10.1057/palgrave.ap.5500121.

Fraser, N. 1990. "Rethinking the Public Sphere: A Contribution to the Critique of Actually Existing Democracy." *Social Text* 25/26: 56–80.

Fuerstein, M. 2014. "Democratic Consensus as an Essential By-Product." *Journal of Political Philosophy* 22 (3): 282–301. doi:10.1111/jopp.2014.22.issue-3.

Fung, A. 2003. "Survey Article: Recipes for Public Spheres: Eight Institutional Design Choices and Their Consequences." *Journal of Political Philosophy* 11: 338–367. doi:10.1111/1467-9760.00181.

Gilbert, M. 1987. "Modelling Collective Belief." *Synthese* 73 (1): 185–204. doi:10.1007/BF00485446.

Goodin, R. E. 2005. "Sequencing Deliberative Moments." *Acta Politica* 40: 182–196. doi:10.1057/palgrave.ap.5500098.

Goodin, R. E., and J. S. Dryzek. 2006. "Deliberative Impacts: The Macro-Political Uptake of Mini-Publics." *Politics & Society* 34 (2): 219–244. doi:10.1177/0032329206288152.

Hamlett, P. 2003. "Technology Theory and Deliberative Democracy." *Science, Technology & Human Values* 28 (1): 112–140. doi:10.1177/0162243902238498.

Jasanoff, S. 2005. *Designs on Nature: Science and Democracy in Europe and the United States*. Princeton: Princeton University Press.

Kadlec, A., and W. Friedman. 2007. "Deliberative Democracy and the Problem of Power." *Journal of Public Deliberation* 3 (2), Article 8: 1–26

Kleinman, D., J. Delborne, and A. Anderson. 2011. "Engaging Citizens: The High Cost of Citizen Participation in High Technology." *Public Understanding of Science* 20 (2): 221–240. doi:10.1177/0963662509347137.

Knight, J., and J. Johnson. 1997. "What Sort of Equality Does Deliberative Democracy Require?" In *Deliberative Democracy: Essays on Reason and Politics*, edited by J. Bohman and W. Rehg, 279–320. Cambridge, MA: The MIT Press.

Lafont, C. 2014. "Deliberation, Participation, and Democratic Legitimacy: Should Deliberative Mini-Publics Shape Public Policy?" *Journal of Political Philosophy*. Article first published online: 22 Jan 2014. doi:10.1111/jopp.12031.

MacKenzie, M. M., and M. E. Warren. 2012. "Two Trust-Based Uses of Minipublics in Democratic Systems." In *Deliberative Systems: Deliberative Democracy at the Large Scale*, edited by J. Parkinson and J. Mansbridge, 95–124. Cambridge: Cambridge University Press.

Mansbridge, J., J. Bohman, S. Chambers, T. Christiano, A. Fung, J. Parkinson, D. Thompson, and M. Warren. 2012. "A Systemic Approach to Deliberative Democracy." In *Deliberative Systems:

Deliberative Democracy at the Large Scale, edited by J. Parkinson and J. Mansbridge, 1–26. Cambridge: Cambridge University Press.

Mansbridge, J., J. Bohman, S. Chambers, D. Estlund, A. Follesdal, A. Fung, C. Lafont, B. Manin, and J. L. Marti. 2010. "The Place of Self-Interest and the Role of Power in Deliberative Democracy." *Journal of Political Philosophy* 18 (1): 64–100. doi:10.1111/j.1467-9760.2009.00344.x.

Mansbridge, J., 1999. "Everyday Talk in the Deliberative System." In *Deliberative Politics*, edited by. S. Macedo, 211–239. New York: Oxford University Press.

Moore, A. 2010. "Public Bioethics and Deliberative Democracy." *Political Studies* 58 (4): 715–730. doi:10.1111/post.2010.58.issue-4.

Moore, A., and K. O'Doherty. 2014. "Deliberative Voting: Clarifying Consent in a Consensus Process." *Journal of Political Philosophy* 22 (3): 302–319. doi:10.1111/jopp.2014.22.issue-3.

Moore, A., and J. Stilgoe. 2009. "Experts and Anecdotes: The Role of "Anecdotal Evidence" in Public Scientific Controversies." *Science, Technology & Human Values* 34 (5): 654–677. doi:10.1177/0162243908329382.

Nullmeier, F., and T. Pritzlaff. 2010. "The Implicit Normativity of Political Practices. Analyzing the Dynamics and Power Relations of Committee Decision-Making." *Critical Policy Studies* 3 (3–4): 357–374. doi:10.1080/19460171003619758.

Parkinson, J. 2006. *Deliberating in the Real World*. Oxford: Oxford University Press.

Rescher, N. 1993. *Pluralism: Against the Demand for Consensus*. Oxford: Oxford University Press.

Richardson, H. 2002. *Democratic Autonomy: Public Reasoning about the Ends of Policy*. Oxford: Oxford University Press.

Richardson, H. 2012. "Relying on Experts As We Reason Together." *Kennedy Institute of Ethics Journal* 22 (2): 91–110. doi:10.1353/ken.2012.0007.

Schudson, M. 1999. *The Good Citizen: A History of Civic Life*. Cambridge, MA: Harvard University Press.

Steiner, J., A. Bächtiger, M. Spörndli, and M. Steenbergen. 2004. *Deliberative Politics in Action: Analysing Parliamentary Discourse*. Cambridge: Cambridge University Press.

Steiner, J., and R. H. Dorff. 1980. "Decision by Interpretation: A New Concept for an Often Overlooked Decision Mode." *British Journal of Political Science* 10 (1): 1–13. doi:10.1017/S0007123400001988.

Sunstein, C. R. 1999."Agreement without Theory". In *Deliberative Politics: Essays on Democracy and Disagreement*, edited by S. Macedo, 123–150. Oxford: Oxford University Press.

Thompson, D. F. 1999. "Democratic Secrecy." *Political Science Quarterly* 114 (2): 181–193. doi:10.2307/2657736.

Thompson, D. F. 2008. "Deliberative Democratic Theory and Empirical Political Science." *Annual Review of Political Science* 11: 497–520. doi:10.1146/annurev.polisci.11.081306.070555.

Turner, S. P. 2003. *Liberal Democracy 3.0*. London: Sage.

Urbinati, N. 2010. "Unpolitical Democracy." *Political Theory* 38 (1): 65–92. doi:10.1177/0090591709348188.

Urfalino, P. 2006. "Apparent Consensus and Voting: Two Modes of Collective Decision-Making." Presented at the workshop on The Mechanisms of Collective Decision-Making, Adriano Olivetti Foundation, Rome, April 29.

Urfalino, P. 2012. "Reasons and Preferences in Medicine Evaluation Committees." In *Collective Wisdom: Principles and Mechanisms*, edited by H. Landemore and J. Elster, 173–202. Cambridge: Cambridge University Press.

Warren, M. E. 1996. "Deliberative Democracy and Authority." *The American Political Science Review* 90 (1): 46–60. doi:10.2307/2082797.

Warren, M. E., and H. Pearse. 2008. "Introduction: Democratic Renewal and Deliberative Democracy." In *Designing Deliberative Democracy: The British Columbia Citizen's Assembly*, edited by M. E. Warren and H. Pearse, 1–19. Cambridge: Cambridge University Press.

Wynne, B. 1989. "Sheepfarming after Chernobyl: A Case Study in Communicating Scientific Information." *Environment: Science and Policy for Sustainable Development* 31 (2): 10–39. doi:10.1080/00139157.1989.9928930.

Reflections on the theory of deliberative systems

John S. Dryzek

ABSTRACT
I address some of the strengths and weaknesses of the deliberative systems approach identified by the contributors to this special issue on the theory of deliberative systems. Their contributions signal significant advance in the approach. These papers show once again that deliberative democracy as a field is very good at recognizing and remedying its own shortcomings, as well as reformulating itself in response to critics.

Alternative histories

According to Elstub, Ercan, and Mendonça in their introduction to this two-part symposium, we can understand the history of deliberative democracy in terms of its generations. I seem to be placed in their first, second, and fourth generations – though I think I would be equally at home in their third. Being a member of my intellectual great-grandfather's generation (as well as my grandfather's generation, and great-grandson's generation) could make life a little confusing for me, though I'm sure a Dr. Who scriptwriter could make sense of it. The 'generations' terminology suggests to me a neat periodization and classification of particular works. Closer examination might reveal a more nuanced story, but simplification has its uses (especially in pedagogy).

This is not the place to reflect on the details of intellectual history (which will be the topic of one chapter of the *Oxford Handbook of Deliberative Democracy*, now in preparation). But in this journal in particular, it should be noted that the way Elstub, Ercan, and Mendonça characterize the first generation as involving 'an emphasis on normative theorizing' does not do justice to the important role for deliberative democracy played by work in the development of critical policy studies in the 1980s. At that time, the vocabulary of 'deliberative democracy' did not exist, but a lot of work at the critical end of the policy field pointed in its direction (for example, Torgerson 1986; Fischer and Forester 1987). Some of the key people involved have more recently played editorial parts in this *Critical Policy Studies* journal.

Anyway, ever since the field began to take more explicit shape under the deliberative democracy title after 1990, there has been an ambition to render whole political systems more deliberatively democratic. This ambition soon extended beyond the nation-state to the global level. At the same time, real-world experimentation often involved the design and close study of micro-level forums, such as mini-publics and (often in less explicitly deliberative terms) exercises in dispute resolution. The attractions of the micro level are easy to understand; it is so much easier to innovate piecemeal rather than changing whole systems, and empirical study is so much more straightforward when one can exercise some control over conditions and gather data that is well bounded in time and place. Whatever their limits, when it comes to contributing to political transformation, mini-publics in particular have provided most of the empirical analyses that make deliberative democracy exemplary across political theory and social science for its integration of normative theoretical concerns and sophisticated empirical analysis. When it comes to practical impact, many practitioners and most observers of mini-publics agree that we must attend closely to their place in larger processes, to whose transformation and deliberative capacity they ought to be able to contribute.

To the deliberative system

The deliberative systems approach represents the latest phase of the field's macro concerns. First introduced by Mansbridge (1999) in somewhat tentative fashion (mainly to establish the importance of 'everyday talk' in deliberative politics), there has been an explosion of work in this idiom in recent years. The papers in this two-part *Critical Policy Studies* symposium all contribute to further development of what Elstub, Ercan, and Mendonça tell us is the fourth generation of deliberative democracy (though the earlier generations have not died yet). Rather than just celebrating the systemic turn, these papers also identify some of the limitations and problems of systems thinking – suggesting perhaps the seeds of a fifth generation. These papers confirm the fact that deliberative democracy as a field is actually very good at recognizing and remedying its own weaknesses, as well as reformulating itself in response to critics. In this, at least the field compares well with other normative theories of democracy such as agonism, which (at least when its adherents criticize deliberative democracy) forgets nothing and learns nothing. Another contrast along these lines can be made with the old-fashioned electoralist models of democracy still deployed by most democratization scholars in the field of comparative politics, oblivious to developments in thinking about the meaning of democracy, and with no idea that they may have missed something important (such as deliberation).

In this spirit, I will take up some of the weaknesses of the deliberative systems approach identified by the contributors to this first part of the *Critical Policy Studies* symposium on the theory of deliberative systems.

Recognizing deliberative systems and their boundaries

How do we recognize a deliberative system when we see one? It is possible to specify what a deliberative system should look like in some normatively ideal sense – though even here there is little consensus among theorists. When it comes to the empirical study of real-world phenomena in deliberative system terms, I believe there is no escape from interpretive judgment in the definition of the system. And in defining the system, one should not make the mistake of thinking it has to be already deliberative – or meet some minimum threshold of deliberativeness to be analyzed in these terms. Rather, it is best to think of a particular system as being potentially deliberative. It is then possible to look at the actual performance of the parts – and the whole – in light of some deliberative standards about what they ought to be doing. With this idiom of inquiry in mind, it might be possible to identify deliberative systems with particular governments; or with governance arrangements; or with governance arrangements on particular issues. So, we could treat the entire government structure of a country as a deliberative system. Or, we could look at (say) the global governance of intellectual property rights in these terms.

This sort of interpretive view is not exactly the approach to defining deliberative systems taken in the article on 'The Boundaries of a Deliberative System' by William Smith, who wants to be much more discriminating when it comes to what is allowed into the system, and what needs to be excluded. Smith's title suggests it is trying to figure out how to draw the boundaries of deliberative systems. However, I think what he is really doing is providing an admission test for particular components of a system, which is not exactly the same as drawing boundaries (because such drawing also requires other judgments concerning, for example, the jurisdiction, level of governance, substantive area, and time that a particular system covers). For Smith, deliberative potential is not enough for a component to be admitted into the system; instead, he demands deliberative actuality. In this light, only truly deliberative action belongs in a deliberative system; though non-deliberative components can be recognized in the environment of a system and as having an influence upon it. Here, Smith appears to reject what is to many others (for example, Mansbridge et al. 2012, 3) a core axiom of the deliberative systems approach: that non-deliberative practices can have positive systemic deliberative consequences, and as such should be treated as part of the system. On closer inspection, however, Smith does actually allow the kind of effect in question – he just wants to put it in a box outside the system as he defines it. In the end, I think it matters little whether non-deliberative practices with positive systemic consequences are defined in or out, provided they can still be connected with the system.

Now, comprehensively and uncontroversially deliberative actions are always going to be in short supply in this imperfect world (why else would the normative project of deliberative democracy be needed?). So, judgment must be exercised as to whether or not particular parts merit categorization as deliberative enough to be included – as Smith puts it, 'to embody paradigmatic features of deliberative conduct to an appropriate degree'. If the judgment is too stringent, the deliberative system loses all empirical purchase if we follow Smith's path. It will also be hard to know what to make of a system where one or two bits are deliberative – but other crucial bits (such as connections between different forums that might be internally deliberative – for example, the scientific assessments and citizen forums described in the article by Moore) do not seem to be. Presumably, we should then just discard the case. If the judgment is too forgiving – and this is a definite danger in taking a deliberative systems approach – then the deliberative system loses its distinctiveness, and the normative project fails. So, the precise content of standards for judgment becomes crucial.

To qualify as deliberative action for Smith, a practice must embody all the deliberative virtues: reflection, respect, and dialogue. This is actually not a complete list (missing out, for example, justification and inclusion). But a sequencing account of a deliberative system could (rightly) point out that not all the virtues need to be displayed to equal extent – or even at all – in different locations in a deliberative system, defined now by time as well as space. Seeking justification and reflection in (say) two different chambers of parliament, or two different rooms in a jury trial, is perfectly defensible.

A real puzzle arises once we recognize the corollary of the fact that non-deliberative practices can have positive consequences for the deliberative system: for it is also the case that intrinsically deliberative practices can have negative consequences for the system as a whole (as Smith recognizes). So, for example, some theorists (notably Rawls 1993, 231) point to the US Supreme Court as an exemplary deliberative institution. But, assuming the Court works in this fashion (a big assumption in these days when it divides along predictable partisan lines), might not its existence free members of Congress to engage in irresponsible demagoguery, secure in the knowledge that there is a deliberative institution elsewhere in the system that will save them from themselves? Though he does not discuss this particular kind of case, I think Smith's answer would have to be that the Supreme Court belongs in the deliberative system, but Congress does not (on this stylized account). But, does that then suggest Congress need not be held to deliberative standards of the sought that would apply if it were treated as potentially part of the system?

The critics noted in passing by Smith and discussed at greater length by Moore in his article who charge expert bodies and mini-publics with 'deliberative elitism' also believe that intrinsically deliberative practices can have non-deliberative or even anti-deliberative systemic consequences. For these bodies might be internally deliberative, but they might detract from the deliberative qualities of the political system as a whole, by preventing deliberation in the larger public sphere that is consequential in the political system. Moore has a good answer to such critics concerning how to integrate such bodies to good effect into the system (which I will return to below), but it seems all Smith says is that they should be accepted as part of the system on the grounds that they embody deliberative action.

Dangers and connectors

Ricardo Mendonça in his paper on 'Mitigating Systemic Dangers' joins Smith in worrying about casual use of the deliberative systems approach. The first of his worries is plausible, involving potential disempowering of weak actors by requiring that they spread their limited resources across too many locations in a system. It would be possible to see this problem as simply the flip side of having a lot of opportunities for influence, which is not such a bad democratic thing; Mendonça's first worry would apply to the degree a democracy provides multiple opportunities for input. His second worry is that decision makers in a deliberative system have discretion concerning which bit or bits of public opinion to pay attention to. This seems like something that could conceivably happen in real-world politics (though how often?), but also something that is readily criticized in a deliberative systems framework, as a deliberate obstruction of communication by refusal to listen on the part of the powerful. Mendonça's third worry is that different discourses may dominate different bits of a deliberative system, obstructing communication between them. Mendonça gives no examples of this third possibility, but it is very easy to see when, for example, radical antiglobalization discourses are present in the public sphere – but are ignored in decision-making.

The problems identified by Mendonça are real and his proposals in the form of 'inducers of connectivity' (why not just 'connectors'?) are compelling. Indeed, his proposals are really just reiterations of the need to take a systemic approach: there cannot be a system without connectivity. Yet it is not entirely clear how the proposals actually speak to the first two problems. The third problem is easy: if we have no connectivity because of different discourses dominating different places, it needs to be induced, and someone needs to do it. But even here, connectivity may not be enough. With antiglobalization discourse, for example, it is not that decision makers do not hear it and need to be reminded of it. They are probably aware of the counter-discourse, but do not want to act or cannot act upon it because they are imprisoned by their location in the political economy (to use the language of Lindblom 1982). What this suggests is that not all the problems identified with deliberative systems can be solved by connectivity: instead, this particular one requires wholesale critique of the political economy in which deliberative systems are embedded.

Experts and citizens

Once we get past his 'Deliberative Elitism' title (which once again fails to do full justice to the content of the paper), Alfred Moore provides a compelling way to think about how to integrate expert knowledge into a deliberative system in a way that is true to core commitments of deliberative democracy. Mini-publics prove especially useful in enabling deliberative citizen scrutiny of expert judgments, and here, Moore joins a number of authors who have recently contemplated the role that mini-publics can play in deliberative systems (see, for example, Hendriks 2006; Niemeyer 2014), as opposed to seeing them as substitutes for deliberative systems, which is what a number of critics both inside and outside the field seem to fear. The broader citizenry can then judge the conclusions of experts and mini-publics alike. Of course we then need to think about connections between these three sorts of locations in a deliberative system – and what Mendonça has to say about agents of connectivity could be drawn upon here, though Moore himself identifies a number of different mechanisms. Moore has less to say about the exercise of formal public authority in the system, but there would be little to stop an application of what Moore says about expert bodies to repositories of public authority such as legislatures or international organizations, which could also be linked to the broader public sphere via mini-publics.

In light of the roles and connections Moore portrays, mini-publics complement rather than displace broad citizen deliberation in the public sphere, and we can see how expertise can be linked in defensible fashion to the broader public sphere in the deliberative system. In addition, the internal workings of expert bodies can themselves be deliberative, thus passing Smith's test for inclusion. Scientific Assessments – such as those of the Intergovernmental Panel on Climate Change (noted by Moore) and the Millennium Ecosystem Assessment – come to mind as bodies that can feature deliberation because experts have to persuade people from different fields (Norgaard 2008). But, even if expert bodies are not especially deliberative, it is still possible to think about the place they might occupy in the system (Smith would object here).

Moore's argument is a vast improvement over other attempts to specify a division of deliberative labor in the system between experts and lay citizens – for example, naive suggestions that citizens should deliberate about the aims of public policy, leaving experts to deliberate about means to those ends (Christiano 2012).

Moore does eventually come round to the elitism in his title, showing that recognizing the place of expert bodies and mini-publics in deliberative democracy does not mean that they need to be treated as deliberative elites

From theory to empirical study

Theory does of course have its place, and the three articles I have discussed make significant contributions to development of the theory of deliberative systems. The deliberative systems approach does, however, currently feature a lot of theorizing (though this theorizing does have empirical illustration) and relatively little close study of actual deliberative systems in the terms that theorists specify. Many of the theoretical worries raised by critics ought to be capable of amelioration (or at least illumination) by close analysis of actual cases. Yet again we are reminded of the wisdom of Nike: 'Just do it!' And that is where the pieces collected in the second part of this *Critical Policy Studies* symposium will come in.

Disclosure statement

No potential conflict of interest was reported by the author.

Funding

This work was supported by funding from the Australian Research Council, Laureate Fellowship [FL140100154].

References

Christiano, T. 2012. "Rational Deliberation Among Citizens and Experts." In *Deliberative Systems: Deliberative Democracy at the Large Scale*, edited by J. Parkinson and J. Mansbridge, 27–51. Cambridge: Cambridge University Press.

Fischer, F., and J. Forester, eds. 1987. *Confronting Values in Policy Analysis: The Politics of Criteria*. Newbury Park, CA: Sage.

Hendriks, C. M. 2006. "Integrated Deliberation: Reconciling Civil Society's Dual Role in Deliberative Democracy." *Political Studies* 54: 486–508. doi:10.1111/j.1467-9248.2006.00612.x.

Lindblom, C. E. 1982. "The Market as Prison." *The Journal of Politics* 44: 324–336. doi:10.2307/2130588.

Mansbridge, J. 1999. "Everyday Talk in the Deliberative System." In *Deliberative Politics: Essays on Democracy and Disagreement*, edited by S. Macedo, 211–238. New York, NY: Oxford University Press.

Mansbridge, J., J. Bohman, S. Chambers, T. Christiano, A. Fung, J. Parkinson, D. F. Thompson, and M. E. Warren. 2012. "A Systemic Approach to Deliberative Democracy." In *Deliberative Systems: Deliberative Democracy at the Large Scale*, edited by J. Parkinson and J. Mansbridge, 1–26. Cambridge: Cambridge University Press.

Niemeyer, S. 2014. "Scaling Up Deliberation to Mass Publics: Mini-Publics in a Deliberative System." In *Deliberative Mini-Publics: Involving Citizens in the Democratic Process*, edited by K. Grönlund, A. Bächtiger, and M. Setälä, 177–202. Colchester: ECPR Press.

Norgaard, R. B. 2008. "Finding Hope in the Millennium Ecosystem Assessment." *Conservation Biology* 22 (4): 862–869. doi:10.1111/cbi.2008.22.issue-4.

Rawls, J. 1993. *Political Liberalism*. New York, NY: Columbia University Press.

Torgerson, D. 1986. "Between Knowledge and Politics: Three Faces of Policy Analysis." *Policy Sciences* 19: 33–59. doi:10.1007/BF02124483.

Message received? Examining transmission in deliberative systems

John Boswell, Carolyn M. Hendriks and Selen A. Ercan

ABSTRACT
With the systemic turn in deliberative democratic theory, there is renewed and broadened emphasis on the inclusion of all affected by a political decision in the making of those decisions. The key enabler of inclusion at a system level is *transmission*: theoretically, a deliberative system is more democratic if it can foster the transmission of claims and ideas across different sites, especially between informal sites of public deliberation and the more formal institutions of political decision-making. Yet little is known about the mechanisms of transmission in deliberative systems. How, and to what effect, is transmission facilitated in practice? This paper draws on case studies of three promising mechanisms of deliberative transmission: institutional, innovative and discursive. We discuss the key factors that enable or hinder different forms of transmission, and reflect on the ways in which they might be strengthened in deliberative systems. Our analysis suggests that the systemic turn in deliberative democracy should go hand-in-hand with a nuanced understanding of how transmission occurs across different sites. As such, our discussion has important implications for deliberative scholars and practitioners as they go about conceptualizing, studying and steering deliberative democracy at the large scale.

Introduction

The 'deliberative system' has become an increasingly popular theme among theorists, researchers and even practitioners of deliberative democracy – as this special issue attests. The central notion of a deliberative system is that deliberation is conceived of as an activity occurring in differentiated ways across a range of interconnected communicative sites. Though there may be little or no perfect democratic deliberation in any site, the collective work done across the system may still produce a suitably deliberative democratic whole (see Mansbridge et al. 2012; Parkinson 2006; Dryzek 2009). The systemic turn expands the range of spaces and institutions that can be understood in deliberative democratic terms and opens up new areas of focus for policymakers, reformers and researchers. Certainly, thus far, the idea of the deliberative system has been closely associated with the search for, or infusion of, crucial aspects of deliberation in unexpected places (e.g. Mansbridge 1999; Chambers 2012).

However, beyond ideal theoretical prescriptions, we still know very little about if and how these different deliberative sites link together, and how they constitute an inclusive deliberative system in practice. This paper fills this gap: it asks how, and to what effect, ideas and claims are transmitted in practice between different sites across deliberative systems.

Building on previous work outlining the value of interpretive research in understanding deliberative systems (Ercan, Hendriks, and Boswell 2015), we approach this task by drawing across three interpretive case studies of deliberative systems in different policy areas, each illustrating a different mechanism of deliberative transmission at work. The first case exemplifies the prospects for transmission within existing democratic institutions through a study of public deliberation on 'honor killings'; the second case considers how transmission works in the context of a novel democratic institution where a mini-public on energy policy was coupled with a parliamentary inquiry; the last case considers how narratives about the issue of obesity facilitate the transmission of claims across sites and institutions. Combined, these studies provide rich insights into how transmission occurs in practice, how it can be enabled but also distorted and what this means for inclusion across deliberative systems.

The paper proceeds in four sections. First, we define the concept of transmission and outline the key mechanisms that deliberative democrats hold hope for enabling effective transmission. Second, we outline our case-based approach and justify its value in examining transmission across deliberative systems. Third, we present an analysis of transmission in each of the three cases. Fourth, we discuss the implications of our empirical insights on recent debates on deliberative systems.

Theorizing transmission

Transmission is a central concept underpinning the shift to a deliberative systems perspective. The idea is that claims must be proliferated across and among sites so that they can be challenged and 'laundered' through the system. Transmission places the emphasis on the connections between the various components that make up deliberative systems, particularly between public and empowered (decision-making) sites.

Especially important are the works of Habermas (1996), which prefigures deliberative systems, and Dryzek (2009), which builds on this account to provide the most comprehensive account of deliberative transmission to date. Habermas (1996) constructs a 'two-track' model of democratic legitimation. In the first track, deliberation in the public sphere fosters 'opinion formation', where affected publics reach agreement on how to deal with complex and contested matters. The resulting opinions are then transferred, via the media, social movements and election campaigns, to the second track, comprised of binding assemblies of 'will formation' where laws are debated and passed. Dryzek (2009) subsequently points to weaknesses in this model – most noticeably its simplistic representation of communication in contemporary politics, especially given the absence of many of the new sites and forms of deliberation associated with the move toward a more deliberative form of governance – but builds on it to produce an account of transmission more attuned to the complexities of deliberative systems. For him, there should be a multiplicity of sites on a spectrum from 'public' to 'empowered' space, with the work of the deliberative system to transmit ideas and claims from the former to the latter. Dryzek accepts the need for some process of filtration – indeed, the role of intermediary sites is to sift and sort appropriate public claims to be presented in empowered sites. Nevertheless, the thrust of his account is that transmission should primarily involve the movement of claims from more informal, open sites to the more formal, closed institutions. Transmission, as envisaged by Habermas and augmented by Dryzek, is what conceptually makes the proliferation of deliberative sites a *system*, and a *democratic* one at that.

But, as with much of the emerging deliberative systems' account, the extent to which this theoretically elegant vision plays out in reality remains unclear. This is not to say that the way in which ideas and opinions shift through democracies is a complete 'black box'. There is a growing body of literature on the affinities (or lack thereof) between key democratic sites, especially on the links between mass media coverage and legislative attention (e.g. see Gamson and Modigliani 1989; Ferree et al. 2002; Yanovitzky 2002; McCombs 2005). There is a larger body of scholarship still on policy responsiveness to public opinion (see Shapiro 2011 for an overview). However, neither body of literature encompasses the broad array of sites and institutions through which claims travel in a deliberative system. More importantly, neither focuses at all on whether, and to what extent, such transmission is *deliberative* in nature.

Understanding transmission, in these terms, requires more than studying whether claims flow through institutions. Transmission is a complex political process. It cannot be equated with legislative responsiveness to public opinion. This might occur, but more important from a deliberative standpoint is that there is recognition of claims raised in public space and careful consideration of them within more empowered settings. Understanding transmission, from a deliberative systems perspective, must involve a deeper analysis of how diverse viewpoints are expressed, acknowledged and facilitated, and whether the claims associated with these viewpoints cross-pollinate different deliberative sites. Knowledge of transmission in these terms undoubtedly remains a significant gap.

The nascent literature on deliberative systems points to at least three key mechanisms of transmission, each involving interplay between individual agency and institutional structure.[1] One is 'middle democracy' (Gutmann and Thompson 1996), whereby actors throughout the system can pursue matters of common interest through existing democratic spaces or conventional institutional links between public and empowered space (e.g. public hearings, legislative inquiries). Two is democratic innovation, with emphasis on the 'coupling' of inclusive participatory forums to empowered institutions (see Hendriks 2016). Three is discourses, understood as broad ensembles of ideas, categories and metaphors, which Dryzek (2009) in particular hopes can enable actors across the system to draw on as shared argumentative resources.

In this paper, we draw together three different case studies, focused on each of these proposed mechanisms, to shed greater light on deliberative transmission in practice. We show how these mechanisms work (or don't) in practice.

Transmission in practice: approach and case studies

This paper brings together empirical insights from three research projects, each conducted separately by the contributing authors. Each project focuses on a particular policy controversy and offers an analysis of that controversy with focus on a particular mechanism of transmission. Nevertheless, there is considerable value in placing these studies side by side and laying bear the commonalities and discrepancies among them.

First, though the studies emphasize different transmission mechanisms – the 'honor killings' case focuses on transmission via existing democratic spaces; the energy case focuses on transmission via democratic innovation; the obesity case focuses on transmission via narrative – all are concerned with the interplay between institutional and discursive conditions within which deliberation takes place. Furthermore, all recognize that transmission depends on both existing structures and individual agency. Accordingly, the analytical difference in the empirical accounts is more one of accent than of substantive distinction. The findings augment each other.

Second, the deliberative systems that surround each issue have common characteristics that can permit comparison. While the institutional and discursive conditions surrounding these cases are different, these seemingly unrelated issues share important features. Each is complex, in that its implications cross an array of public silos and involve a multiplicity of actors. Each involves significant uncertainty, in respect to both the suite of options available to deal with the issue and the perceived legitimacy of any intervention. And each is politically intractable, in that it has a tendency to mobilize fierce interest or identity politics.

Third, all three analyses share an overarching interpretive orientation, in that they are fundamentally interested in examining how transmission is enacted in practice, taking into account the broader institutional and sociopolitical contexts, as well as the key actors involved. As such, shared themes across the three cases were developed through an iterative process of both individual and communal interpretation of our data and its implications on deliberative scholarship. The overall philosophy is, in this sense, consistent with the interpretive tradition within which each of the projects belongs, and which elsewhere we have argued has much to offer the empirical study of deliberative systems (see Ercan, Hendriks, and Boswell 2015).

What this inductive, mixed-case comparison facilitates is a linking of contextual understanding of political phenomena with broader theoretical ideas (see Flyvbjerg 2006 on the accretion of rich insights from case material). The result is a collective account that is suggestive of 'plausible conjectures' (see Rhodes 2014) that apply across deliberative systems in respect to different jurisdictions, issues and mechanisms, but that still achieves some of the richness and vividness associated with single case research. Taken together, then, these cases offer timely insights into emerging ideas about deliberative systems. Our exploration sheds light not just on whether transmission occurs but on how, under what conditions and to what effect.

Case 1: honor killing debate and the role of the institutional transmission mechanisms

The first case focuses on how transmission occurs through conventional institutions of representative democracies. More specifically, it examines the extent to which existing mechanisms and tools (such as parliamentary inquiries) can facilitate the transmission of 'problem definitions' and possible solutions from various sites of public debate and deliberation. The case concentrates on the institutional tools that inhabit the area between the informal and formal spheres of democracy. It illustrates the importance of institutional links for enabling the transmission of claims from public to empowered spaces.

The case discussion here draws on a comparative broader study of deliberative systems surrounding 'honor killing' debates in two democracies, Britain and Germany (Ercan 2012). 'Honor killing' is usually defined as the murder or attempted murder of young women by family members on 'cultural grounds' for behavior said to offend the principles of family or community honor. In recent years, there were heated debates over these murders in both Britain and Germany in similar sites including media, parliaments and courts. When seen from a deliberative system perspective, these debates can be seen as diffuse and collective 'meaning-making processes' characterized by the contestation of discourses of what an 'honor killing' is and what needs to be done about it.

In line with this, this study involved mapping the key sites, actors and discourses around these murders and analyzing whether and how certain discourses moved across different sites, and identifying the factors that enabled the movement and transmission of discourses from one site to another. In doing so, the study drew on a variety of sources including documents produced by government agencies (such as police reports, court verdicts, national plans and strategies, reports from government inquiries into 'honor killings' and written consultation responses); documents produced by civil society organizations and advocacy groups (such as strategy papers and campaign information from various women's organizations); transcripts of parliamentary debates and motions on 'honor killing', which are consistently well documented in both countries; selected media coverage; and published academic research on the issue of 'honor killing'. The study used these documents to reconstruct the 'honor killing' debates in Britain and Germany from a deliberative systems perspective.

A close analysis of public and policy debates over the issue of 'honor killing' revealed that these murders came to the political agenda in both Germany and Britain around the same time (in Britain in 2003 after the murder of Heshu Yones, and in Germany in 2005 after the murder of Hatun Sürücü) and debated in similar ways. In both countries, two particular discourses of these murders gained traction: culture-based and gender-based discourses. Those employing culture-based discourses defined 'honor killing' as a culturally specific type of murder that occurs only in minority cultures. Such discourses were particularly evident in the case of German public and policy debates. Here, 'honor killing' is predominantly framed as an indicator of failed integration of minorities in Germany (Ercan 2015). The below excerpt from a press release of the Christian Democratic Union (CDU) provides a clear example of culture-based discourses of these murders:

> The concept of so-called multicultural society has failed. It supported the establishment of parallel societies and the segmentation of cultural groups with their own value systems. This also entails the worst form of self-justice: the so-called honour killing.[2]

Similar culture-based discourses were obviously present also in the case of Britain. The alternative 'problem definition' of 'honor killing' was suggested by gender-based discourses, which depicted these murders under the broader paradigm in terms of domestic violence, or 'violence against women' in general (Ercan 2014, 2016). The gender-based discourse emphasized the patriarchal roots of 'honor killing' that occur worldwide: *whenever a man regards a woman as his property and seeks to uphold that false assumption by cruel and abusive force.*[3] In his parliamentary speech on 'honor killing', Lord Giddens, for instance, suggested mainstreaming these murders under the umbrella of violence against women. He argued that that Britain is *by no means free of the impulsions and imperatives which underline* honour *killings more generally.*[4]

In both Britain and Germany, the discursive contestations over the meaning of 'honor killing' occurred mainly between culture-based and gender-based frames of these murders and yielded different kinds of outcomes. What is particularly instructive for the purposes of this paper is that although the gender-based frames were evident in the public space in both countries, their transmission to empowered space was possible only in the case of Britain. In other words, the deliberative system that emerged around the issue of 'honor killing' in Britain allowed the alternative 'problem definitions' developed in one sphere to flow to others, whereas this was not the case in Germany. This was largely due to the fact that the institutional transmission mechanisms that were present in the case of Britain were absent in Germany.

The British 'honor killing' debate draws our attention also to the importance of institutional transmission mechanisms located at the intersection of public space and empowered space. In this context, two transmission mechanisms that were present in British case and absent in the German case deserve particular attention: *semiformal institutions* and *government sponsored inquires* that are designed to address the issues around honor-based violence including 'honor killings'. In terms of the former, the Women's National Council (WNC) was particularly instrumental in terms of enabling transmission of 'gender-based frames' from public space to empowered space. The WNC represented more than 450 partners including women and women's organizations in England, Northern Ireland, Scotland and Wales (Donaghy 2007). The presence of umbrella organizations such as the WNC provided feminist counter publics with the incentives to coordinate their strategies within more encompassing frames. The WNC also offered an important institutional opportunity structure for marginalized groups, most notably for women in minority communities to articulate their concerns and influence state policies on violence against women. The WNC steered a number of public consultations with women in ethnic minorities with the aim of informing government policies (e.g. see She Who Disputes: Muslim Women Shape the Debate 2006). Women's organizations have successfully utilized the WNC and the public consultations it has facilitated with women in minority communities to influence state policies and establish a gender-based definition of domestic violence and 'honor killing' (Predelli 2009).

The second institutional transmission mechanisms, namely the government-sponsored enquires over the issue of 'honor killing', assumed a similar function of deliberative transmission. In July 2007, the House of Commons Home Affairs Select Committee launched an inquiry into issues around violence against women, which consisted of a series of consultations with key personnel and survivors, visits to women's organizations and refuges, oral evidence from expert witnesses and survivors and an online consultation that ran for 6 weeks from January 2008. This inquiry was particularly influential in changing the terms of the 'honor killing' debate in Britain. The final report of this inquiry characterized 'honor killing' as gender-based violence and called government to tackle these crimes through the prism of gender (Home Affairs Committee 2008).

Both institutional mechanisms discussed here, semiformal institutions and government inquiries focusing particularly on the issue of 'honor killing', were missing in the case of Germany. Here, the main transmission mechanism between public space and empowered space has been political parties and party-affiliated organizations (*Parteinahe Stiftungen*). Political parties serve as the central mechanisms for 'political linkage' between civil society and formal decision-making institutions. They are responsible for transmitting the political will into political action (so called *Transmissionsriemen der Politik*). Although this is a role typically attributed to all political parties, what merits particular attention in the German context is the lack of any other institutionalized mechanisms enabling the transmission of public opinion into decision-making. Insofar as other actors, such as women's or migrant organizations, seek a policy voice in Germany, the primary route is through political parties and party organizations. Even strong civil society movements cannot rely exclusively on 'extraparliamentary politics' (Rucht 1996, 201). Put differently, the German political system privileges individuals and organizations with close ties to political parties. Only they have the potential to access and influence the decision mechanisms.

In the case of 'honor killing' debate, the party-dominated institutional structure in Germany hindered the possibilities for direct interaction and transmission between counterpublics in the public space and formal decision-making circles in the empowered space. Unless such actors were tied to political parties, their 'problem definitions' and policy proposals remained unheard. Also, what weakened the chances of gender-based discourses to be transmitted to the empowered space in the case of Germany was that here feminist groups did not employ 'gender-based' discourses of 'honor killing'. In contrast with Britain, German feminists defined 'honor killing' as an issue that concerned solely the members of patriarchal cultures, most notably Islamic cultures (Ercan 2015; Ferree 2012).

A close analysis of the British and German 'honor killing' debates over time reveals that there are several factors that affect the prospects of transmission across different sites. In this sense, it would be mistaken to reduce the differences between these two cases to the differences in the institutional settings of these countries. In other words, although crucial, the institutional linkage between different spheres alone does not guarantee a successful transmission. Besides the presence of institutional channels, the transmission of ideas or discourses from one site to another also depends on the discursive opportunity structures in a given society at a given time. The discursive opportunity structures are about the 'established notions of who and what are considered reasonable, sensible and legitimate' over the issue at stake (Koopmans 2004, 451). In other words, such structures are about the question of who is recognized as the main meaning-making body on the issue at hand. In the British 'honor killing' debate, counterpublics organized around women's organizations have had a 'discursive advantage' as they have been recognized by the government as the main meaning-making institutions. Government agencies openly acknowledge their expertise in this field and emphasize the need for collaboration to address 'honor killing' effectively. Several policy documents such as White Papers and consultation reports point to the preferred role and legitimacy of women's organizations. Similarly, most media reports have included their views on the issue of 'honor killing'. The discursive establishment of women's organizations as central actors in policy reports, in the media as well as in the course of the parliamentary debates, provided a conducive context for their claims to be transmitted to decision-making cycles and ultimately changing the terms of the 'honor killing' debate in Britain. This is particularly manifest in the way 'honor killings' have been debated in the empowered sites, most notably in the parliament (Ercan 2016). The subsequent shift of framing of 'honor killing' in the key government documents (such as the strategy papers of the Association of Chief Police Officers of England, Wales and Northern Ireland or Crown Prosecution Service) as a gender-based violence can be seen as an indicator that the transmitted arguments were seriously considered with a view to revising views and opinions in the empowered sites.

Overall, the comparison of how the institutional differences between Germany and Britain played out in the public and policy debates over 'honor killing' shows that many of the mechanisms located in and around existing democratic institutions assume an important role in enabling transmission of ideas from public to empowered spaces.

Case 2: energy debate and the role of innovative transmission mechanisms

The second case examines transmission between an innovative democratic process engaging 'everyday citizens' and a conventional empowered deliberative institution. More specifically, it draws on an empirical study of a mini-public that was formally embedded in a parliamentary inquiry in 2012 on energy policy in the state of New South Wales, Australia (see Hendriks 2013).

Mini-publics stand at the heart of the debates on democratic innovations. Many scholars hold great aspirations for the capacity of mini-publics to act as 'deliberative transmitters' (see Grönlund, Bächtiger, and Setälä 2014). For example, mini-publics are advocated as a means: to indicate how an informed public would vote (Fishkin 2009); to link informal and formal deliberative sites (Hendriks 2006); to transmit information on public views on complex issues to executive agencies and to the voting public (Mackenzie and Warren 2012), to promote mass public deliberation by distilling, constraining and synthesizing discourses (Niemeyer 2014). In all these proposals, it is assumed that the process and outcomes of mini-publics are transferred into the broader deliberative system. Yet some empirical research suggests that in practice many mini-publics are poor transmitters because they lack any institutional or political connection to relevant and significant deliberative sites in empowered spaces, such as the media, elite committees and parliaments (Ercan and Hendriks 2013; Goodin and Dryzek 2006).

In what follows, we consider how transmission occurs when a mini-public is intentionally established as a mechanism for transmitting ideas from the public into the empowered deliberative space of a parliamentary committee, and then onto parliament. Under deliberation is the dry and technical issue of energy around which there is seldom an active public sphere. While some energy-related topics such as climate change and local infrastructure projects can generate public interest, the complex and more mundane business of generating, distributing and selling energy typically lacks public interest and broad deliberation.

To compensate for this deliberative void, the NSW Parliament's Public Accounts Committee (PAC) took a more proactive approach to soliciting public input into its inquiry into the economics of energy generation.[5] In addition to its conventional consultative activities that included public hearings and written submissions, the PAC incorporated a mini-public process into its Energy Inquiry. The participatory design involved two concurrent citizens' juries involving a total of 54 randomly selected citizens: one run in an urban center (Sydney) and the other in a rural center (Tamworth) (see Hendriks 2013). This was the first consultative exercise of its kind for the NSW parliament. The citizens' juries were asked to consider the financial and public perception aspects of alternative forms of energy generation. Both juries met 4–5 times over a 10-week period between June and August 2012. After several months of deliberation, the juries each produced a report, which were considered by the PAC in the preparation of its own report to parliament that was released in late 2012 (for details, see PAC 2012).

The discussion here draws on a study that examined if, and how, transmission occurred between the mini-public and the relevant elites and their institutions (see Hendriks 2013, 2016). This qualitative study involved semistructured interviews with committee members (six members of parliament (MPs)), direct observations and document analysis of minutes, relevant reports and policy documents. No data was collected to examine transmission between the mini-public and the broader public debate. The analysis suggests that transmission (between the mini-publics and elites) took place on several levels.

First, according to the committee members interviewed, the citizens' recommendations were considered and discussed at length (Hendriks 2013). A number of MPs stated that they particularly valued the citizens' reports because they offered fresh 'common sense' insights into a highly polarized and technical issue. Some MPs interviewed strongly believed that the citizens' recommendations received more weight than other submissions, for example:

> Why the citizens' feedback received such a weighting is because they're not the usual suspects. They're delivering, without any vested interest, their circumstances, their opinions, their impacts, based on the way they see it. And it is valuable because it's happened in this format in a structured and more detailed way than we see often when policies are being debated or reports are being delivered.

Second, there is evidence that some of the citizens' ideas and suggestions shaped the committee's formal report (see PAC 2012). For example, the citizens' reports were included as appendices in the main PAC report, and their recommendations were summarized in Chapter 5. Various elements of the citizens' recommendations were also integrated and taken up throughout the PAC report. For example, recommendation 8 (of 24) explicitly calls on the NSW government to convene more deliberative democracy processes, and recommendation 12 (of 24) explicitly refers to a recommendation of the Sydney citizens' jury '*that electricity network extensions to renewable energy resources should be funded by Commonwealth Government's Clean Energy Finance Corporation*'. Several other recommendations made by the citizens were also incorporated in the PAC report particularly issues of concern to consumers, such as demand management and providing greater opportunities for consumers to participate in the market.

But while the committee may have considered all the citizens recommendation, not all ideas were accepted. As one MP explained:[6]

> The citizens' reports certainly did have an impact and when there's no complicating factors, then it often finds its way into the recommendation or part of the recommendation as well.

In other words, the citizens' reports had an impact on the MPs' recommendations to the extent that they did not compromise existing government policy or party positions. Moreover, some of the more controversial or more radical proposals were noted but not explicitly accepted, others were noted and rejected. For example, the PAC report does not address the broader issue of market distortion that the citizens were concerned about including the long-standing advantage that coal-fired power stations have had in terms of low-cost capital, subsidized supporting infrastructure (such as rail, ports, etc.), and low-cost coal contracts that emerging renewable technologies have not had. More problematic was that some issues of 'public concern' were reduced to 'lack of public information'. For instance, some themes of concern to the citizens, such as their rejection of coal seam gas production due to their lack of confidence in the technology, were addressed in terms of providing the public with more accurate information. Other more politically controversial topics were explicitly avoided altogether such as the role of the state in regulating the electricity market. This watering down or omission of some of the citizens' recommendations suggests a certain kind of blockage in the deliberative system. How severe this blockage is depends on how seriously the MPs considered the citizen ideas and claims in their own deliberations. Best case, they may have considered them at length and then excluded them for particular reasons, or worst case they simply ignored them. The problem with parliamentary committees for this kind of research is that their deliberations are typically behind closed doors, so instead of studying transcripts of committee deliberations, we have to rely on self-reporting. According to the committee members interviewed, all the citizens' recommendations were fully considered and discussed at length.

Third, apart from the selective transmission of substantive policy ideas, in this case there was also some transmission of democratic norms from the mini-public into the parliamentary space. In particular, the mini-public process facilitated a rethinking of how the MPs typically engage with the public in formal parliamentary processes. Most of the PAC committee members (MPs) interviewed were very positive about the mini-public experience, describing it variously as 'a great initiative', an 'interesting exercise' and a 'terrific success'. Several interviewees explicitly stated that the citizens' reports had made significant impact on the committee's internal deliberations. For example, according to one MP:

> It's definitely played a role and I think it's heightened the awareness of a direct democratic approach ... Members of Parliament do have that direct involvement with community members, but this is done in a structured way and I think, when I read the recommendations ... there's no doubt that it's had a good influence, bottom up, into many of the recommendations and the commentary within the report that will ultimately be tabled at Parliament.

Overall then, in this case deliberative transmission was not entirely seamless, but in comparison with other mini-public projects, the citizens' juries and their recommendations here did have an impact on policy recommendations and democratic norms (cf. Goodin and Dryzek 2006). In terms of inclusion, there was an attempt to consider the views of both urban and rural publics, which can differ considerably on energy matters. There is also some evidence that more marginalized ideas were considered and included. For example, the PAC's report seized on some of the more publically controversial recommendations that one of the citizens' juries proposed, such as the need to 'start a discussion about nuclear technology'. Such an idea, though likely to be unpalatable in a wider unreflective public setting, made its way from the mini-public into parliamentary deliberations.

What were some of the factors that aided transmission in this case? First, the process was perceived as novel and welcomed by almost all the elected representatives on the PAC. Most openly admitted in the interviews that they did not know how to best represent their constituents on the issue of energy – it is too dry and technical. So the idea of intentionally forming a public to elicit their views that would then inform their own empowered deliberations was a welcomed one. The MPs not only valued the process, but what the citizens had to say. The process was also strongly supported and championed by the chair of the committee. He not only commissioned the newDemocracy Foundation to undertake the innovation, but he encouraged his fellow committee members to observe the citizens' juries and consider the citizens' recommendations.

Transmission in this case was also facilitated by relationships established between deliberators from different deliberative sites. In this case, the empowered deliberators (MPs) personally met most of the citizen deliberators on several occasions (e.g. when they attended one of the juries) and they witnessed their hard work. The MPs also realized that these ordinary citizens were wrestling with a topic that they (as elected representatives) also had little expertise on. This manifested itself in a sense of obligation that the MPs felt to act on the citizens' input. As one MP explained: 'I think there was an obligation to treat the process and output with respect'. Another MP explained how he wanted to send a message of gratitude to the citizens in the report.

Finally, transmission was aided in this case by the public context of parliament. For example, when the PAC tabled their report in parliament, five of the six PAC members (including those most skeptical of the juries) stood up in the chamber and congratulated the committee, and the citizens for their contributions to the report. In other words, in the public arena of parliament all the MPs were keen to be seen to be supporting the use of the mini-public in this instance.

Overall, this case presents an example of how transmission between an intentionally formed public and an empowered deliberative site might be facilitated. But institutional designs alone are not enough. Effective transmission needs champions who are willing to invite the public into their deliberations, and empowered deliberators willing to welcome and listen to public input.

Case 3: obesity debate and role of discursive transmission mechanisms

The final case also encompasses a range of deliberative settings, but its accent is on a discursive rather than institutional mechanism of transmission: it explores how narratives – broad chronological accounts that actors rely on to make sense of and communicate about complex and contested matters (see Boswell 2013) – transmit ideas, claims and evidence across a range of deliberative sites, from the mass media in public space, via expert and stakeholder settings, to the empowered institutions of policy-making. The particular focus of the case is the issue of obesity in Australia and the UK, where a so-called 'epidemic' of this condition over the last decade or so has prompted considerable policymaking concern, confusion and conflict. Drawing on over 1000 documents, 25 h of video footage and 36 interviews with relevant policy actors across the complex deliberative systems on obesity in both countries, the analysis focuses not just on whether narratives move across sites in the deliberative system, but *how* they move, with a particular focus on how the competing narratives on obesity are performed across public and empowered space.

At a superficial level, the analysis shows that narrative is indeed a key mechanism of transmission in deliberative systems. Most narratives on obesity prevalent in public space – studied here through an analysis of mass media coverage – are transmitted all the way to empowered spaces of policy decision-making. Narrative, in this sense, facilitates a 'communicative miracle' of sorts (see Hajer 1995), allowing lay actors, scientists, professionals, policymakers, NGO and industry representatives a common language with which to assess the problem of obesity and prescribe policy solutions. Indeed, many of the actors interviewed as part of the project spoke of the value of being able to engage across different sites to transmit key ideas and claims to different audiences.

However, the analysis reveals that the extent of this 'communicative miracle' is limited. There is, importantly, significant distortion in the process of transmission. It shows how the critical narratives on obesity that emerge in public space, demanding significant policy change and challenging existing assumptions and practices of policy-making on this issue, are invariably blunted, muted and emptied of specificity as they enter or approach empowered space.

This dynamic is apparent in both deliberative systems, but it is in Australia that it is most stark, never more so than in the wake of the incoming Rudd government's decision to make tackling obesity a priority in its first term. The government seeded deliberation on the issue across a range of expert and stakeholder settings, including a far-reaching Parliamentary Inquiry, a specialist taskforce, and as an important part of the health stream at the innovative 2020 Summit in which Australia's Parliament was opened up to the ideas and engagement of 1000 of the nation's 'best and brightest'. These developments were especially welcome at the time, coming after the conservative Howard-led coalition government's reluctance to prioritize this issue or engage with experts and stakeholders about it. All of these sites elicited impassioned, radical performances of key critical narratives on obesity. Most often this was in the form of the predominant counter-narrative, transmitted from deliberative sites in public space, which sees obesity as an environmental issue created and sustained by the insidious influence of 'Big Food'. All these radical internal deliberations, which typically invoked demands for much stronger regulation of the food sector, then fed into composite outputs, which performed this counter-narrative on obesity in a way that was far more moderate and generic, on the basis that this would be a more 'realistic' way of influencing the status quo. The results were sets of recommendations that worked to 'reduce exposure to food marketing' or 'make healthier choices easier', formulations of this account that permitted plenty of 'wriggle room' in how they could be interpreted. All were then met with an official government response, which, though it continued to feature these key markers of the counter-narrative and some other critical accounts, reinterpreted and reproduced them in such a way as to almost entirely empty them of their original meaning. The policy outcome has been a series of 'soft', moderate and voluntary measures around food reformulation, marketing restrictions and labeling requirements. These moves, and the discussions that surrounded them, provide the veneer of taking seriously the concerns expressed in public spaces. They serve both to avoid deliberation of the substance of these ideas in empowered spaces and to neutralize the broader issue by pushing it down the public agenda (see Boswell 2016).

Some civil society actors spoke with immense frustration about this less miraculous side of transmission via narrative. One commented on his dismay at the manner in which the critical counter-narrative he subscribed to was delivered to empowered space:

> Everything is getting watered down, even the existing documents that have been put together the whole thing about reducing the intake of the unhealthy food and junk foods has been cleansed out of it.[7]

Another argued that the narrative was reflected back from empowered space with distortion:

> Look at the official government response. It's unbelievable. Everything gets watered down, becomes much less than it was this. A few things they're not going to do, but a lot of things, well, 'this will be addressed by this', 'this will be addressed by that'. Oh, a little bit, maybe. And some of those bigger ideas just don't even get addressed![8]

While another, more resigned to this inevitability rather than upset because of it, tried to make sense of this broader dynamic:

> [Decision-makers] need room to move. That's what they need. Even if they've got a frame themselves, they perhaps prefer not to make it too explicit…. There has to be enough space in the frame for the people that they want to participate in this to play, as it were. So you can't set the boundaries too explicitly, and too clearly, and too ideologically, too early.[9]

The point is important because it highlights that transmission cannot be a one-way process. An important complement to Habermas and Dryzek's theoretical ideas about deliberative transmission, in this sense, is Neblo's (2005). He reverses the direction of transmission and places particular emphasis on the need for actors in empowered space to convince those in public space that their claims and actions map onto the public's expressed beliefs and preferences. His account accepts that *transmission* must inevitably involve some *transformation*, encountering formal obstacles and technical elements as 'opinion' is translated into 'will'. This is certainly what we see in the obesity case where administrative, legal and, above all, political obstacles engender a significant transformation of the critical narrative in question. Yet Neblo also stresses the importance of actors in empowered space explicitly addressing and justifying this process in order to sustain their representative claims in a dynamic process. Here, we see a lack of any such public accountability; powerful interests worked to neutralize the issue as the critical narrative became diffused across sites and over time. The obesity case highlights, then, how problematic it can be when distorted transmission goes under-acknowledged and unchecked.

So, although the analysis shows that narrative can operate as a useful discursive mechanism for transmitting claims and ideas across sites of various kinds, its attentiveness to how narratives are performed across these deliberative systems tempers enthusiasm for their democratizing potential in deliberative systems. Indeed, the result is that actors in public space are unaware of, or at least feel powerless to challenge, the muting and moderation of claims as they approach empowered space. In spite of superficial appearances, they do not feel their narrative is adequately represented in empowered space.

Discussion

So, what do these cases collectively tell us about deliberative transmission? Aggregating the insights from across the studies, we can ascertain both potentials and pitfalls, and use them to underpin some suggestions for how deliberative transmission might be strengthened.

On the one hand, the studies highlight the transmission that can and does occur in deliberative systems. Indeed, they show that deliberative transmission occurs in multiple, interrelated ways. While in each case there was some evidence of transmission for policy impact, this is not the only or sometimes even the most important type of transmission on display. In particular, echoing Goodin and Dryzek's (2006) account of the multiple potential impacts of micro citizen deliberation, all three cases highlight the importance of transmission as a form of acknowledgment, legitimating the political value of identities (respectively activist, citizen and expert) that had been excluded or under-acknowledged.

On the other hand, the three studies highlight problems that can inhibit or distort transmission across deliberative systems. They show that transmission is vulnerable to the vagaries of the institutional and political context in which it occurs. Given that all contexts will pose challenges, what can be done to strengthen deliberative transmission to ensure that the claims raised in public space can have a greater influence on deliberation in empowered space? Below we outline three ways in which deliberative transmission can be strengthened.

Enabling transmission

A key message from the case on honor killings is that existing institutions can play an important role in facilitating deliberative transmission from public space to empowered space. When the idea of transmission first emerged, deliberative democrats, such as Habermas (1996) and Dryzek (2009), placed great emphasis on communicative mechanisms, such as the media, protests and boycotts, to connect informal and formal deliberative spheres. Yet our first case shows that some of the semiformal deliberative spaces that are embedded in our existing institutions of representative democracy (such as commissions of inquiry or parliamentary committees) offer crucial mechanisms of transmission between informal public opinion (public space) and formal decision-making cycles (empowered space). In fact, without such spheres and procedurally guaranteed links between informal and formal spheres, 'the legitimacy generated by the former cannot reasonably be claimed by the latter' (Squires 2002, 134). The institutional architecture of deliberative systems must be able to accommodate the variety of affected actors and organizations in public space, providing them with the means to transmit ideas and claims to more formal sites in empowered space.

Yet one important lesson from this case, and that on energy policy, is that relying on the existing institutional architecture may not always be sufficient. Some deliberative systems, like those surrounding the issue of 'honor killings', will continue to feature exclusionary discourses and norms that do not recognize the legitimate meaning-making power of counter publics, and for which there is no easy institutional fix. Other systems, for example, those pertaining to nonsalient issues or technical topics, may lack an active public that is available to mobilize citizens at the grassroots and engage in institutional opportunities to represent their claims. For nonsalient issues, we need not only to seed opportunity structures for engagement, but we also need to create opportunities for publics to form.

The second case study provides insights into how this process of seeding can be done. The key is not that democratic innovations, such as mini-publics, are better than established institutions. Indeed, the limitation with mini-publics, typically, is that they risk being disconnected from many of the elite sites that dominate deliberative systems (Papadopoulos 2012). We show that institutional designs may be needed in some deliberative systems to encourage connections between public spaces and empowered spaces (Hendriks 2016). In this case, a novel democratic innovation, a mini-public, was used to bring together a group of randomly selected citizens to deliberate on a complex issue who then made a series of recommendations for decision makers. Here, a participatory innovation was able to open up an elite and expert-dominated policy issue like energy, and in doing so it offered a vital dose of democratic inclusivity, rendering the otherwise hidden or implicit value assumptions more visible, and transmitting lay perspectives on these that can challenge the status quo.

Amplifying transmission

All three cases demonstrate the importance of agency in amplifying (or muffling) transmission across the deliberative system. While theorists such as Habermas (1996) and Dryzek (2009) might celebrate the role of social movements in deliberative transmission, there is little specific recognition of the role individual actors can play in both assisting, and in some cases distorting, transmission. The Habermasian definition of deliberation as a broad and 'subjectless communication' tends to divert the attention away from the individuals who might facilitate or hinder transmission across different sites. Yet in our second and third cases, we saw how a few particular policy actors were crucial in shaping what voices were heard and how messages were transmitted into more empowered sites. In some instances, as we saw in the energy mini-public, actors play an important mentoring role by encouraging others to listen to the voices of weaker publics and then ensuring that these publics' preferences are transmitted (with greater legitimacy) into empowered spaces.

We also saw in these two cases how actors with privileged access to empowered space could choose not to amplify particular claims. This is not, in itself, problematic. After all, not every claim expressed in public space can or should make it to empowered space. But we might hope to encounter justification for these choices. Indeed, such minimal accountability is a long-held criterion in deliberative democratic theory (Gutmann and Thompson 1996).

The results on this front were mixed. In the energy case, all the recommendations proposed by the citizens were included in the MPs' report and a few made it into the MPs' final recommendations to parliament. The reasoning for why certain proposals from the citizens – especially more radical and politically unpalatable suggestions – did not make it into the MPs' recommendations could have been much more transparent. In the obesity case, there was very little explicit recognition of public claims let alone discussion. There was instead a tacit muting and moderation of claims and ideas in line with *realpolitik* assumptions about what would be feasible given the perceived preferences of powerful stakeholders.

One important ingredient in effective amplification appears to be the connectivity and accountability between the empowered actors and those whose claims they might amplify. In the obesity case, the relationships between the various deliberative sites have been ad hoc, ambiguous and unstructured; as a result, the accountability ties are weak. In contrast, the deliberate coupling of the energy mini-public with the parliamentary committee (PAC) or the parliamentary inquires in the case of British 'honor killing' case certainly facilitated a sense of accountability that the MPs felt toward the citizens or relevant stakeholders (even though there were no formal representative ties). Nevertheless, as in the other cases, the citizens' views were filtered to a certain degree as they made their way into the more empowered space of the parliamentary committee. In our opinion, a more robust deliberative system should strive to make this filtering process as transparent as possible; for example, in the energy case the MPs could have publicly defended why they accepted only some of the citizens' recommendations and, more importantly, why they rejected others.

The overall implication here is that the two-way relationship between actors engaged in empowered spaces and those they represent ought to be structured in deliberative systems so as to better ascertain the strength of their 'representative claims' (Saward 2009).

Sustaining transmission

Finally, the importance of sustaining transmission between public and empowered spaces over time is a theme of all three cases. In the obesity case, we saw how the narratives in public space progressively lost strength and specificity as they moved toward empowered space, highlighting the potential for mere surface transmission in deliberative systems. This points to a need for transmission from public to empowered spaces to work equally well the other way, ensuring that the claims and actions of empowered actors are subject to scrutiny and challenge in public space. Institutional architecture that permits greater deliberative transmission throughout the long journey from public deliberation to policy action can help to shed greater light on, and allow greater public influence over, the inevitable 'wriggle room' that empowered actors rely on.

In the energy case, transmission was not long-lived and it was largely in the direction from public to empowered space. The mini-public served as an 'anticipatory public' not so much to guide executive agencies, as Mackenzie and Warren (2012) suggest, but to inform the specific deliberations of elected representatives. Once the MPs had produced their own report, the citizens' recommendations had served their purpose. Two-way transmission in this case was also minimal. For example, the citizens were not brought together to scrutinize the MPs' recommendations and hold them 'to account' as is the case in some mini-publics (see Hendriks 2005). The mini-public in this case was also not designed to stimulate the sustained mass public deliberation in the way that Niemeyer (2014) envisages.

The 'honor killing' case shows that sustaining transmission between public space and empowered space depends on various factors. Besides the presence of semiformal organizations such as the WNC, transmission depends on discursive legacies, on the established notions of what makes sense, and whose voice is considered reasonable and legitimate in a given society. Furthermore, the chances of transmission of ideas and discourses from public space to empowered space seem to be significantly higher in democracies characterized by the presence of strong and vocal counter publics and where these counter publics are acknowledged as the legitimate participants of meaning-making processes over contested issues.

Conclusion

This paper makes a significant contribution to ideas about transmission in the deliberative system. It shows what kinds of deliberative transmission take place in practice, which mechanisms and features can enable it, but also what institutional or discursive features can distort or inhibit it. The paper therefore contains important lessons both for theory and practice.

For deliberative scholars, the observations lend a more nuanced hue to the notion of transmission. Firstly, our case studies illustrate that deliberative transmission can occur in multiple ways – via existing institutions, via democratic innovations as well as via discourses. It is important to acknowledge that these are not mutually exclusive alternatives, and in many cases when they occur simultaneously, they could potentially generate competing legitimacy claims. An important question for future research is to think about what happens in deliberative terms when transmission mechanisms transmit contesting messages to empowered spaces. There are also many other transmission mechanisms operating in deliberative systems that deserve empirical attention such as social movements, voting and social media.

Secondly, our cases demonstrate that deliberative transmission should not just be thought of as occurring if claims correspond across public and empowered space. This is at once too restrictive – there are other important forms of transmission besides policy impact – and too naïve – discursive affinity does not imply a substantive impact. These findings should encourage theorists of deliberative systems to think harder about what deliberative transmission does and should entail.

For empirical scholars, the cases presented here demonstrate a variety of ways to study deliberative transmission. They begin a scholarly conversation about how claims travel reciprocally among sites on a dynamic spectrum from public to empowered space. Further research is needed, both to confirm the features of transmission in deliberative systems that we uncover and to test the efficacy of enabling, amplifying and sustaining transmission in the ways that we suggest. Our analysis provides different pathways to parse these out – focusing on different mechanisms or compiling insights from across them to produce a cumulative account. It therefore represents an important contribution along the way.

Notes

1. We acknowledge that there are other potential transmission mechanisms that none of our analyses pick up on – in particular, elections, referenda and social movement activism – but justify this approach on the basis that the three mechanisms emphasized here represent the major ones around which most theoretical and empirical scholarship has centered.
2. Nicolas Zimmer, Press Release, The CDU Fraction Berlin, 14 September 2005.
3. Hansard texts, 14 March 2002. All Hansard texts that are referenced in this paper are available at www.parliament.uk.
4. Hansard texts, 15 December 2005.
5. The Public Accounts Committee (PAC) of the NSW Parliament is concerned with issues of public accountability. One of its primary functions is to follow-up on reports from the Auditor General. From time to time, the PAC is also asked by the parliament or by a minister to examine a particular policy issue.
6. The names of the interviewees in this study are not included to protect their anonymity. All interviews for this study took place at the NSW Parliament, Sydney on 15 November 2012.
7. Professor Boyd Swinburn on *SBS Insight*, March 24, 2009.
8. Interview with Australian clinician and advocate, June 2011.
9. Interview with Australian public health researcher, July 2011.

Disclosure statement

Part of this research was funded by the newDemocracy foundation. This was an independent grant research awarded to Carolyn M Hendriks and there was no potential conflict of interest. There were no potential conflict of interest reported by Boswell or Ercan.

Funding

Part of this research was funded by the newDemocracy foundation. This was an independent grant research awarded to Carolyn M Hendriks and there was no potential conflict of interest.

ORCID

Carolyn M. Hendriks http://orcid.org/0000-0002-9734-3610
Selen A. Ercan http://orcid.org/0000-0002-3649-2882

References

Boswell, J. 2013. "Why and How Narrative Matters in Deliberative Systems." *Political Studies* 61 (3): 620–636. doi:10.1111/post.2013.61.issue-3.
Boswell, J. 2016. "The Performance of Political Narratives: How Britain and Australia's 'Fat Bombs' Fizzled Out." *British Journal of Politics and International Relations*. Advance online publication. doi:10.1177/1369148116630232.
Chambers, S. 2012. "Deliberation and Mass Democracies." In *Deliberative Systems: Deliberative Democracy at the Large Scale*, edited by J. Parkinson and J. Mansbridge, 52–71. Cambridge: Cambridge University Press.
Donaghy, R. 2007. *Light Touch Review, Report*. London: The Women's National Commission.
Dryzek, J. S. 2009. "Democratization as Deliberative Capacity Building." *Comparative Political Studies* 42 (11): 1379–1402. doi:10.1177/0010414009332129.
Ercan, S. A. 2012. "Beyond Multiculturalism: A Deliberative Democratic Approach to 'Illiberal' Cultures." PhD thesis, School of Politics and International Relations, Australian National University, Canberra.
Ercan, S. A. 2014. "Same Problem, Different Solutions: The Case of 'Honour Killing' in Germany and Britian." In *'Honour' Killing and Violence: Theory, Policy and Practice*, edited by A. Gill, C. Strange, and K. Roberts, 199–218. London: Palgrave Macmillan.
Ercan, S. A. 2015. "Creating and Sustaining Evidence for 'Failed Multiculturalism': The Case of 'Honor Killing' in Germany." *American Behavioral Scientist* 59 (6): 658–678. doi:10.1177/0002764215568988.
Ercan, S. A. 2016. "From Polarization to Pluralisation: A Deliberative Democratic Approach to Illiberal Cultures." *International Political Science Review*. Advance online publication. doi:10.1177/0192512115619465.
Ercan, S. A., and C. M. Hendriks. 2013. "The Democratic Challenges and Potential of Localism: Insights from Deliberative Democracy." *Policy Studies* 34 (4): 422–440. doi:10.1080/01442872.2013.822701.
Ercan, S. A., C. M. Hendriks, and J. Boswell. 2015. "Studying Public Deliberation after the Systemic Turn: The Crucial Role for Interpretive Research." *Policy and Politics*. Advance online publication. doi:10.1332/030557315X14502713105886.
Ferree, M. M., W. A. Gamson, J. Gerhards, and D. Rucht. 2002. *Shaping Abortion Discourse. Democracy and the Public Sphere in Germany and the United States*. Cambridge: Cambridge University Press.
Ferree, M. M. 2012. *Varieties of Feminism. German Gender Politics in Global Perspective*. Stanford, CA: Stanford University Press.
Fishkin, J. 2009. *When the People Speak: Deliberative Democracy and Public Consultation*. New York: Oxford University Press.
Flyvbjerg, B. 2006. "Five Misunderstandings about Case-Study Research." *Qualitative Inquiry* 12 (2): 219–245. doi:10.1177/1077800405284363.
Gamson, W. A., and A. Modigliani. 1989. "Media Discourse and Public Opinion on Nuclear Power: A Constructionist Approach." *American Journal of Sociology* 95 (1): 1–37. doi:10.1086/229213.
Goodin, R. E., and J. S. Dryzek. 2006. "Deliberative Impacts: The Macro-Political Uptake of Mini-publics." *Politics & Society* 34: 219–244. doi:10.1177/0032329206288152.
Grönlund, K., A. Bächtiger, and M. Setälä. 2014. *Deliberative Mini-Publics: Involving Citizens in the Democratic Process*. Colchester: ECPR Press.

Gutmann, A., and D. Thompson. 1996. *Democracy and Disagreement*. Cambridge: The Belknap Press.
Habermas, J. 1996. *Between Facts and Norms: Contributions to a Discourse Theory of Law and Democracy*. Cambridge: Polity Press.
Hajer, M. A. 1995. *The Politics of Environmental Discourse: Ecological Modernization and the Policy Process*. Oxford: Clarendon Press.
Hendriks, C. M. 2005. "Consensus Conferences and Planning Cells: Lay Citizen Deliberations." In *The Deliberative Democracy Handbook: Strategies for Effective Civic Engagement in the 21st Century*, edited by J. Gastil and P. Levine, 80–110. San Francisco, CA: Jossey-Bass.
Hendriks, C. M. 2006. "Integrated Deliberation: Reconciling Civil Society's Dual Role in Deliberative Democracy." *Political Studies* 54 (3): 486–508. doi:10.1111/j.1467-9248.2006.00612.x.
Hendriks, C. M. 2013. *Elected Representatives and Democratic Innovation: A Study of Responses to Citizens' Juries Embedded in the NSW Parliament's Public Accounts Committee*. A Research Report prepared for The newDemocracy Foundation. Sydney: The newDemocracy Foundation.
Hendriks, C. M. 2016. "Coupling Citizens and Elite in Deliberative Systems: The Role of Institutional Design." *European Journal of Political Research* 55 (1): 43–60.
Home Affairs Committee. 2008. "Domestic Violence, Forced Marriage and 'Honour' Based Violence, Sixth Report of Session 2007-08." Accessed July 14, 2014. http://www.publications.parliament.uk/pa/cm200708/cmselect/cmhaff/263/263i.pdf
Koopmans, R. 2004. "Migrant Mobilisation and Political Opportunities: Variation Among German Cities and a Comparison with the United Kingdom and the Netherlands." *Journal of Ethnic and Migration Studies* 30 (3): 449–470. doi:10.1080/13691830410001682034.
Mackenzie, M. K., and M. E. Warren. 2012. "Two Trust-Based Uses of Minipublics in Democratic Systems." In *Deliberative Systems: Deliberative Democracy at the Large Scale*, edited by J. Parkinson and J. Mansbridge, 95–124. Cambridge: Cambridge University Press.
Mansbridge, J. 1999. "Everyday Talk in the Deliberative System." In *Deliberative Politics: Essays on Democracy and Disagreement*, edited by S. Macedo, 211–242. New York: Oxford University Press.
Mansbridge, J., J. Bohman, S. Chambers, T. Christiano, A. Fung, J. R. Parkinson, D. F. Thompson, and M. E. Warren. 2012. "A Systemic Approach to Deliberative Democracy." In *Deliberative Systems: Deliberative Democracy at the Large Scale*, edited by J. Parkinson and J. Mansbridge, 1–42. Cambridge: Cambridge University Press.
McCombs, M. 2005. "A Look at Agenda-Setting: Past, Present and Future." *Journalism Studies* 6: 543–557. doi:10.1080/14616700500250438.
Neblo, M. 2005. "Thinking through Democracy: Between the Theory and Practice of Deliberative Politics." *Acta Politica* 40: 169–181. doi:10.1057/palgrave.ap.5500102.
Niemeyer, S. 2014. "Scaling up Deliberation to Mass Publics: Harnessing Mini-Publics in a Deliberative System." In *Deliberative Mini-Publics: Involving Citizens in the Democratic Process*, edited by K. Grönlund, A. Bächtiger, and M. Setälä, 177–202. Colchester: ECPR Press.
PAC. 2012. *Report on the Economics of Energy Generation*. Sydney: Legislative Assembly of the NSW Parliament, Public Accounts Committee. Accessed August 2, 2013. http://www.parliament.nsw.gov.au/Prod/Parlment/committee.nsf/0/6e0c25bf50c6aa0dca257abd00196735/$FILE/Report%206%2055%20-%20Economics%20of%20Energy%20Generation%20v4.pdf
Papadopoulos, Y. 2012. "On the Embeddedness of Deliberative Systems: Why Elitist Innovations Matter More." In *Deliberative Systems: Deliberative Democracy at the Large Scale*, edited by J. Parkinson and J. Mansbridge, 125–150. Cambridge: Cambridge University Press.
Parkinson, J. R. 2006. *Deliberating in the Real World: Problems of Legitimacy in Democracy*. Oxford: Oxford University Press.
Predelli, L. N. 2009. *'Women's Organisations and Claims-Making in the United Kingdom, with a Focus on Policies Addressing Violence against Women'* First European Conference on Politics and Gender (ECPG). Belfast: Queen's University Belfast.

Rhodes, R. A. W. 2014. "Genre Blurring' and Public Administration: What Can We Learn from Ethnography?'" *Australian Journal of Public Administration* 73 (3): 317–330. doi:10.1111/aupa.2014.73.issue-3.

Rucht, D. 1996. "The Impact of National Contexts on Social Movement Structures: A Cross-Movement and Cross-National Comparison." In *Comparative Perspectives on Social Movements. Political Opportunities, Mobilizing Structures, and Cultural Framings*, edited by D. McAdam, J. D. McCarthy, and M. N. Zald, 185–205. Cambridge: Cambridge University Press.

Saward, M. 2009. "Authorisation and Authenticity: Representation and the Unelected." *Journal of Political Philosophy* 17 (1): 1–22. doi:10.1111/jopp.2008.17.issue-1.

Shapiro, R. Y. 2011. "Public Opinion and American Democracy." *Public Opinion Quarterly* 75 (5): 982–1017. doi:10.1093/poq/nfr053.

She Who Disputes: Muslim Women Shape the Debate. 2006. London: Report, Women's National Commission/Muslim Women's Network.

Squires, J. 2002. "Deliberation and Decision-Making: Discontinuity in the Two-Track Model." In *Democracy as Public Deliberation: New Perspectives*, edited by M. P. d'Entreves, 133–155. Manchester: Manchester University Press.

Yanovitzky, I. 2002. "Effects of News Coverage on Policy Attention and Actions: A Closer Look into the Media-Policy Connection." *Communication Research* 29: 422–451. doi:10.1177/0093650202029004003.

Brazilian Social Assistance Policy: an empirical test of the concept of deliberative systems

Debora Rezende de Almeida and Eleonora Schettini Cunha

ABSTRACT
Recently, the systemic approach to deliberative democracy has set forth a new way of thinking about the legitimacy of non-electoral forms of representation based on the connection of different discursive spheres. Despite its theoretical potentials, the theory has not been able to either indicate what fosters this connection, or understand the impacts of articulation on the representative process. We present some results of a research study focusing on the Brazilian Social Assistance System and its main participatory and deliberative institutions. We argue that at least two dimensions are responsible for the connection between arenas – institutional design and the circulation of participant – and that these dimensions also present contradictory effects in terms of the legitimacy of representation, including problems related to public accountability and the inclusion of different discourses.

1. Introduction

Representation is not just a necessity given the size of modern politics, but it is crucial for constituting democratic practice (Plotke 1997; Urbinati 2006). Although this claim may be accepted by very different approaches without major controversies, recently, what we mean by political representation is under reconsideration due to, at least, two pressing conditions. First, complaints about the quality of representation and the limits of the people's authoritative voice during elections have been extensively discussed in contemporary politics. Second, the criticisms directed at representative democracy have been accompanied by emerging forms of non-electoral representation that go beyond territorial borders and elected representatives. Such dynamics include civil society actors that claim to represent the interests, opinions, and ideas of individuals and groups that they consider to be under-represented (Mendonça 2008). In extending the scope of representation to non-electoral forms, political theorists have to think about how representation can be legitimate (Dryzek and Niemeyer 2008; Urbinati and Warren 2008; Saward 2008).

In this article, we defend the idea that establishing a dialog with the literature on deliberative systems can help advance our comprehension of representation as a dynamic relationship. So, an evaluation of the democratic legitimacy of spaces that reflect civil society representation needs to consider that these spaces do not operate in an isolated manner, but rather belong to a group of deliberative spheres which have a close connection to specific areas of public policy. The legitimacy of decisions, however, occurs in a deferred and diffuse manner and stems from a continuous process of interaction among different spaces, where various types of representatives are present and different groups are being represented (Parkinson 2003; Bohman 2012). Our intention is not to discuss the idea of a deliberative system itself, but rather show how a systemic approach paves the path for rethinking the democratic legitimacy of representation. However, while this perspective presents interesting reflections on the legitimacy of the processes of participation and social representation, there are many questions left unanswered, requiring a concomitant revision of its principles. We do not know what factors promote the articulation between spaces and actors, nor do we know what impact this connection has on democratic representation.

Our objective is to reflect on these two questions based on a Brazilian empirical case of non-electoral representation, in order to test the effectiveness of the systemic approach for analyzing representation in practice. It is important to note that Brazil has developed an extensive range of participatory institutions, which connect State and society in the process of formulating public policies and redistributing public goods and services (Avritzer 2009). The most well-known experience is that of participatory budgeting, yet there are also the policy councils, national conferences, river-basin committees, among others. Many researchers have pointed towards a type of representation that originates in these participatory arenas given that civil society organizations are speaking for others and participating in public policy decision-making processes (Almeida 2015; Avritzer 2007; Gurza Lavalle, Houtzager, and Castello 2006). In addition, several areas of public policy were constituted as national systems for the purpose of ensuring unified attention to the rights of citizens, particularly considering the continental dimensions and specificities of Brazilian federalism.[1] Participatory institutions, such as policy councils and conferences, have a central role in enabling the formulation of shared decisions among federal unities and in articulating the political representatives of civil society and the state inside these national systems.

In order to advance the deliberative systems discussion, we will present a case study of the Brazilian Social Assistance Unified System (SUAS). We consider two factors that influence deliberative connection and may have impact on democratic representation, namely, institutional design and the circulation of actors (Almeida and Cunha, 2012; Mendonça 2013). First, institutional design must be considered because participatory processes that occur at the municipal, state, and national levels in Brazil are connected to the political system and to each other as a result of the design of certain public policy systems (Avritzer 2013). SUAS is an exemplar case of analysis because its organizational structure is responsible for integrating public deliberations and civil society innovations into the political system as a whole. It is important to point out that this decentralized and participatory national system was not structured from a pre-existing policy, and its implementation was strongly guided by the normativity.[2] Thus, the deliberative interaction in SUAS occurs by an institutionalized manner (Mendonça 2013), which imposes to understand how institutional design can both connect civil society actors to distinct spheres and impact the representability of social actors. We believe that the study of SUAS may be useful for understanding how other structured contexts of deliberation may influence the way interactions occurs.

Second, we argue that the actors play a fundamental role in the interaction of spheres in SUAS since they become highly engaged in several formal and informal arenas and end up linking diverse moments of a broad deliberative process. They frequently act across different spaces, helping some themes and discourses to be taken into consideration within the system. There are many studies highlighting the close connection and the blurring of lines among civil and political society in Brazil, given the multiple roles played by civil society actors, who often establish alliances with political parties or occupy space within state institutions (Abers and von Bülow 2011; Wampler 2012; Avritzer 2009; Abers, Serafim, and Tatagiba 2014). We intend to consider how the circulation of actors through different spaces may enhance the legitimacy of representation once these representatives have many opportunities to establish contact with other actors. Moreover, it will be worth analyzing if the participants of the main participatory institutions of SUAS serve as mediators between the discourses present in public sphere and the political system. The reflection on the connection among spheres will take the council and conferences as references in order to understand their interaction with macro and micro spheres (Hendriks 2006).

This article presents a brief review of the recent transformations to the concept of political representation and the contributions and limitations of the systemic approach to deliberation in order to consider the democratic legitimacy of civil society's representation. The second part deals with the aforementioned factors considered important for deliberative articulation and representativity through the lens of the SUAS. It is important to note that greater attention will be given to social assistance's two main participatory and deliberative arenas: the councils and the national conferences.

The data is based mainly on documentary analysis of the system's organization in order to understand the role of institutional design as a factor of connectivity. The institutional analysis will be also considered so as to understand how SUAS's rules and norms influence the circulation of actors. Complementary data includes interviews carried out with 19 national council members (IPEA 2012) and 410 delegates present at the IX Social Assistance National Conference that took place in 2013.[3] In addition, we conducted participant observations at the National Conferences occurred in 2011 and 2013 and at the National Council meetings occurred in 2013. We hope that this variety of sources may provide us with a more accurate picture of the actors' engagement and their circulation among spaces. Lastly, some of the conclusions point to the impact that these variables have on deliberative articulation and the possible contradictory effects for both the process of representation and deliberative democracy.

2. Rethinking political representation: a systemic approach to democratic legitimacy

The concept of political representation was generally associated with the topic of representative government and the logic of representation in the spheres of the State (Vieira and Runciman 2008). Recent research has gone beyond the study of parties, parliaments, and electoral rules to focus on the transformations in representation, considering the emergence and empirical confirmation of non-electoral forms. These would include the diffusion of more informal structures and opportunities for democratic representation and influence, as well as the increase in demands for group recognition (Castiglione and Warren 2006; Young 2000). Until recently, the main analytical tools for understanding these experiences focused on participatory and/or deliberative democratic theory. However, given the limits related to the number of participants in real-world deliberation, some authors agreed that democracy is inherently representative, which, in turn, presented several theoretical challenges for them (Bohman 2012; Parkinson 2006; Urbinati 2006). We focus on the transformations of the normative understanding of democratic legitimacy, recognizing that this type of representation lacks formal mechanisms of authorization and accountability.

Urbinati's work (2006, 2011) goes in this direction, when she defends that elections are one of the many dimensions of both representation and the relationship between the State and society. There are many forms of communication and influence that citizens activate through the media, social movements, and political parties that constitute political representation. Political representation is a circular and dynamic process that allows for the mediation between the diverse partialities of social life and state institutions. The legitimacy of representative democracy depends on both free regular elections and the activation of permanent communication between civil and political society.

It is worth recalling that an interpretation of representation as a dynamic phenomenon was already present in Pitkin (1967). She defined representation as a creative activity, a substantive acting for others that necessarily involves an overlapping of activities, a plurality of arenas and publics (221–222). She points out other modes of representation, the descriptive and the symbolic, and different agents who do the representing, such as State officials, interest groups, lobbyists, and people who act before government agencies. Despite this theoretical advance, the last chapter of the book heavily focuses on one specific type of action: speaking on behalf of others in an established institutional context.

There are significant differences among the authors who seek to understand this emerging scenario but, in common, they shift the evaluation of legitimacy of representation from its exclusive focus on the foundational act, i.e. authorization, and situate it in the representative process (Urbinati 2006; Rosanvallon 2009; Saward 2008). Therefore, it does not make much sense to think about legitimacy as an element acquired in a specific moment and through some kind of mechanism, it seems more fruitful to speak of processes of legitimation, where legitimacy is established over time, through the critical examination of political action (Almeida 2015). This change forces us to seriously think not only about the alternative ways civil society representatives should be open to public judgment, but also the different relationships established with the represented (Young 2000). As Saward (2006, 312) states 'a political claim, is nothing if it is not heard, seen, or read by its intended audience, those whom it is meant to attract and convince'.

The contemporary theory of representation highlights various possibilities regarding the democratic relationship between representatives and whom they claim to represent. There are different sources of authority for democratic representatives (institutional affiliation, intangible goods, social location, and formative experience), different ways to hold democratic representatives accountable (public justification, membership democracy, performance indicators, public exposure in the media), and different ways to authorize (retrospectively, through organizational means, such as membership or followership, attendance at meetings, participation in programs) other than elections (Dovi 2012; Castiglione and Warren 2006; Saward 2006; Gurza Lavalle, Houtzager, and Castello 2006; Montanaro 2012). While these dimensions present corresponding forms of authorization and accountability, they fail to understand the democratic representation in a relational way that goes beyond a microanalysis of spaces and actors.

Recent systemic approaches of deliberation seem to be promising for evaluating democratic legitimacy, since accountability and responsiveness is not restricted to isolated actions or individuals, but may be fomented in public deliberation that occurs among different arenas. Democratic legitimacy becomes less personalized in the actors and more dynamic, or in other words, focused on the connection among different spheres and deliberative moments (Parkinson 2006; Dryzek 2009; Mendonça 2008; Bohman 2012).

Many authors have devoted themselves to further developing the concept of deliberative system since it was first systematized by Mansbridge (1999). Recently, Mansbridge (2012) propose that there are no forum, even if ideally constituted, has the sufficient deliberative capacity to make the majority of the decisions and policies adopted in democracies legitimate. A proposal for a systemic approach emerges from this perspective: 'we suggest that it is necessary to go beyond the study of individual institutions and processes to examine their interaction in the system as a whole' (Mansbridge *et al*, 2012, 2). Deliberative system is defined as 'a set of distinguishable, differentiated, but to some degree interdependent parts, often with distributed functions and a division of labor, connected in such a way as to form a complex whole' (4). For Parkinson (2006), once deliberative functions are distributed in various subsystems, one expects that the interdependence and interaction of spaces will facilitate the process by which arguments are tested in different parts. This dynamic has the potential of producing forms of checks and balances, since the system should be capable of combining and recombining judgments, as well as producing self-correcting tendencies.

Despite these efforts, there are still problems with the operationalization of the concept. Owen and Smith (2013) argue that the systemic approach may risk 'flattening out' the concept of deliberation by attempting to include all forms of political engagement. They question if there should be a deliberative minimum by which it would be possible to judge the parts or if everything should be considered in the deliberative system. Mendonça (2013) also presents some criticisms regarding the fluidity of the legitimacy principle. He claims that the process may become so disperse it might lead to the strengthening of the decision-makers' discretionary powers.

In our opinion, one of the risks regarding the legitimacy of representation from a systemic view is that the dispersion of deliberation over time and space may exclude perspectives within the deliberative system. This may happen either by weakening actors who do not have the resources to make their positions present in many arenas (Mendonça 2013), or by weakening the relationship between civil society representatives and whom they claim to represent, since linkages between discourses and action are opaque to citizens, and may thus be manipulated by powerful insiders (Papadopoulos 2012). Agreeing with Castiglione and Warren (2006) that the practice of political representation should be seen as a two-way relationship, which can be used to exclude people from politics or to include them, it is important to consider not only how connections exist, but also how the system promotes such connections.

Parkinson (2012) is critical of the possibility for connectivity. For him, it is necessary to use a variety of different communication channels between citizens and representatives. Even in non-electoral forms of representation where there are no clear lines of responsibility and accountability, or fixed and pre-existing constituencies, representatives need to call constituencies to recognize their claims. Parkinson defends that responsiveness is a matter of mutual co-creation between citizens and representatives, although there will always be some gap between demands and outcomes in a deliberative system.

Dryzek (2009) considers that deliberative systems would be composed of five elements in order to develop the deliberative capacity of a political system. First, it would include a public space with a plurality of viewpoints and few restrictions on who can participate. Second, it needs empowered spaces for actors to produce collective decisions. Third, there should be mechanisms of transmission set up to ensure that the public space can influence empowered spaces. Fourth, empowered spaces should be accountable to the public sphere. Finally, a deliberative system must present decisiveness, in the sense that these first four elements are consequential, namely, that they exert influence on collective decisions.

We rely upon Parkinson and Dryzek's inspiration to understand how actors in SUAS's participatory institutions, which are considered empowered spaces, may be accountable to the public sphere and connected to decision-making processes. Here it is essential to understand and identify the 'transmission' mechanisms or channels that help civil society representatives connect with the plurality of perspectives and ideas present in the social assistance system. Following Mendonça (2013), we defend that in order to avoid the laudatory perspective of the theory, it is important to discuss its theoretical limits and understand what promotes the connection among the arenas, given that the articulation is not natural. We propose to deal with these challenges and analyze the role of two factors in the articulation of the deliberative system, that is, institutional design and the circulation of actors (Mendonça 2013; Almeida and Cunha 2012). We argue that there is also a mutual influence among these variables, such as the interaction between the rules and the circulation of actors.

By relying upon Hendriks' (2006) typology, we will evaluate how actors from participatory institutions (mixed spheres) articulate themselves with macro (informal spaces that attract different civil society organizations and individuals) and micro spheres (formal spaces composed of parliamentarians, government employees, specialists, etc.). This typology is very useful since it helps considering the multiplicity of SUAS's spaces, and their specific compositions and purposes, which has influence on both the connection and possible incompatibilities between the deliberative spheres. The focus on political representation exercised in mixed spheres is attributed to the fact these arenas include representatives from organized civil society and have more restrictive processes of authorization and inclusion. In addition, they share the power to produce binding decisions with the state, which makes these arenas very dependent on systemic articulation in order to guarantee the process of democratic legitimacy.

3. Social assistance's deliberative system and the representation of civil society

Brazil's 1988 Constitution instituted, for the first time, social assistance as a social right, in which the State had a role in guaranteeing the public and social protection of all Brazilian citizens. The Constitution provisions also call for both democratic planning and decentralization, sustained by the creation of collegiate bodies composed of representatives from the government and society, and the establishment of broad processes for revising the respective policies. These processes should involve those responsible for the policies' implementation along with social actors and service providers (Cunha 2013). The decentralized and federal format of the Brazilian state, which is organized into three levels of government, introduced many challenges for the coordination of public policies in the country. In order to implement the national policies, agreements among the governments were established, generating a new model in the federal system. This context set up the normative and empirical bases for the institution and organization of the social assistance policy in Brazil.

The Organic Law of Social Assistance (LOAS)[4] was enacted in 1993, delimiting and defining the format and relative content of the policy's operationalization. The Law brought some important innovations in terms of policy design, such as a division of responsibilities and functions among the federal entities, and the creation of participatory and deliberative spaces – councils and conferences – composed of representatives from the State and civil society at each level of government. However, it was only in the mandate of President Lula (2003–2010), a member of Workers' Party (PT), that most of the guidelines was implemented and considered as reference for governmental action (Sátyro and Cunha 2014). The creation of SUAS[5] in 2005 was part of a broader attempt by the Lula administration to introduce more participatory and inclusive forms of governance in Brazil.[6]

The SUAS was responsible for articulating the efforts and resources of the three levels of government for funding and implementation of the National Social Assistance Policy. Coordinated by the Ministry of Social Development and Fight against Hunger (MDS), the system establishes competences for the government' levels, in decentralized manner, and the civil society' participation directly in the shared management process, thus reinforcing existing participatory and deliberative arenas.

Thus, the SUAS is composed of a complex system of institutionalized spaces that deliberate on social assistance policy. Considering Hendriks' typology of deliberative spheres, the System is made up of: (a) macro discursive spaces, such as civil society forums, which discuss issues related to politics and exert influence on the decision-making process; (b) micro discursive spaces, known as intergovernmental commissions, set up at the state and federal levels and expected to carry out the role of negotiating and producing agreements that guarantee the organization and implementation of articulated social assistance actions, and (c) mixed spheres, namely, the policy councils and conferences in the three levels of government, consisting of government representatives and civil society, which should discuss and decide general guidelines, proposals, and plans for the policy in its entirety. This is a complex system that both associates formal and informal arenas of participation and deliberation and includes other spaces and actors such as Legislative Assemblies, which are legally responsible for approving

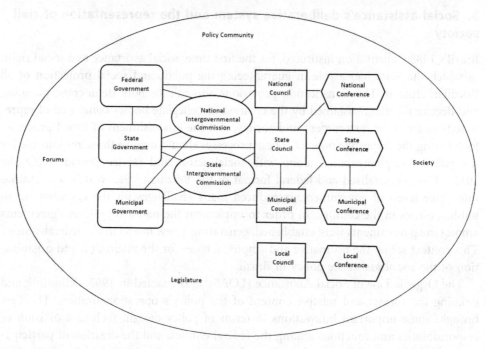

Figure 1. – Relationship among spheres in SUAS.

the budgets for the policy area, research and educational institutions, among others (Figure 1).

We analyze the interaction among these spaces, considering that they are primarily structured on the basis of representation and produce deliberative content impacting the System. In the next subsections we will present two factors that have the potential to impact deliberative connection: institutional design and the circulation of participants within the system.

3.1. *Institutional design*

Institutional design refers, here, to a 'purposeful and deliberate intervention that succeeds in establishing new institutional structures and processes, or rearranging existing ones, thereby achieving intended outcomes and improvements' (Olsen 1997, p. 205). The design of Brazilian participatory institutions, such as councils and conferences, in the phases of public policy establishes the level of decision-making power, the way they interact with other forums, the forms of inclusion and authorization, and mechanisms for accountability. A systemic articulation in these cases is shaped and regulated by a group of rules that creates and organizes these institutions, rather than randomly or occasionally found (Mendonça 2013).

The rules and norms that constitute participatory institutions, as a component that affects the behavior of actors and the level of deliberative effectiveness or decision-making power, is a recurrent theme in the literature on the matter (Button and Ryfe 2005; Fung 2007; Avritzer 2009). However, these analyzes generally focus on the internal dynamics of these spaces, ignoring the role of institutional design and its relation to the articulation among different fora of the system – micro, macro, and mixed.

The so-called macro discursive spheres, such as the fora and other participatory mechanisms for collective actors and citizens, organized by civil society, have characteristics and designs that are quite differentiated amongst each other as a result of the context in which they were created and of the actors who compose them. They all promote the articulation of a policy community[7] and bring issues into public debate with the objective of influencing agendas and the deliberations occurring in other spheres of the system, mainly in the micro and mixed spheres. The variation in the design of the macro spheres makes it difficult to describe and analyze them through a single perspective. However, it is worth emphasizing their important role in absorbing, condensing, and channeling issues that emerge from the public sphere and are presented in the political sphere (Habermas 2003).

Among the micro discursive spheres, the intergovernmental commissions are worth considering more carefully. Their deliberations on the operational aspects of SUAS influence the System as a whole, when decisions are made at the federal level, or influence the System partially, when decisions are made at the state level. Some of the rules that pertain to the organization and operation of the commissions also establish the forms of interaction with the other spheres in the System. The first of these guidelines is related to the composition of the commissions. At the federal level, it is made up of governmental representatives from federal, state, and municipal secretaries and the state commissions (one for each state) are integrated by state secretaries and representatives from the municipalities. The federal commission, when it is called upon, advises the state commissions and creates a strategy of permanent dialog with them. The commissions' composition and attributes are what facilitate a flux of ideas, themes, and discourses stemming from macro and micro discursive spheres at the three levels of government. Another rule establishes that the agreements made by the public administrators in the commissions should be sent to the councils that belong to that specific level of government. This is important for disseminating knowledge and/or for deliberating on issues that are within that council's scope of action, reflecting, henceforth, a connection among the micro and mixed spheres at each government level.

The mixed spheres, councils and conferences, have very specific designs and deserve more attention. The 1988 Constitution opened space for participatory practices in social assistance policy. During the 1990s, a set of participatory institutions were created, such as policy councils, that have been disseminated in different policy areas, and nowadays there are social assistance councils in almost all Brazilian municipalities. The councils are established at the federal, state, and municipal levels, and have the responsibility of formulating, evaluating, controlling, and regulating the policy. In social assistance, these councils also have the responsibility of setting goals and budget priorities.

The National Council specifically deals with advising the councils at the state level, while the state councils are responsible for advising the municipalities with the support of the National Council when necessary. The councils are defined as hybrid institutions, to the extent that they are made up equally of government and civil society actors (divided according to groups, such as workers, service providers, and service users),[8] who are either elected or appointed by those organizations. The institutional design of councils are defined by state and municipal legislation, but in social assistance there are national guidelines regarding their composition and main functions in policy decision-making processes. Due to the characteristics of local legislation and the difference in the associational life in Brazilian cities, there is great variation in what can be designated as civil society organizations in the hybrid institutions, which may or may not include a plurality of perspectives and ideas. Considering these differences in institutional design and paying attention to the relationship that civil society actors establish among arenas, especially with society as a whole, is fundamental for discussing the plurality of discourses, ideas, and opinions that emerge from these experiences.

Conferences are also a space where government officials and civil society representatives collaborate in the formulation of public policy and the realization of conferences expanded in number and in public policy areas (Avritzer 2013; Pogrebinschi and Samuels 2014). However, there are differences in relation to the conferences' origins, how participation is structured, and what functions these participatory institutions have in the public policy cycle.

In SUAS, the conferences have been stimulated by the National Council for Social Assistance, which together with its correspondent Ministry[9] defines the issues, rules, the flows and procedures for the National Conference. In addition, it encourages the other two levels of government to organize its own conferences (Faria and Cunha 2012). The conferences begin at the municipal level, reflect a sequenced deliberative flux in which the policy is evaluated, guidelines are defined for this level of government, and other guidelines are highlighted as worthy of debate at the state and national level. The main role of the state conferences, and consequently the national conference, is to debate on the issues and concerns brought forth from the previous level, therefore defining the guidelines that should direct the actions at the state and national levels. At federal level, the conference involves a wide range of participation – an average of 2000 people participates at the national level – and occur periodically every two or four years.

Generally, the conferences should evaluate the policy situation and define which guidelines are to be discussed and formulated by the area in the subsequent years. Considering that the legitimacy of civil society representation is our focal point, it is necessary to include the questions of how conferences' rules are open to a plurality of discourses, opinions, and ideas and how the participation process facilitates the relationship between this mixed space and the whole system.

The analysis of SUAS's institutional design allows us to make some additional inferences about the connection among the spheres. First, it is important to note that there is a close relationship between councils and conferences. The councils call the conference meeting and play a central role in the organization of the entire process. After the conference is debated on at the three levels of government, the final and decisive deliberations are taken to the councils at each level so that they can approve and send off the decisions to the sector responsible for acting upon such measures. The council is also responsible for ensuring that the other actors in the System carry out the deliberations from the conferences.

Second, the rules and norms that instituted the National Conference on Social Assistance prescribe the interaction with micro and macro spheres, since these processes occur with the administrative body and rely upon the participation of members from the council, the government, the intergovernmental commissions, the fora, and civil society organizations. In addition, the conferences allow for the inclusion of citizens during the policy formulation process at the municipal level, since anyone who shows up can potentially be elected as a representative to participate in the next level.

Third, in the SUAS, the different spheres may also have the role and/or responsibility of eventually or regularly interacting with the other arenas. This is the case of the intergovernmental commissions and councils, where the decisions from the commissions should be submitted for deliberation at the councils, or when there is a need for some kind of legislative production and the entire system (or a great part of it) mobilizes itself to support or pressure the Legislative Branch.[10]

Finally, the hybrid characteristic of councils provides a great opportunity for civil society representatives in mixed spheres to be connected with state actors and society. First, the establishment of these channels requires the presence of civil society organizations that can sustain and legitimate the actors which represent the interests of different social sectors (Côrtes 2006). The councils must not only involve the policy community, linked to the policy's professionals, but also integrate associations and social movements. The problem is that more democratic forms of social representation will be present especially where social movements and organizations are more organized (Avritzer 2009). Second, social assistance councils in Brazil are institutionalized spaces of permanent interaction between society and government officials that produce binding decisions. The institutional design serves as transmission mechanism by which deliberation may ends up being consequential.

SUAS' institutional design offers us opportunities to understand the connection among the mixed spheres, such as councils and conferences, the political system, and society. The institutions, by proposing rules that regulate the spheres, produce both incentives and obstacles with regard to systemic connection. This occurs because they normatively establish the relationship that social and state actors should have in order to influence decision-making processes. Nevertheless, one cannot ignore the conflicting interaction with the State, as indicated by classic deliberation studies (Habermas 2003). Some of these studies have shown how the creation of intergovernmental commissions in health policy[11] negatively affected the capacity of councils to consolidate themselves as central decision-making fora in the policy area (Côrtes et al. 2009).

Another conflict that emerges from the institutionalized context of mixed spheres relates to their difficulty in becoming connected to macro contexts. The involvement of a plurality of civil society organizations depends on specific legislation and the organizations' comprehension of who counts as representatives in these spaces. Moreover, it depends on how the inclusion is made, as seen in the next subsection. These dilemmas suggest that, in practice, the fact that the spheres connect with each other does not mean there is immediate democratic representation, since norms and rules are not sufficient for deliberation that occurs in councils and conferences to be translated into other spheres, and vice versa.

3.2. Participants

The second dimension analyzed and considered as a catalyst of connectivity refers to the participants and their circulation among the spaces. It has been shown that the articulation of discourses and perspectives in the deliberative system is often the result of the circulation of certain individuals who are profoundly engaged and active within the system (Cunha and Almeida 2013). Frequently, these actors – workers, users, service providers, or individuals with acknowledge experience in the area – act across different spaces, helping some themes and discourses to be taken into consideration inside and among the spheres of the system. It is worth emphasizing that many scholars have noticed the multiple roles taken on by civil society actors inside and outside the government institutions in Brazil. Wampler (2012) suggested that civil society leaders in participatory institutions act both as participants and representatives, and as linkages or intermediaries between elites and masses, beyond traditional institutions like parliament. Abers and von Bülow (2011) discusses the close relationship between social movements and State, given that their activists frequently occupy state positions. In our case study, we evaluate if the circulation of the participants from councils and conferences in state and social spheres may help foster connectivity and enrich their representativity. However, it is important to consider not only those participants, but also how SUAS provides opportunities for the connection of different actors in the system as a whole.

First, in SUAS, civil society actors that make up the macro and mixed spheres sometimes occupy public posts or have access to government officials and vice versa. In interviews[12] with six bureaucrats of the National Secretary for Social Assistance of MDS, responsible for the implementation of SUAS, three of them declared previous participation in NGOs, social movements, civil society organizations, and in municipal councils. On the one hand, these previous experience may influence the way they interact with State and participate in the policy's formulation. On the other hand, participatory institutions also help government officials identify key problems, and grievances among the population, especially the most organized sectors. By relying on leaders' expertise, government officials can better target both the citizens' policy priorities and the policy issues most important to community leaders (Wampler 2012).

Second, it has been noted that there are councils that are composed of representatives from intergovernmental commissions and civil society fora. There are even Working Groups that are made up of council members, technical staff from the government and/or specialists, some of whom belong to academia. These groups operate for a determined period and articulate themselves with arenas of continuous deliberation.

Third, there are innumerous other actions that articulate and mobilize the entire system, ranging from scientific and/or cultural events to the conferences themselves. These processes seem to not only strengthen the policy community and their identity, but also create opportunities for mutual recognition and the establishment of confidence, all of which tend to increase as the actors regularly cross paths. These encounters equally allow for the construction of discourses and counter discourses, bringing people, and organizations closer together.

Fourth, when considering the participants of the main participatory institutions in Social Assistance Policy, our interviews present interesting data about the multiple roles that actors play in the system. Almost half of participants of the 2013 National Conference (49.6%) claimed to be members of social assistance municipal councils. Among them, 25% claimed to also participate in councils of other policy areas. In relation to the National Council for Social Assistance, IPEA (2012) data shows that 79% of the council members claim to have already attended (47%) or are still participating

(32%) in another policy council. The actors' engagement among the distinct mixed spheres of the system may facilitate the process by which arguments are tested in different parts, considering that an actor can be a representative of different discourses.

It is worth highlighting, however, that the flow of different discourses and perspectives cannot be evaluated only through a perspective based on the individual, who transfers his/her experience to other fora. One must consider the representativity of the spaces in the System. In order to evaluate representation, we look at whether the circulation of actors influences the processes of inclusion (authorization) and accountability between actors and fora from different arenas, and how institutional design influences this process.

The rules establish that the process of choosing representatives from civil society for SUAS' mixed spheres begins with voluntary nominations. The organizations that seek to serve terms in the councils or to participate in the conferences need to introduce themselves to the other members of the policy community, whether it is through instituted electoral or indication processes set up by the councils, or during the conferences in the moments reserved for choosing representatives. All those participating and who have a vote can elect the representatives. These selective processes create a type of authorization, even if this occurs among a restricted public. Both State and society recognize these representatives as valid interlocutors. The social representatives are generally authorized by their organizations and the selection process may or may not include all of the associations concerned with the issue or even those groups that are not organized in associations (Avritzer 2007). Social Assistance includes the possibility for the citizen who uses the system to run for a position in the council. The government administrators also give social actors the authority to act, therefore, endorsing the selection process and the final decisions made by these actors.

On the one hand, observing these processes has revealed that the networks the participants belong to during their trajectory are important for the moments when they select who shall represent them (Cunha 2013). On the other hand, the council members themselves consider that their representative legitimacy is derived from their experience, since this reaffirms not only their history of dealing with public policy, but also the recognition they have received from their peers. Research among social assistance[13] council members, distributed in capital and medium-sized cities of four Brazilian regions, revealed that 53.5% believe that the legitimacy of their representation stems from their experience in the field and the recognition from peers. Another 13.2% of council members attribute their legitimacy to the advocacy of some issues in the area, and 33.3% considered that legitimacy emerges from the electoral process by which they were submitted (Cunha and Almeida 2013).

Hence, the interaction of actors in deliberative arenas plays a relevant role, since it is what allows the members of the policy community to maintain contact with each other (regularly or eventually) and share convictions and identities. The connections transcend the State (at the three levels) and reach the informal and formal deliberative spheres, which may be micro, macro, or mixed in scope. Furthermore, these articulations straighten personal and professional ties that are then transferred over into broader networks. These interactions seem to produce enough mutual knowledge for establishing relationships based on trust and identification that will eventually influence the process of choosing representatives.

With regard to conferences, the councils define how the participants will come together, taking into account that these participants are citizens who have either an elected or innate representative connection[14] with the right to voice and vote (Faria and Cunha 2012). Generally, the process of defining the participants parallels the structure of representation in the councils. In other words, it assumes a format of parity among the members of the government and civil society (workers, service providers, and service users). In the state and national conferences, the criterion for selection also considers the size of the municipalities (small, medium, and large cities) and states. There are different phases for choosing the representatives, who are then selected among the participants at each stage of the conference in order to represent the subsequent level. This format for choosing the conference delegates has generated criticism with regard to how it deals with inclusion. According to Teixeira, Leite de Souza, and Fiuza Lima (2012), it is important to examine how there is the lack of greater concern during the conferences with the qualitative criteria for including social perspectives, such as quotas for gender and race. Despite the fact that the territoriality criterion is relevant, in a country representing a continental dimension such as Brazil, this creates an imbalance in terms of regions, given that the southeast region is overrepresented, for example.

Although there is a positive relationship between the flow of actors and the authorization of representatives, based on trust established among the members of the policy community, it is worth examining some contradictory effects. Councils and conferences should include social and political actors considered relevant for the social assistance policy area, particularly those who are sub-represented in formal political arenas (such as the service users and workers). Nevertheless, studies have shown that, in general, the service users in social assistance have not been able to express their voices in councils and, in some situations, they are not even represented by their own organizations, but rather by the institutions that are their service providers (Cunha 2013). Hence, the necessary engagement in the social assistance policy community may exclude other voices that do not belong to such networks. However, it is important to note there is a great difference between the representatives from conferences and councils. Conferences quantitatively involve more actors and allow for both deliberation at different levels of the federation and participation of citizens who are not organized in social movements or associations, which, in turn, may qualitatively improve the connection between mixed and macro spheres.

In addition, the circulation of actors generates a flow of information, which can then contribute to the association between representatives and the represented on a long-term basis. Another important aspect is how the loyalty to one's trajectory and one's experience with the issue at hand seem to be relevant factors for generating accountability. This keeps representatives and the represented, who belong to the same policy community, associated with one another (Almeida and Cunha 2012). However, it is still important to consider the controversial relations that arise from the experience and expertise acquired by the actors. While being associated to a policy community contributes to the establishment of identity ties and the circulation of ideas and reasons, it can also exclude other perspectives or limit accountability. This is an essential point when considering the relationship between mixed spheres and the macro context, particularly when focusing on the fact that citizens, who are neither associated to civil society organizations nor to a policy community that encourages interactions, tend to be excluded from political representation if accountability fails to succeed.

Council members have already recognized the lack of interaction among the mixed and macro spheres – particularly with the policy's beneficiaries – and with the mixed and micro context – particularly with the state institutions directly linked to the implementation of the policy. Regarding the connection between the National Council and macro context, IPEA's interviews indicate that, in the council member's perception, the Council exerts little or no influence on the issue in public opinion (impression of 58% of respondents). Moreover, when council members were questioned about the forms of communication they use to publicize their actions, it became clear that homepages and profiles on social networks have little expressiveness (only one response among 19 interviews). The main way for council members to keep in touch with those they represent is through meetings (cited by 14 respondents) and informal conversations with the organizations (13 respondents). Accountability seems to develop in an endogenous manner, within a mixed context, and be directed at the base of movements and social organizations (IPEA 2012).

Regarding the relationship with spaces of policy decision-making, the National Council members consider that they have little or no influence on the agenda of Congress (69% of respondents); the Ministry of Social Development and Fight Against Hunger (52%); and other ministries related to CNAS (48%). This is a worrying conclusion when considering that a notion of deliberation needs to be consequential (Dryzek 2009).

These findings suggest that although actors work as a fundamental transmission mechanism of deliberation, they also put tremendous constraints on representativity, particularly if one considers the inclusion of a plurality of perspectives. Moreover, further qualitative research may point out how the engagement of actors among spheres may lead to a change in one's position regarding the very issues these actors have defended. Ultimately, this adds more complexity to our understanding of the relationship established between the actors and those they represent.

4. Final considerations

The idea of a deliberative system has been quite useful for studying Brazil's experience in social assistance and the challenges towards democratic legitimacy that involve the representation of civil society. However, we showed that further theoretical and empirical development is needed in order to understand which factors can contribute to systemic interaction. This study sought to contribute to this debate by discussing the role of two variables that act as catalysts in deliberative connection: institutional design and the circulation of actors. Indirectly, the study also called attention to how the forms of articulation taken on by these variables impact both connection among spheres and accountability of civil society representatives.

The analysis of the Social Assistance Unified System allowed us to identify a high degree of institutionalization and analyze the influence of rules and norms on deliberative articulation, which is different from more informal systems of deliberation. It is possible to state then that with regard to this policy, the different spheres of deliberation articulate amongst themselves, producing intricate and complex connections of actors and institutions. Given the federal organization in Brazil, the institutional design defines the interactions which should occur separately at the three levels of government, as well as among them, further increasing the complexity of the System and the deliberative flux. Then, institutional design may work as a transmission mechanism through which there is interaction between the public sphere and empowered spaces, such as councils, and allows them to be consequential. Furthermore, SUAS's rules provide opportunities for civil society representatives to establish a relationship with public sphere and State institutions, which may foster accountability.

The circulation of actors and their representativity also seem to be promising for systemic connection. The recurrent interactions of representatives and the represented, both within and outside of the System, are conveyed in the manner in which the actors move among the spheres, which can be reflected in the process of holding certain posts, the composition of the spaces themselves, and the existence of fora, events and groups that connect the distinct representatives. These characteristics reflect a form of legitimacy that is derived from the actual dynamic of the System. The legitimacy is derived from the links, which are constructed by the representatives and the represented through other forms of action – participation and deliberation – and that happen continuously and daily in the System. The circulation of actors can also contribute to the control of representatives, since actors are expected to publically inform and justify their actions during articulation.

These are the characteristics that highlight the movement of different discourses through the perspective of the individual, who transfers his/her experience to other fora once he/she is recognized within a policy community as a legitimate actor. The article also emphasized how it is necessary to go beyond just considering the circulation of actors, focusing then on the representativity and plurality of the spaces in this System. This dimension allows us to evaluate which representatives are being included and how they are able to articulate themselves with those who do not directly participate in deliberation or who do not authorize these representatives. In this case, we drew attention to how the rules and norms also indirectly impact the circulation of actors and their representativity, by establishing a set of characteristics that define who the participants should be and which public they should be held accountable to. Among the dimensions of representation influenced by the rules of the SUAS, we should include: (a) the origin of all the representatives, once they are bound to a certain public policy area; (b) the necessary association of civil society representatives with organizations and/or social movements, reflecting a certain experience in dealing with that specific issue; (c) the differentiated processes for choosing representatives – elections in specific plenary sessions, elections in conferences, elections and indications among peers; and (d) the establishment of 'representatives who represent the representatives', which occurs when delegates are chosen for conferences or when council members are chosen to act at the state and national levels.

The results presented here allow us to make at least two affirmations regarding the impact of the deliberative connections on the representativity of the fora and actors in the Social Assistance System. First, we verified that the two factors considered contribute to delimiting and establishing the connections among the System. However, there are contradictory effects or moments of displacement in the interaction of these variables as proposed by deliberative theorists (Mansbridge 2012). While the rules and norms allow for the circulation of actors and their connection in specific moments, this is still not enough for stimulating the articulation of mixed fora, particularly with regard to the articulation of councils and conferences with other institutions in the System. Empirical studies have shown how difficult it is to articulate councils and conferences with decision-making and policy implementation spheres, as well as with the population (IPEA 2012). Hence, the problem of deliberative interaction is not limited to the circulation of individuals and institutional design.

Second, another impact resulting from the contradictory relations between institutional design and representativity refers to the process of including different discourses. By guaranteeing the institutionalization of the articulation within the SUAS, the rules can also simultaneously restrict the type of actor or discourse that enters the deliberative fora, and consequently influence the type of actors with which the representatives need to be held accountable. While there are stakes on the plurality and diversity of Brazilian participatory institutions, they confront obstacles when dealing with the rules of inclusion that privilege a type of public, which seems to distance itself from the macro context, as is the case of excluding social assistance service users.

By considering the impact of the connections in the representativity of social actors, this study highlighted some of this theory's limits and potentials for evaluating the legitimacy of representation. While the relative flexibility of deliberative ideals contributes to rethink the process of legitimation of representation over time and among spaces, it puts some doubts about the possibility of effective democratic deliberation. In other words, systemic theorists are betting on strong sense of deliberation, discussions aimed at the common interest and with a practical guidance – 'what is to be done' – but do not respond adequately how a weak or limited connection, such as provided by institutional design and participants, can generate this kind of result. In addition, we showed that systemic approach needs to think in the conflicts resulting from the potential inducers of connectivity, considering the difficult art of connecting representatives and the represented. Comparative studies in other policy areas with institutionalized systems and different historical of organization and participation may be useful in order to test the explanatory strength of these factors in promoting connectivity. We hope to have pointed towards possible research agendas, as we continue working on the reflections presented in this debate.

Notes

1. Brazil is divided into 5570 municipalities, 26 states, and the Federal District, all of which possess political and administrative autonomy.
2. The Brazilian Unified Health System (SUS), by contrast, was structured from a preexisting policy, which had a tradition of civil society participation over time in various experiments before its establishment.
3. The National Council for Social Assistance is composed of 18 members and an equal number of alternate members. At the IX National Conference of Social Assistance, there was an average of two thousand (2000) delegates. The interviews were carried out with civil society and government actors.
4. The Organic Law on Social Assistance, Nº 8.742, established in 1993, was recently changed by Law Nº 12.435, in 2011.

5. Created from the deliberations of the Fourth National Conference on Social Assistance, occurred in 2003, and foreseen in the Organic Law of Social Assistance (Loas) – Nº 8.742/93, SUAS had its implementation bases consolidated in 2005.
6. Other policy areas have also experienced, for the first time, the expansion of participatory arenas and the institutionalization of governmental spaces to deal with their demands, such as woman rights, and racial equality.
7. For Côrtes (2006, 83), a 'policy community refers to a community of political players, who are organized on behalf of a common social policy project'. In the case of Social Assistance in Brazil, the sectorial political elite, made up of professionals, service providers, along with some social movements and civil society organizations, are important players in the system.
8. In health councils, however, users' representatives occupy half of the seats, and the other half should come from representatives of the government, health care providers, and health professionals.
9. The Ministry of Social Development and Fight Against Hunger (Ministério do Desenvolvimento Social e Combate à Fome – MDS).
10. An example of this was the recent approval of Law 12435/2011, which deals with the organization of social assistance in Brazil.
11. Social Assistance systematically organizes itself similar to the Health System.
12. This refers to preliminary research on the relationship between bureaucrats from MDS and social movements and organizations. These interviews were conducted in 2013 by the undergraduate student Gabriella Kashiwakura with the author's supervision.
13. A research conducted with 159 council members in the northeast, southeast, south, and center-west regions in Brazil.
14. The National Council members and the Organizing Committee are considered innate representatives, since they have right to participate in conferences without a further selection process.

Disclosure statement

No potential conflict of interest was reported by the authors.

Funding

This article presents the partial results of research financed by FAPEMIG, the Pró-Reitoria de Pesquisa da Universidade Federal de Minas Gerais (PRPq/UFMG), and the Conselho Nacional de Desenvolvimento Científico e Tecnológico (CNPQ) through the Programa de Iniciação Científica (PROIC/UnB). We would like to express our gratitude for their support.

References

Abers, R., L. Serafim, and L. Tatagiba. 2014. "Repertórios de interação Estado-sociedade em um Estado heterogêneo: a experiência na era Lula." *Dados* 57 (2): 325–357. doi:10.1590/0011-5258201411.

Abers, R., and M. von Bülow. 2011. "Movimentos sociais na teoria e na prática: como estudar o ativismo através da fronteira entre Estado e sociedade?" *Sociologias* 13 (28): 52–84.

Almeida, D. R. 2015. *Representação além das eleições: repensando as fronteiras entre Estado e sociedade*. Jundiaí: Paco Editorial.

Almeida, D. R., and E. S. M. Cunha. 2012. "As dinâmicas da representação: a complexidade da interação institucional nas cidades brasileiras." In *Congress of the Latin American Studies Association*, May 23–26, San Francisco, CA. Available from https://lasa.international.pitt.edu/members/congress-papers/lasa2012/files/29398.pdf.

Avritzer, L. 2007. "Sociedade civil, instituições participativas e representação: da autorização à legitimidade da ação." *Dados – Revista de Ciências Sociais*. Rio de Janeiro. 50 (3): 443–464.

Avritzer, L. 2009. *Participatory Institutions in Democratic Brazil*. Washington, DC: Woodrow Wilson Center; Johns Hopkins University.

Avritzer, L. 2013. "Conferências nacionais: ampliando e redefinindo os padrões de participação social no Brasil." In *Conferências nacionais: atores, dinâmicas participativas e efetividade*, edited by L. Avritzer and C. H. L. Souza, 125–140. Brasília: IPEA.

Bohman, J. 2012. "Representation in the Deliberative System." In *Deliberative Systems: Deliberative Democracy at the Large Scale*, edited by J. Parkinson and J. Mansbridge, 72–94. Cambridge: Cambridge University Press.

Button, M., and D. M. Ryfe. 2005. "What Can We Learn from the Practice of Deliberative Democracy?" In *The Deliberative Democracy Handbook: Strategies for Effective Civic Engagement in the 21st Century*, edited by J. Gastil and P. Levine, 20–33. San Francisco, CA: Jossey-Bass.

Castiglione, D., and M. E. Warren. 2006. "Rethinking Democratic Representation: Eight Theoretical Issues." In *Rethinking Democratic Representation Workshop*, May 18-19, 2006. Columbia: University of British Columbia.

Côrtes, S. V. 2006. "Building up User Participation: Councils and Conferences in the Brazilian Health System." *Sociologias* 1 (Selected Edition): 1–23.

Côrtes, S. V., et al. 2009. "Conselho Nacional de Saúde: histórico, papel institucional e atores estatais e societais." In *Participação e saúde no Brasil*, edited by S. V. Côrtes, 41–72. Rio de Janeiro: Fiocruz.

Cunha, E. S. M. 2013. *Efetividade deliberativa de conselhos de assistência social*. Jundiaí: Paco Editorial.

Cunha, E. S. M., and D. R. Almeida. 2013. "Sociedade civil e representação nas arenas deliberativas da Assistência Social no Brasil." LASA's XXXI International Congress, Washington, DC, 29 May–1 June.

Dovi, S. 2012. *The Good Representative*. West Sussex: Blackwell.

Dryzek, J. S. 2009. "Democratization as Deliberative Capacity Building." *Comparative Political Studies* 42 (11): 1379–1402. doi:10.1177/0010414009332129.

Dryzek, J. S., and S. Niemeyer. 2008. "Discursive Representation." *American Political Science Review* 102 (4): 481–493. doi:10.1017/S0003055408080325.

Faria, C. F., and E. S. M. Cunha. 2012. "Formação de agenda na política de assistência social: o papel das conferências como um sistema integrado de participação e deliberação." In *36° Encontro Anual da Associação de Pós-graduação em Ciências Sociais (ANPOCS)*. 21–25 Outubro. Águas de Lindóia-SP. http://www.anpocs.org/portal/index.php?option=com_content&view=article&id=505%3Aanais-do-encontro-sps-mrs-e-gts-&catid=161%3A36o-encontro-anual-da-anpocs&Itemid=76

Fung, A. 2007. "Minipublics: Deliberative Designs and Their Consequences." In *Deliberation, Participation and Democracy: Can the People Govern?* edited by S. W. Rosenberg, 159–183. New York: Palgrave Macmillan.

Gurza Lavalle, A. G., P. P. Houtzager, and G. Castello. 2006. "Democracia, pluralização da representação e sociedade civil." *Lua Nova: revista de cultura e política* São Paulo 67: 49–103. doi:10.1590/S0102-64452006000200004.

Habermas, J. 2003. *Direito e democracia*: entre facticidade e validade. Tradução de Flávio Beno Siebeneichler. Vol. 2, 2nd ed. Rio de Janeiro: Tempo Brasileiro.

Hendriks, C. 2006. "Integrated Deliberation: Reconciling Civil Society's Dual Role in Deliberative Democracy." *Political Studies* 54: 486–508. doi:10.1111/j.1467-9248.2006.00612.x.

IPEA. 2012. Relatório Final de Pesquisa (Conselho Nacional de Assistência Social), 2012. Accessed February, 20 2013. http://ipea.gov.br/participacao/estudos-do-ipea/conselhosnacionais

Mansbridge, J. 1999. "Everyday Talk in Deliberative System." In *Deliberative Politics: Essays on Democracy and Disagreement*, edited by S. Macedo, 211–239. NY: Oxford University Press.

Mansbridge, J. 2012. "A Systemic Approach to Deliberative Democracy." In *Deliberative Systems: Deliberative Democracy at the Large Scale*, edited by J. Parkinson and J. Mansbridge, et al. 1–26. Cambridge: Cambridge University Press.

Mendonça, R. F. 2008. "Representation and Deliberation in Civil Society." *Brazilian Political Science Review* 2 (2): 117–137.

Mendonça, R. F. 2013. "The Conditions and Dilemmas of Deliberative Systems." Paper presented at American Political Science Association annual meeting, Chicago, IL, August 29–September 1.

Montanaro, L. 2012. "The Democratic Legitimacy of Self-Appointed Representatives." *The Journal of Politics* 74 (4): 1094–1107. doi:10.1017/S0022381612000515.

Olsen, J. P. 1997. "Institutional Design in Democratic Contexts." *The Journal of Political Philosophy* 5 (3): 203–229. doi:10.1111/1467-9760.00032.

Owen, D., and G. Smith. 2013. "Two Types of Deliberative System." Paper presented at American Political Science Association annual meeting, Chicago, IL, August 29–September 1.

Papadopoulos, Y. 2012. "On the Embeddedness of Deliberative Systems: Why Elitist Innovations Matter More." In *Deliberative Systems: Deliberative Democracy at the Large Scale*, edited by J. Parkinson and J. Mansbridge, 125–150. Cambridge: Cambridge University Press.

Parkinson, J. 2003. "Legitimacy Problems in Deliberative Democracy." *Political Studies* 51: 180–196.

Parkinson, J. 2006. *Deliberating in the Real World: Problems of Legitimacy in Deliberative Democracy*. Oxford: Oxford University Press.

Parkinson, J. 2012. "Democratizing Deliberative Systems." In *Deliberative Systems: Deliberative Democracy at the Large Scale*, edited by J. Parkinson and J. Mansbridge, 151–172. Cambridge: Cambridge University Press.

Pitkin, H. F. 1967. *The Concept of Representation*. Berkeley and Los Angeles: University of California.

Plotke, D. 1997. "Representation is Democracy." *Constellations* 4 (1): 19–34. doi:10.1111/cons.1997.4.issue-1.

Pogrebinschi, T., and D. Samuels. 2014. "The Impact of Participatory Democracy: Evidence from Brazil's National Public Policy Conferences." *Comparative Politics* 46 (3): 313–332. doi:10.5129/001041514810943045.

Rosanvallon, P. 2009. *La legitimidad democrática: imparcialidad, reflexividad, proximidad*. Buenos Aires: Manantial.

Sátyro, N., and E. S. M. Cunha. 2014. "The Path of Brazilian Social Assistance Policy Post-1988: The Significance of Institutions and Ideas." *Brazilian Political Science Review* 8 (1): 80–108. doi:10.1590/1981-38212014000100004.

Saward, M. 2006. "The Representative Claim." *Contemporary Political Theory* 5: 297–318. doi:10.1057/palgrave.cpt.9300234.

Saward, M. 2008. "Representation and Democracy: Revisions and Possibilities." *Sociology Compass* 2 (3, May): 1000–1013. doi:10.1111/j.1751-9020.2008.00102.x.

Teixeira, A. C., C. H. Leite de Souza, and P. P. Fiuza Lima. 2012. "Arquitetura da Participação no Brasil: uma leitura das representações em espaços participativos nacionais." In *Textos para discussão 1735*. Brasília: IPEA.

Urbinati, N. 2006. *Representative Democracy*. Chicago: University of Chicago.

Urbinati, N. 2011. "Representative Democracy and Its Critics." In *The Future of Representative Democracy*, edited by S. Alonso, et al. 23–49. Cambridge: Cambridge University.

Urbinati, N., and M. E. Warren. 2008. "The Concept of Representation in Contemporary Democratic Theory." *Annual Review of Political Science* 11: 387–412. doi:10.1146/annurev.polisci.11.053006.190533.

Vieira, M. B., and D. Runciman. 2008. *Representation*. Cambridge: Polity.

Wampler, B. 2012. "Participation, Representation, and Social Justice: Using Participatory Governance to Transform Representative Democracy." *Polity* 44 (4): 666–682. doi:10.1057/pol.2012.21.

Young, I. M. 2000. *Inclusion and Democracy*. Oxford: Oxford University.

Deliberative networks
Andrew Knops

ABSTRACT

Deliberative systems have been proposed as a way of conceiving the complexity of real-world policymaking in deliberative terms. However, there is a concern that in doing so they blunt the critical edge of deliberative ideals. This paper advances an alternative concept – the 'network' of deliberative exchanges – that can encompass real-world complexity without sacrificing deliberation's normative bite. It sets out the components of a network approach, making clear how these are grounded in deliberative principle. It then shows how the network model can apply to actual policy processes, with an extended case study – a critique of the key stages in the Thatcher government's decision to adopt a poll tax in the UK.

The 'practical turn' in deliberative theory concerns the vexed question of how abstract deliberative ideals might guide practical policymaking in large and sophisticated democracies (Dryzek and Niemeyer 2010, 8). Without such guidance, deliberative theories risk being dismissed as irrelevant or ineffective. Much has been learned from studying single initiatives designed to reproduce these abstract ideals as closely as possible and assessing existing institutions for correlates of better deliberative practice. But both approaches have been criticized for failing to provide a fuller description of the wider policymaking process (Chambers 2009). A 'systems' account of deliberation has recently been proposed to address this deficit (Mansbridge 1999; Mansbridge et al. 2012). Different aspects of the policymaking process are seen as contributing to a broader deliberative whole, even when they may not appear deliberative in isolation. However, the wider coverage this model seems to offer may have been bought at the price of blurring the boundary between what counts as deliberation and what does not. This could weaken the critical purchase of the principles underlying the deliberative project.

This paper advances an alternative, network, approach to deliberation, designed to inject greater analytic and critical precision into the systems approach. It will show how a network model gives practical effect to deliberative ideals in a way that mobilizes their critical potential even in the face of the formidable problems of scale and complexity posed by modern democratic polities. The paper begins by briefly outlining the principles that comprise the abstract specification of the deliberative ideal. The challenges posed by operationalizing these ideals in large, real-world democracies are then considered. In Section 2 the deliberative systems approach is introduced as a recent attempt to address these challenges. Yet even some advocates of the systems model recognize it risks diluting the deliberative ideal. These difficulties are examined before introducing a network concept of deliberation as a possible remedy.

The fundamental elements of a deliberative network – a deliberative exchange, and the relation between two such exchanges – are then explained in detail in Sections 3 and 4, respectively. The broader notion of a network composed of these elements is characterized in Section 5, including the insights this formulation offers into the practical application of deliberative principles. With the benefit of this greater detail, Section 6 relates the network model back to the systems approach. Systems conceptions of deliberation can be given a more precise focus within a network frame.

Having clarified the key conceptual elements of a deliberative network, the next section demonstrates their application to practice. This is illustrated in Section 7 with an extended case study of real-world policymaking – the UK government's decision to adopt a poll tax. The example illustrates the relevance of a deliberative network approach to policy processes carried on at the heart of the modern nation-state in all their complexity, while retaining a clear critical edge. It also brings out some of the limitations of the deliberative network model.

With the benefit of these conceptual and practical insights, the paper concludes that a network account of deliberation not only clarifies how deliberative principles can inform practice in modern polities, but has the potential to address the problems of scale and limited resources that such polities raise.

1. Deliberative principles

Initially, advocates of deliberative democracy concentrated on specifying its 'theoretical principles' (Guttmann and Thompson 1996, 1). These aimed to establish deliberation's normative credentials as an alternative theory of democratic legitimacy (e.g. Habermas 1988; Cohen 1997). The most influential statements stipulated the components of 'an *ideal deliberative procedure*' (Cohen 1997, 68). All those affected by a decision should be free to participate in deliberation to determine its outcome (72–75). All participants in deliberation should be free to make and challenge any assertion, and to express their 'attitudes, desires and needs' (Habermas 1990, 88–89). While recognizing moral diversity and pluralism (Cohen 1997, 72; Guttmann and Thompson 1996, Chapter 1), such an exchange should aim at consensus about the common good (Cohen 1997, 75). Reasons offered should therefore be 'public' in the sense they are both comprehensible, and designed to be acceptable, to all others affected by a decision (74; Guttmann and Thompson 1996, 52). Above all, deliberation should promote 'no force except that of the better argument' (Habermas 1988, 108).

Later contributions pay attention to the risk the style of speech adopted in deliberation might exclude (Young 1996, 2000; Dryzek 2000) and to the space available for relatively powerless groups to develop their positions (Fraser 1992). Others have argued for broadening the type of reasons that can be legitimately deployed, to embrace private interests (Mansbridge et al. 2010) and the goal of a deliberation, to include meta-consensus – agreement on the *nature* of the issue in hand, in addition to agreement on the substantive issue itself (Dryzek and Niemeyer 2007).

But deliberation is more than merely an exercise in integrating abstract moral principles such as freedom, equality and reason. As a *political* theory, deliberation owes an account of how it guides practical action, which confronts real-world issues of scale and constraints on time and knowledge. The 'systems' model of deliberative democracy has recently been developed to address these matters (Mansbridge 1999; Warren 2007; Parkinson and Mansbridge 2012).

2. Deliberative systems

A deliberative systems approach recognizes it is impossible for all issues to be agreed in a single deliberative exchange: 'no single forum, however ideally constituted, could possess deliberative capacity to legitimate most of the decisions and policies that democracies adopt' (Mansbridge et al. 2012, 1). Instead, we should envisage deliberation as a system comprising interrelated parts. While individual elements might not be deliberative in themselves, taken together they contribute to a whole, which is. Division of labor amongst a system's parts can thus resolve issues of scale and complexity, which would otherwise make implementing deliberation in modern democratic polities intractable (Mansbridge et al. 2012, 2–3).

A deliberative system is defined as one in which talk is the basis for collective decision (Mansbridge 1999, 5). The systemic framework is designed to be applicable to any set of procedures, from informal chats through parliamentary debates to international institutions, although most versions retain a focus on the nation-state as the primary locus of collective decision (Mansbridge et al. 2012, 2, 7–10; Parkinson 2006; Habermas 1996). Further definition takes two forms, both operating at the functional level.

(1) *Procedural-functional* definitions focus on the different tasks to be undertaken in deliberation. Provided these are performed at some point, by some mechanism, the system as a whole is deemed deliberative. For example, Parkinson argues that a deliberative system must define, discuss, decide and implement – with different actors, including activists, experts, the media and elected assemblies playing different parts in these processes (2006, 169). Goodin's sequential model looks at the roles played by different institutions – caucus room, parliamentary debate, election campaign and postelection bargaining – in contributing to a system that is over time more fully deliberative (2008). On a broader scale, the 'twin-track' approach of Habermas, which sees deliberation delivered through a 'wilder' public sphere of opinion-formation that is transmitted to formally tighter deliberative mechanisms of state government, provides a further functional differentiation within a broader deliberative system (1996). However, these procedural definitions must be supplemented by a broader notion of what deliberation aims for: defining, discussing, deciding and implementing are not enough in themselves to distinguish a deliberative system in Parkinson's model; Goodin's institutions require a further standard against which their partial contribution can be assessed, as does Habermas's 'wild' public sphere.

(2) *Outcome-functional* definitions supplement procedural-functional definitions by specifying the benefits claimed for any form of deliberation. If a practice contributes to these benefits in some way, it is part of a deliberative system. Epistemically, deliberation should produce better informed and more thoroughly reasoned decisions. Ethically, it should encourage mutual respect between citizens (Mansbridge et al. 2012, 10–12). Democratically deliberation should include all those who are affected by a decision. A good deliberative system is defined as one that promotes these goals (13). Their achievement might be impeded by a series of systemic failings. Actors in one part of the system may colonize or distance their critics, in either case stifling challenge. One institution may dominate others, overruling dissent. Or a particular social group may dominate institutions, ensuring that the group's perspective receives preferential treatment (Mansbridge et al. 2012, 22–23).

Despite these efforts at definition, even advocates confess 'the deliberative systems approach is based on a loosening of what counts as "reasoning together"' (Parkinson 2012, 167). There is a danger that this approach could lead to 'concept stretching' (Steiner 2008), blurring the boundaries between what is and is not legitimate deliberation. Practices might count as deliberative even though they provide only a very weak link between issues of collective concern, arguments pertinent to those issues, the individuals they affect and those charged with taking a decision. This link is not specified in current versions of the systems model, beyond the relatively imprecise criteria that all elements should be committed to using 'talk' to resolve disputes, and the outcome-functional epistemic, ethical and democratic goals of deliberation, which in themselves provide an insufficient teleological formulation, and on which procedural-functional definitions ultimately depend. At the same time, the critical point of a deliberative analysis is its impact on practice. To provide a viable guide to real-world political action, abstract statements of deliberative ideals do need to be supplemented by more detailed guidelines. Without such detail, it is unclear whether deliberative theories have an answer to the challenge posed by problems of scale and economy of knowledge in modern, complex polities.

This paper explores a way of strengthening the systems model. It first specifies a tighter notion of a deliberative *network*. This differs from existing definitions of a deliberative system as components of a network are conceived as discrete deliberative exchanges. Such exchanges may be partial in terms of their subject matter and the parties that engage in an exchange, but each exchange is regarded as comprising all the elements of deliberation. This contrasts with the systems account of deliberation, where different elements of the system can provide different aspects of an exchange – for example, the media might present a range of views on an issue, which is ultimately decided in parliament. The tighter network version of deliberation is still able to address issues of scale, in that not everyone has to decide everything in a single face-to-face episode. However, using this model we can specify with much greater precision the link between elements in the network and how the network mobilizes the principles in the abstract ideal. Thus, a network approach preserves deliberation's critical edge, while making it serviceable to guide real-world practice.

3. Deliberative exchange

The basic activity involved in deliberation is an exchange of reasons. This, in turn, takes place in the medium of language, or meaningful interaction. Specifying the types of interaction that count as deliberative is therefore an important first step in defining an exchange. Interaction also presupposes the existence of different acting parties. We can describe these parties in relation to the type of interaction they perform by identifying a set of deliberative roles, some or all of which participants in deliberative exchange perform.

3.1. Deliberative interaction

The basic activities[1] that constitute any deliberative exchange can be divided into stages. Deliberation commences with a disagreement about the validity of a claim – to truth or moral rightness. Parties offer reasons for and against acceptance of the claim in issue. Finally, deliberation is resolved by agreement between the parties on the reasons that have been offered in argument for either the acceptance or rejection of the claim in question (van Eemeren and Grootendorst 2004, 59–62).

Such an account represents the most basic version of the components of an argument or deliberative exchange. However, combinations of these fundamental elements can be used to describe and analyze much more complex structures. So, an attempt might be made to counter one validity claim by replacing it with an alternative[2] (van Eemeren and Grootendorst 2004, 60 note 41). Another form of linked structure is where the argument for acceptance of an initial claim depends on acceptance of a subsidiary claim (119). The stages of the basic specification can be combined to account for much more complicated aspects of real-world exchanges.

3.2. Deliberative roles

Corresponding to these interactions, we can enumerate a series of deliberative roles. In the simplest version, we have just two parties. One party – the proponent – makes a claim that the other – the opponent – challenges. The proponent proceeds to offer reasons for the opponent to accept the claim, while the opponent provides reasons for the proponent to reject it. The argument is resolved when they both agree on the basis of the reasons exchanged to either reject or accept the claim (van Eemeren and Grootendorst 2004, 141–142).

Just as the actions in the simplest version may be combined in more complicated ways, so we can have different combinations of individuals performing particular roles. There may be more than one proponent or opponent of the claim in issue. Different participants may then offer reasons for or against the acceptance of the claim in issue, assuming the roles of defenders or attackers of the claim respectively. And these reasons may be addressed to an audience made up of a separate group again, whose job it is to evaluate the arguments offered to arrive at a reasoned decision on the claim in dispute. Individuals may also change sides, offering arguments both for and against a claim at different points. These variations may be combined with the more complex structures of interaction and argument outlined in Section 3.1.

Whatever the combination of roles, and whoever fills them, it is vital to the proper functioning of any deliberative exchange that they are unimpeded in their exercise. So in addition to an issue in dispute and participants, an exchange requires procedures that specify how the exchange should be conducted in a way that ensures that the different roles can be exercised freely by all those taking part in an exchange.[3]

4. Deliberative exchanges related

The key to identifying a single exchange is that, regardless of the other protagonists involved, members of the same group have responsibility for taking the decision, which terminates the exchange, on the basis of the reasons advanced to them by any parties. If a different group takes a decision, then we have a separate exchange. Having outlined the components of a single deliberative exchange, we can now specify the simplest relation between two such exchanges. For this, we posit

(1) a single deliberative exchange, which has concluded;
(2) a third party, who has not been involved in the first exchange; and
(3) a second deliberative exchange, of which the third party is to be part, but which has not yet begun.

In order to determine the relevance of the first exchange for the second, this third party must evaluate the first exchange. The evaluation is external to that undertaken by those involved in the first exchange in reaching their decision. It does not involve a complete revisiting of all the reasons mobilized in that exchange. In this sense, it is 'vicarious'. Although undertaken at 'one remove', the evaluation of the previous exchange is not a matter of accepting the decision completely on trust.[4] Instead, it involves an indirect assessment of the deliberative merits of the earlier exchange on the basis of its scope and strength.

4.1. Scope

The *scope* of a deliberative exchange is indicated by the decision taken on the claim in issue and the reasons for that decision. A clear statement of a decision allows a third party to assess whether they, and any deliberation they might take part in, are affected by the earlier decision. A clear statement of the reasons for that decision will allow the third party to determine the scope of the deliberative exchange that led to it. Reasons for the acceptance of a claim consist of the claim itself – the conclusion of the argument – and a further set of claims, known as the premises of the argument. Premises are advanced in the hope that they will make acceptance of the conclusion more likely. Much of what is involved in reaching an agreement through argument comprises establishing a set of premises that all parties can accept, which support a common conclusion. Such shared premises comprise the reasons for that conclusion.

The core activity of deliberation is the challenging of claims. Because the premises for the conclusion of a deliberative exchange are accepted by all, the premises themselves are not challenged. So the premises on which the conclusion of a deliberative exchange is justified mark the limits of that exchange. The scope of a deliberative exchange can thus be defined by specifying the conclusion reached – in simplest form, the decision to accept or reject the claim in issue – and the premises from which that conclusion was derived. This indicates to a third party the factors that were deemed relevant to the decision, and by implication, those that were not.

For example, a commission on benefit reform might have been convinced to exempt lone parents from proving they are seeking work before they can receive state benefits, on the grounds that this was the most cost-effective way of ensuring childcare. A later review of government expenditure, seeking economies, seeing this exemption might consult the finding of the earlier commission. Realizing that in this respect the scope of the two investigations overlapped, as they shared the assumption that costs are paramount, it could decide to accept the reasoning of the earlier group and reject the withdrawal of this exemption as a cost-cutting option.

If the premises of an earlier exchange cover all the factors that those in a later exchange deem relevant to a determination of the same or a narrower issue, this suggests there is no need to replicate the earlier exercise. Reinvestigation is likely to produce a similar conclusion. However, if there are elements a third party deems relevant beyond the scope of the earlier deliberation, which it failed to consider, a further exploration in the later exchange is warranted. As no single exchange can deal with every topic, all exchanges are, in this sense, partial in their coverage. Determining the scope of a previous exchange allows the extent of that partiality to be specified in relation to the proposed subject matter of a later exchange. So, in our example, it might be that the earlier commission's decision to retain exemptions was based not on the relative economic efficiency of parental childcare but rather on arguments about the need for the state to support the moral primacy of parents' duty to care for their children. Considering the economic dimension, a later review might recognize the lack of overlap in its scope with that of the earlier commission, prompting it to seek further argument about economic implications of the exemption.

4.2. Strength

In addition to evaluating the scope of an earlier deliberative exchange, it is also important to assess *membership* – who filled the roles in that earlier exchange – and *procedures*. Although an exchange has ranged widely, its conclusions might be biased if the participants did not reflect a balanced cross section of those likely to be affected, technical issues were not adequately addressed or the exchange of reasons was not free and equal. Again, all deliberative exchanges will be constrained in some way along these dimensions – time and resources are limited. The important point is to determine in what way they have been so constrained. On any claim in issue, a balanced cross section of people whose interests are likely to be affected should be represented. While a third party will want to check there are representatives of their own position, they will also want opposing positions to be represented to ensure robust challenge. Similarly, if the claim relates to areas of specialist knowledge, participants should have access to relevant expertise, and such knowledge itself should have been exposed to challenge, for example, through expert review processes. It is also important to ensure that the procedures for conducting the previous deliberative exchange permitted free and equal participation by all concerned, and to clearly recognize any limitations on this.

Such limitations do not invalidate the earlier exchange per se. But they do weaken it in respect of those whose participation has been compromised. Returning to our example, the initial commission's conclusion that lone parents should be exempt from actively seeking work would be strengthened if that commission had consulted those in the opposing camp in a process where they were free to state their position or expert studies on childcare and its costs that were open to peer review.

Based on knowledge of the decision taken in a deliberative exchange, the reasons for it, the participants and the procedures for their interaction, a third party who was not involved in that exchange can arrive at a deliberative evaluation of it in relation to a claim in issue in a second deliberative exchange in which that third party is proposing to engage. Both the scope of the earlier deliberative exchange and its strength may be gauged. These elements will determine the relative impact of the earlier deliberative exchange on the later. If the scope of the earlier decision covers issues seen as relevant to the claim under scrutiny in a second exchange, the participants are judged representative and balanced and the procedures robust, it would be unusual for a second exchange to rehash the ground covered by the earlier. By considering the limits of the earlier decision's scope, representation or procedures, participants in a later exchange can identify any areas that were not covered properly and limit themselves to discussing these. In the process, they may challenge these aspects of the earlier decision. By defining the deliberative limits of a previous decision, therefore, participants in a later exchange can articulate the relationship between that exchange and their own, and act accordingly.

4.3. Transparency

Obviously such an evaluation requires that the information it is based on is made available to the third-party evaluator. Where details of the decision taken, the reasons for the decision, the parties involved and the procedures followed are clearly stated, a deliberative exchange may be termed deliberatively transparent. Transparency is thus an important property of deliberative relations. A deliberatively transparent exchange is open to evaluation in other deliberative exchanges. This may result in that exchange influencing other deliberative exchanges, or it may result in that exchange being challenged in later exchanges. In either case, however, transparency facilitates a continuing open dialogue. On the other hand, if elements of transparency are lacking, it becomes more difficult for others to gauge the relevance or weight that one deliberative exchange has for another.[5]

Note also that just as any single deliberative exchange is partial, so is the way it is evaluated. Such an evaluation will always be from another, limited, perspective. No evaluation can take into account all the matters that were not considered in an earlier exchange, or all who might have been included, or all aspects of procedure. A later exchange will focus on those aspects of the earlier decision that are especially relevant to the subsequent decision and those who are going to take it. That does not completely deprive such an evaluation of utility. Any evaluation is helpful as far as it goes. However, it does emphasize the need for transparency in the evaluation itself. Any evaluation of a deliberative exchange should clearly state which exchange it is evaluating, and its premises – the aspects of the scope and strength of that exchange that define its limits, as well as the aspects (if any) of coverage or representation relevant to the later decision that the earlier exchange is felt to lack. This helps specify the way in which the evaluation might be partial too.

5. Deliberative networks[6]

Having specified more clearly the essential elements of a deliberative exchange, and of the simplest form of relation between two such exchanges, we are now able to describe a deliberative network and its dynamics. The relation between one deliberative exchange and another forms the basic unit of a deliberative network. A deliberative network comprises many such relations between many different deliberative exchanges. The relation between each exchange in the network, however, remains in essence one of vicarious evaluation, based on transparency.

As we saw above, transparency permits an open engagement across deliberative exchanges. If the decision of an earlier exchange is relevant to a later exchange – in terms of scope, and adequate – in terms of the reasons offered and the strength of that decision, those in the later exchange can *vicariously* accept the conclusion of the earlier exchange as a premise of the later deliberation. The later exchange is thus spared the effort of (i) assembling the reasons for the conclusion in the earlier exchange from scratch (ii) interrogating them to locate those that should found acceptance of the conclusion – the process of exchanging reasons in argument and (iii) consulting the various parties to the earlier exchange. Instead, they can vicariously accept the conclusion on the basis of the final set of reasons accepted by the earlier exchange, and the strength of the process by which that conclusion was reached. In situations where those in a later exchange are not satisfied with aspects of the earlier exchange, they will characterize it as more partial, along dimensions of scope and/or strength. Even where the conclusions, though relevant, are rejected, the work done by an earlier exchange will often save some effort in assembling, and possibly in interrogating, the reasons for a conclusion.

In this way, while no one forum can undertake to deliberate on every possible issue, it is possible to accumulate the results of multiple exchanges across the network, the findings of one exchange forming premises in another, and so on. A division of labor is therefore possible, while the dialogue across deliberative exchanges remains deliberative, in that it is based on claims that form the conclusions or premises of the arguments that traverse them. The difference is that in a network these claims are accepted or rejected on *vicarious* deliberative criteria for evaluating deliberation carried on in an earlier exchange. This division of labor allows citizens to select the areas on which they wish to concentrate, so that they are not overburdened with the task, and to best mobilize their particular experience, knowledge and motivation, while still contributing to the overall debate.

So the commission in our example might have had their decision to continue to exempt lone parents from the need to actively seek work in order to claim benefits influenced by a group of lone parents. That group may in turn have supported their position with a review they had undertaken of published research into the comparative costs to the state of enforcing or not enforcing this condition. Here, a group of those directly affected draw on the conclusions of others – guided by reference to the scope of any premisses assumed, and the procedures adopted, including openness to the criticism of other experts – in forming their own conclusions. This is then transmitted to inform the commission's conclusions, which incorporates the reasoning in the original research and work done by the lone parent group in summarizing and reviewing it. Finally, the commission's conclusions and the scope of its premises, including all the above material, and the strength of the procedures by which it has been generated, can be taken into account by the final efficiency review. This spares that review considerable effort in assembling these reasons from scratch. And it allows multiple actors to contribute to this final decision, without having to engage constantly in face-to-face exchange, while not compromising the purposes or opinions of any of those actors.

Of course, all this depends on undertaking an evaluation of previous decisions. This is in turn facilitated by the provision of information on which a vicarious evaluation can be based – transparency. Both of these operations take effort. However, the extensive efficiencies of vicarious evaluation for a later exchange – avoiding the need to assemble reasons from scratch, to engage with them in detail to identify those underpinning a conclusion, and to consult a range of parties – provide considerable positive motivation to pursue such information. Conversely, the normative and practical dangers of relying on a decision that is relatively partial – in the assumptions on which it is based, the rigor of the procedures with which it has been deliberated or the range of those affected – but which has not been assessed as such constitute corresponding negative incentives for full transparency and systematic vicarious evaluation.

Given these pressures for a later exchange to demand transparency from an earlier exchange, it is in the interests of those in the earlier exchange to produce as strong and clear a result as possible on the issue under discussion, with robust premisses, since this will carry more weight with a wider audience. It is also in their interests to make the exchange deliberatively transparent to make their deliberations accessible. Without this it will be impossible to assess its scope and weight. If a later exchange is aware of a lack of transparency, they will be reluctant to accept or act on such an opaque decision. Conversely, a strong decision with wide scope clearly stated will have maximum impact, enhancing the practical effectiveness of the originating exchange by extending their influence while minimizing the need for them to engage in further detailed face-to-face deliberation.[7]

Of course, if those in a later exchange are not alert to a lack of transparency about a decision, they might still accept it. So it would still have extended impact. However, by defining a deliberative exchange as a conclusion reached by a particular group of people, a deliberative network model promotes accountability for such a step, which further motivates transparency. Should adverse consequences stem from action based on acceptance of inadequately supported conclusions, they can be traced back to those assumptions, and the process and group by which they were adopted. To the extent their adoption resulted from lack of vigilance on the part of a later exchange, they can be held responsible. To the extent that it was caused by calculated deception or misrepresentation by an earlier exchange, the blame can be allocated them (and see below, pp. 16–18).

In this way, therefore, a deliberative network model relates the principles of the deliberative ideal to the practical exigencies of the real world. The ideal specifies the elements of the activity of deliberation at its highest level of abstraction, conceived as rights that those affected should have to carry out such activities. The basic unit of a network model – a single, actual deliberative exchange – is described in terms of these activities. Having defined a single exchange, aspects of that exchange – the decision taken, its premises, those represented in the exchange and the procedures that governed it – are used to evaluate its scope and strength, from the perspective of another exchange. The potential division of labor and attendant economies this vicarious evaluation promises then provides the motivation for those in the network to both seek and supply the information necessary for the transparency that forms the links between nodes. In turn, the transparency facilitates the continued application of critical deliberative standards by providing the information for vicarious evaluation. Not only does a deliberative network model show that it is possible to apply deliberative principles to inform practice without diminishing their critical bite; it demonstrates how practical motivations can positively drive the critical application of those principles.

6. Deliberative networks related to deliberative systems

This paper started by proposing deliberative networks as a way of strengthening the notion of a deliberative system, in which different interrelated parts functioned together to achieve deliberative goals in a way that could guide decision-making in large, diverse and complex modern democracies. Having developed the conception of a network as a relationship between discrete deliberative exchanges, explained its key features and outlined some of its advantages for this task, it is now possible to describe more precisely the relationship between the concept of a deliberative network advanced here and that of a deliberative system, and the way in which the former strengthens the latter.

There are two main differences between a deliberative network and a deliberative system. First, the elements of a deliberative network are only individual deliberative exchanges. Each exchange contains all the elements of deliberation – a disagreement, exchange of reasons and a decision. However, the components of a deliberative system might perform only one of these functions, as in our earlier example where the media presented a range of reasons, but a decision was taken by another body. The second difference lies in the level at which the two formulations are pitched. A network account models the dynamics of a set of interactions, whereas the systems account has a more functional focus on institutions.

Yet although discussion of deliberative systems has been dominated by an institutional register, it is quite possible to define a system in terms of a particular issue (Mansbridge et al. 2012, 8). To specify a particular deliberative system from this alternative perspective, we would first need to identify a particular claim in dispute, and the parties to that dispute. We would then need to locate the reasons being exchanged, and the parties who carried out the exchange, along with those charged with reaching a decision. Clearly these elements might be fragmented. In particular, there may be many different parties offering reasons, both for and against the relevant questions in dispute. These may also influence decisions across a broad range of individuals, in different forms of association, on this issue. Strictly speaking, the decisions of each association would form separate systems under a network approach (above p. 6). Only if it was possible to identify some overarching decision resulting from these disparate associations on the same issue would it be possible to characterize them as part of the same system, even though they refer to the same reasons, offered by the same protagonists, on the same issue.

Relativizing a deliberative system to a particular issue and the decision by which it is collectively resolved does allow us to integrate the deliberative systems and network approaches. In this light, a deliberative system is conceived with respect to a deliberative exchange. Different institutions making different functional contributions to the system can be redescribed as groups, or associations, performing different roles and hence different aspects of the interactions involved in a single deliberative exchange, without losing anything. The members of those associations, their procedures and their audiences are then simply viewed as aspects of the more comprehensive exchange of which they are part, which is fully characterized by taking together these elements for each of the institutions that are seen as part of the system.

Seen from this perspective, a deliberative system is coterminous with a deliberative exchange in a network. A network comprises two or more deliberative exchanges and the relationship between them. This has the advantage of clearly distinguishing between the components of a particular exchange on a particular issue, and the components of a network – the exchanges themselves. It also gives a clearer focus to the notion of a deliberative system since its elements must be specified in terms of the deliberative activities of making or rejecting claims, supporting or challenging claims with reasons, or evaluating those reasons in order to decide whether or not to accept a claim. Greater clarity on which of these activities, and what specific decision, components of the system contribute to will enhance the analytical rigor of the concept of a system.

7. Application

The dimensions of a network conception of deliberation, and a fuller description of its relation to the notion of a deliberative system, have now been set out. The point of developing such a conception is to bring deliberative principles to bear on political practice. Accordingly, this section demonstrates the utility of the network model for analyzing real-world policy processes by applying it to a particularly significant example of one such process – the UK government's decision to introduce a poll tax. Not only is it possible to describe the key features of this process in network terms, but doing so provides insight into their deliberative quality, demonstrating the critical purchase of deliberative principles on such real-world practices.

The Thatcher government's adoption of poll tax comprised two central elements: a Department of the Environment review, commissioned in late 1984, which recommended it, and a meeting of the prime minister and members of cabinet at Chequers, her country retreat, on 31 March 1985, which endorsed that recommendation. From a network perspective, these two elements represent exchanges linked by a deliberative nexus. A clear decision taken by one body – the review – is evaluated by a separate group – cabinet, led by the prime minister.

Having identified this central deliberative nexus, we can now consider its components: the first exchange – the departmental review – and its representation to the second exchange at Chequers. Deploying the network frame, the decision taken in the first exchange will be analyzed for strength and scope. That decision's presentation to the second exchange can then be assessed for transparency. The analysis will show that on the crucial issues of the fairness and practical feasibility of the poll tax the presentation of the review's findings to the Chequers meeting lacked transparency. The consequences of this deficiency will be traced, demonstrating the considerable incentives for ensuring transparency in a deliberative network.

7.1. Background

Poll tax replaced domestic rates as a source of UK local government revenue. Domestic rates were set by local authorities and paid by householders in the local authority area based on the estimated value of their property. Others, such as many renting accommodation, were not liable to pay (King and Crewe 2013, 44). Tories had long been critical of the rates. They objected to interhousehold inequities: equally valued houses attracted the same liability regardless of the number and income of occupants. Periodic revisions to estimated property values could lead to considerable increases in liability, disproportionately affecting property-owning Tory supporters. Nonhouseholders were not liable for rates, while many had the full amount rebated. Tories felt these voters would support high-spending policies that benefitted them at no personal cost (Butler, Adonis, and Travers 1994, 51–53; King and Crewe 2013, 42, 44). In opposition, Thatcher inserted a promise to abolish rates in the Conservative's unsuccessful 1974 election manifesto (Conservative Party 1974, 6). But a 1975 review found no workable alternative to rates (Butler, Adonis, and Travers 1994, 25), and the 1979 manifesto downplayed their reform (Conservative Party 1979, 14).

With the Tories in power, a 1981 Green Paper (Department of the Environment 1981) reviewed rates, local income tax, local sales tax and poll tax against systematic criteria. Poll tax was rejected as too difficult and expensive to administer (Butler, Adonis, and Travers 1994, 33–34). A subsequent House of Commons Committee enquiry echoed these findings. The 1983 White Paper *Rates* stated the government's commitment to rates 'for the foreseeable future' (Department of the Environment 1983, 14). However, within a year rates reform was back. Central government attempts to control local authority expenditure had met increasingly radical defiance. Opposition to the abolition of the Greater London Council and refusal by some far-left councilors to set a rate had exposed the ineffectiveness of the complex system of local authority grant limitations. In late 1984, Patrick Jenkin, Secretary of State for the Environment – the department responsible for this field – obtained the prime minister's backing for a series of 'studies' into local government finance to address this issue (Butler, Adonis, and Travers 1994, 41–45). The studies recommended adoption of a poll tax. They constitute this case study's first 'deliberative exchange'.

7.2. Initial exchange: the departmental 'studies'

A deliberative exchange will always be partial. As detailed (pp. 6–8), partiality can be characterized along two dimensions: strength – membership and procedures, and scope – the decisions reached, their attendant reasons and premisses.

7.2.1. Strength: membership

The studies were led by two junior ministers: William Waldegrave and Kenneth Baker, both keen to earn Thatcher's recognition as 'One of Us.' Apart from an official seconded from the Treasury and one from the Department of Health and Social Security (DHSS), civil servants were from the Department of the Environment (Butler, Adonis, and Travers 1994, 47–48). Four specialist 'assessors' from outside government advised the team. Lord Rothschild had headed the Conservative's Central Policy Review Staff 'think tank'. He suggested Leonard Hoffmann QC, although Hoffmann left in March 1985 to become a judge. Waldegrave invited Tom Wilson, a retired academic economist from Glasgow University. Christopher Foster, who had been an LSE economist and government advisor, completed this group (48–49).

Of the assessors, only Foster was an expert in local government finance, having coauthored an important survey including an appraisal of poll tax (Foster, Jackman, and Perlman 1980). While team members were acquainted with local government finance, this was only from the perspective of central government design and oversight. Detailed knowledge of its administration lay with local authorities, especially their treasuries. Yet neither had a presence (Butler, Adonis, and Travers 1994, 213, 6, 9; 220–221). Much pressure for rates reform had come from individual rate payers who felt they had suffered financial injustice. Any new system would also be likely to impact individuals. A regressive measure like the poll tax was particularly likely to hit the poor. However, there was no attempt to represent these groups directly by including any of their members, or organizations that lobby on their behalf, on the team. The DHSS secondment was primarily to consider administrative integration of any tax with the benefits system.

7.2.2. Strength: procedure

In line with the 'activist mentality' of officials of the day, the studies united a small, tight, high-quality 'project team' to provide solutions to particular government policy problems in a matter of months (Butler, Adonis, and Travers 1994, 209, 214). There was also a degree of alignment between government and officials' interests. The Department of the Environment administered the cumbersome system of local authority grant controls. The team's proposals promised to replace much of this with pressure from a poll tax paying local electorate (222). This led to an 'unusually strong' shared sense of purpose (50) muting challenges to emerging proposals (King and Crewe 2013, 46).

Internally close, the team's procedures were also relatively closed to outside influence. The absence of members from other government departments, local authorities or citizens' interest groups could have been addressed with sustained dialogue enabling these bodies to fully express their views and raise objections. Advice was sought from outside sources, including other departments, but was limited to specific information points (Foster 2005, 103; King and Crewe 2013, 45). The team's assessors appear to have been sidelined to the extent they disagreed with the emerging consensus behind poll tax within the team. (Butler, Adonis, and Travers 1994, 60, 66).

7.2.3. Scope

The studies proceeded from two basic premises. First: if residents bore more of the cost of local spending currently obscured by central grants and two-tier authorities, they would oppose increases. Second: because they did not pay rates, many local voters received the benefits of expensive policies for free. Making all voters liable for the cost of local services would improve accountability (Butler, Adonis, and Travers 1994, 51–54). The prime minister's opposition to rates was well known, reinforced by a disastrous Scottish revaluation in 1984–1985 (61–65). The rates, and by association any property tax, appear to have been assumed 'beyond the terms of reference of the studies' (study official quoted in Butler, Adonis, and Travers 1994, 55). The other two options – local income or sales taxes – were peremptorily ruled out. The former was contrary to the government's determination to reduce income tax, the latter impractical. (55–56). The team concentrated on the benefits of the remaining choice – poll tax – in light of their two foundational tenets of accountability.

From this perspective, the poll tax held practical, ideological and political appeal. Practically, the increased pressure it was assumed spreading liability through a per capita tax would bring would reduce the need for central controls, allowing considerable simplification. Ideologically, this extension of liability was conceived as the expansion of free-market discipline to the (local) state – the heart of the Thatcher project. Politically the same mechanism would redress the interhousehold and revaluation injustices that had so animated the Tory rank-and-file. The attractions of the tax framed in this way seem to have constrained the team's ability to entertain challenges to this picture and the assumptions on which it was based along two key dimensions (Foster 2005, 106).

7.2.3.1. Unfairness.
The same principle of flat-rate liability per person that held the promise of greater local accountability meant the poll tax regressively bore no relation to ability to pay. Perhaps because of this, the team paid little attention to the fairness of the poll tax as opposed to its capacity to redress inequitable features of the rates. In particular, there would be considerable losses in the switch to the new tax, especially among the 'nearly poor'. We have seen the interests of this group were not represented in the composition or procedures of the team. Whether any attempt was made to calculate these effects or bring them to the attention of team ministers is unclear. They certainly seem to have been accorded little weight (Butler, Adonis, and Travers 1994, 216, 221).

7.2.3.2. Impracticality.
The individual basis of poll tax liability required tracking the people to whom liability attached. As the 1981 Green Paper acknowledged, this is much more difficult than locating property and its ownership. Again, whether or not the team were aware of them, they appear to have glossed over these inconvenient features. This was probably exacerbated by the failure to represent or consult with local authority officials with experience of these issues. The relative difficulties of administering individual versus a property-based liability may also have been obscured by the team's *a priori* dismissal of the latter, ruling out such comparison.

The fairness and practicality of the poll tax were challenged in detail in a paper by Hoffmann, one of the team's assessors, cautioning against the poll tax once it had become clear this was the team's preferred option. That it was ignored (Butler, Adonis, and Travers 1994, 68) provides perhaps the starkest evidence of the critical limitations of the study on both these issues.

So, framing a poll tax within free-market assumptions meant it promised considerable practical, ideological and political advantages. Concentrating on these benefits, the team refused to engage with two main challenges to the free-market model that might undermine them. Concerns about poll tax's fairness could obscure free-market accountability. Problems of practicality threatened to overthrow the tax entirely, in favor of alternatives the team already assumed unacceptable. These assumptions – about the scheme's operation on free-market principles, its fairness and its relative practicality – constitute unquestioned premises that limit the scope of the team's decision to adopt poll tax. These limitations were buttressed by the weaknesses identified in the team's membership and procedures. In these ways, the study was *partial*. It failed to inquire fully into the tax's fairness and practicality, and too readily dismissed alternatives.

7.3. *Transparency*

The findings of the first exchange – the studies – were presented for evaluation by a second exchange, a dedicated 'awayday' at Chequers, the prime minister's country retreat, on Sunday 31 March 1985. That meeting was attended by the prime minister and almost half her cabinet. These included Lord Whitelaw, the deputy prime minister, fresh from an encounter with Scottish Tories making plain their discontent with rates, the Home, Welsh and Northern Irish secretaries. The party chairman and a junior Scottish Office minister arrived late by plane from Edinburgh. The chancellor, Nigel Lawson, was absent. He had been told this was 'a preliminary discussion' where 'no decisions would be taken' (Lawson 1992, 571). Peter Rees, chief secretary to the Treasury, went instead, briefed to register the Treasury's opposition to poll tax. Jenkin attended, along with Waldegrave, Baker, the lead civil servant from the team and the principal secretary for the department. No one else from the study team was present. No local authority representatives were invited, no papers circulated in advance (Butler, Adonis, and Travers 1994, 68, 70–71).

Baker led with an analysis of the problems with the existing local government finance system – the equity and accountability problems outlined (15, 19). Waldegrave followed with solutions – including the poll tax – emphasizing the advantages the studies team identified (19–20). Prompted by Jenkin, he ended by reminding the prime minister its introduction would deliver her pledge to abolish rates (Baker 1993, 122; Crick and van Klaveren 1991, 409). There followed a long discussion. Thatcher declared herself well-disposed to the arguments advanced for poll tax from the start (Foster 2005, 104). Emphasis was again on the tax's potential benefits. The home secretary did worry that constructing a register might have civil liberties implications, and that it might be seen as a tax on voting. Rees presented the Treasury's objections. But they were the minority. The regressive effect of the tax on winners and losers was not interrogated in any detail (104). When asked the cost of administering the tax, the Department of the Environment replied it was 'not a great amount more' than rates. A departmental minister suggested it was 'easily collectable' (Butler, Adonis, and Travers 1994, 75). Again this issue received limited attention (Foster 2005, 104).

The most explicit failure to be transparent about the partiality of the studies related to practical difficulties and costs. Despite being aware of the limitations of their inquiries, team members minimized the problems the tax might face (Foster 2005,

104). Their lack of transparency on fairness involved a failure to alert the Chequers meeting to the salience of the issue for a regressive poll tax, requiring more detailed investigation. The doubts transparency on these two issues would have raised may have thrown the question of their ready dismissal of alternatives into greater relief. Given the Chequers meeting was looking for a workable source of local, domestic revenue, the team's peremptory exclusion of any form of property tax constitutes a further unquestioned premiss the team should have made explicit.

7.4. Consequences

The immediate consequence of this lack of transparency was that the Chequers meeting approved the team's recommendation of a poll tax, with no dissenters, 'not provisionally... subject to overcoming problems of its regressiveness and collectability' but wholesale (Foster 2005, 104). The support given, in particular by the prime minster and her deputy, seems to have been sufficient to counter any subsequent direct opposition, even from the chancellor. The prime minister had been converted (Butler, Adonis, and Travers 1994, 76).

Longer-term repercussions were drastic. The tax was widely perceived as unfair, largely because of its regressive nature and the large amounts those on relatively modest incomes stood to lose. Widespread resistance to payment meant collecting the tax became extremely difficult and costly. Nationwide protests led to some of the worst rioting seen in mainland postwar Britain (Butler, Adonis, and Travers 1994, 126–153). These difficulties were a significant factor in Thatcher being voted out of office by her own party (1, 168–170). Within a year of winning the 1992 election, her successor, John Major, abolished poll tax replacing it with a banded property tax – the Council Tax – still in force today (Butler, Adonis, and Travers 1994, 170–183; King and Crewe 2013, 62–63). Significantly, these dire consequences stemmed from precisely the gaps in their investigation the studies team failed to make clear: fairness, practicality and the failure to explore alternatives (Butler, Adonis, and Travers 1994, 67).

7.5. Insights

In addition to demonstrating a network model can critically apply clear deliberative standards to detailed practical policy processes, this brief case study illustrates the considerable incentives for observing such standards a network model can bring to bear. It clearly links the deliberative failings of limitations in strength, scope and lack of transparency to the political failings of the tax. Through identifying groups of actors with decisions taken, it assists the allocation of responsibility for these shortcomings.

Of course, what it also shows is that, while a deliberative network model can help expose the incentives for transparency, the information required for effective vicarious evaluation, and the mechanism for allocating deliberative responsibility, other factors will affect whether, in any given case, transparency is actually demanded, evaluations are actually carried out and acted upon, and blame is actually allocated. The deliberative network model shows it is possible to do this, and indeed there are motivations. Nonetheless, it is still no guarantee actors will take these opportunities. While an account was finally demanded in our poll tax case study, if deliberative principles had been mobilized earlier it is arguable that much of the waste and harm caused by the tax could have been avoided. That it was not suggests there remain considerable costs involved in deliberating even within a network – in providing, gathering and evaluating, even vicariously, information about a completed deliberative exchange. There are also countervailing pressures – apparent short-term gain, personal ambition and hegemonic assumptions such as the overweening free-market liberalism in our example. A deliberative network has the potential to counter these factors, but it still requires action to realize that potential.

8. Conclusion

No single real-world deliberative exchange can cover all the issues faced by a modern democratic polity. However, a deliberative network model characterizes the partial coverage of those issues achieved in a single exchange by reference to the ideal principles of free and equal challenge in reasoned debate. It then uses this characterization as the link between discrete exchanges that allows for a wider dialogue *across* individual exchanges through which those deliberative ideals can be more closely approached. Integrated with a systems approach, the network model demonstrates there is no need to loosen the standards that constitute 'reasoning together on an issue' in order to conceptualize larger-scale, real-world decision-making processes.

Notes

1. Despite developments in the theory of deliberation (p. 3), these activities remain central.
2. 'Meta-consensus' – agreement on the nature of an issue, rather than its substance, may be seen as an application of this strategy.
3. These should themselves be open to challenge (Knops 2006, 608–609).
4. For an argument for acceptance of deliberative findings based on trust, see Mackenzie and Warren (2012); for an objection, see Parkinson (2012, 160–161).
5. New information technologies greatly enhance the potential to access such information.
6. These are distinct from 'governance' networks, mainly because deliberative networks do not sanction coercive bargaining so legitimacy is derived from a reasoned, not 'rough', consensus (cf. Sørensen and Torfing 2007, 8–11).
7. For empirical evidence that when deliberation results in a clear conclusion this carries more weight, see de Cindio and Schuler (2007).

Acknowledgments

I would like to thank John Dryzek, Marit Böker, Maija Setälä and the anonymous referees for their detailed comments on earlier drafts of this paper. Thanks also to all who discussed versions at conferences or seminars at the Universities of Western Bohemia, Pilsen in the Czech Republic, Newcastle-upon-Tyne, Glasgow and Oxford in the UK and Turku in Finland. In addition, I am grateful to the Academy of Finland project 'Democratic Reasoning' at the Political Science Unit at the University of Turku for generously hosting me on a visiting fellowship during which the paper was finalized.

Disclosure statement

No potential conflict of interest was reported by the author.

References

Baker, K. 1993. *The Turbulent Years*. London: Faber.
Butler, D., A. Adonis, and T. Travers. 1994. *Failure in British Government: The Politics of the Poll Tax*. Oxford: Oxford University Press.
Chambers, S. 2009. "Rhetoric and the Public Sphere: Has Deliberative Democracy Abandoned Mass Democracy?" *Political Theory* 37 (3): 323–350. doi:10.1177/0090591709332336.
Cohen, J. 1997. "Deliberation and Democratic Legitimacy." In *Deliberative Democracy: Essays on Reason and Politics*, edited by J. Bohman and W. Rehg, 67–91. Cambridge, MA: Massachusetts Institute of Technology Press.
Conservative Party. 1974. *Conservative Party Manifesto*. London: Conservative Party Central Office.
Conservative Party. 1979. *Conservative Party Manifesto*. London: Conservative Party Central Office.
Crick, B., and A. van Klaveren. 1991. "Poll Tax: Mrs Thatcher's Greatest Blunder." *Contemporary Record* 5 (3): 397–416. doi:10.1080/13619469108581185.
de Cindio, F., and D. Schuler. 2007. "Deliberation and Community Networks: A Strong Link Waiting to be Forged." Paper delivered to Communities and Action: CIRN Conference, Prato, November 5–7.
Department of the Environment. 1981. *Alternatives to Domestic Rates*. London: HMSO, Cmnd. 8449.
Department of the Environment. 1983. *Rates*. London: HMSO, Cmnd. 9008.
Dryzek, J., and S. Niemeyer. 2010. *Foundations and Frontiers of Deliberative Governance*. Oxford: Oxford University Press.
Dryzek, J. S. 2000. *Deliberative Democracy and Beyond: Liberals, Critics, Contestations*. Oxford: Oxford University Press.
Dryzek, J. S., and S. Niemeyer. 2007. "The Ends of Deliberation: Meta-consensus and Inter-subjective Rationality as Ideal Outcomes." *Swiss Political Science Review* 13 (4): 497–526. doi:10.1002/j.1662-6370.2007.tb00087.x.
Foster, C. D. 2005. *British Government in Crisis, or the Third English Revolution*. Oxford: Hart.
Foster, C. D., R. Jackman, and M. Perlman. 1980. *Local Government Finance in a Unitary State*. London: Allen & Unwin.
Fraser, N. 1992. "Rethinking the Public Sphere: A Contribution to the Critique of Actually Existing Democracy." In *Habermas and the Public Sphere*, edited by C. Calhoun, 109–142. Cambridge, MA: MIT Press.
Goodin, R. 2008. *Innovating Democracy*. Oxford: Oxford University Press.
Guttmann, A., and D. Thompson. 1996. *Democracy and Disagreement*. Cambridge, MA: Belknap Press.
Habermas, J. 1988. *Legitimation Crisis*. Cambridge: Polity Press.
Habermas, J. 1990. "Discourse Ethics: Notes on a Program of Philosophical Justification." In *Moral Consciousness and Communicative Action*. Translated by C. Lenhardt and S. W. Nicholsen, edited by J. Habermas, 43–115. Cambridge: Polity.

Habermas, J. 1996. *Between Facts and Norms: Contributions to a Discourse Theory of Law and Democracy*. Translated by W. Rehg. Cambridge: Polity.

King, A., and I. Crewe. 2013. *The Blunders of Our Governments*. London: Oneworld.

Knops, A. 2006. "Delivering Deliberation's Emancipatory Potential." *Political Theory* 34 (5): 594–623. doi:10.1177/0090591706290780.

Lawson, N. 1992. *The View from No. 11: Memoirs of a Tory Radical*. London: Bantam.

Mackenzie, M. K., and M. E. Warren. 2012. "Two Trust-Based Uses of Minipublics in Democratic Systems." In *Deliberative Systems*, edited by J. Parkinson and J. Mansbridge, 95–124. Cambridge: Cambridge University Press.

Mansbridge, J. 1999. "Everyday Talk in the Deliberative System." In *Deliberative Politics: Essays on Democracy and Disagreement*, edited by S. Macedo, 211–239. Oxford: Oxford University Press.

Mansbridge, J., J. Bohman, S. Chambers, T. Christiano, A. Fung, J. Parkinson, D. F. Thompson, and M. E. Warren. 2012. "A Systemic Approach to Deliberative Democracy." In *Deliberative Systems*, edited by J. Parkinson and J. Mansbridge, 1–26. Cambridge: Cambridge University Press.

Mansbridge, J., J. Bohman, S. Chambers, D. Estlund, A. Føllesdal, A. Fung, C. Lafont, B. Manin, and J. L. Martí. 2010. "The Place of Self-Interest and the Role of Power in Deliberative Democracy." *The Journal of Political Philosophy* 18 (1): 64–100. doi:10.1111/j.1467-9760.2009.00344.x.

Parkinson, J. 2006. *Deliberating in the Real World: Problems of Legitimacy in Deliberative Democracy*. Oxford: Oxford University Press.

Parkinson, J. 2012. "Democratizing Deliberative Systems." In *Deliberative Systems*, edited by J. Parkinson and J. Mansbridge, 151–172. Cambridge: Cambridge University Press.

Parkinson, J., and J. Mansbridge, eds. 2012. *Deliberative Systems*. Cambridge: Cambridge University Press.

Sørensen, E., and J. Torfing. 2007. "Governance Network Research: Towards a Second Generation." In *Theories of Democratic Network Governance*, edited by E. Sørensen and J. Torfing, 1–21. Houndsmills: Palgrave Macmillan.

Steiner, J. 2008. "Concept Stretching: The Case of Deliberation." *European Political Science* 7: 186–190. doi:10.1057/palgrave.eps.2210186.

van Eemeren, F. H., and R. G. Grootendorst. 2004. *A Systematic Theory of Argumentation: The Pragma-dialectical Approach*. Cambridge: Cambridge University Press.

Warren, M. E. 2007. "Institutionalizing Deliberative Democracy." In *Can the People Govern? Deliberation, Participation and Democracy*, edited by S. W. Rosenberg, 272–288. Houndsmills: Palgrave Macmillan.

Young, I. M. 1996. "Communication and the Other: Beyond Deliberative Democracy." In *Democracy and Difference: Testing the Boundaries of the Political*, edited by S. Benhabib, 120–135. Princeton, NJ: Princeton University Press.

Young, I. M. 2000. *Inclusion and Democracy*. Oxford: Oxford University Press.

Reflections on how to empirically ground the deliberative system's theory

Leonardo Avritzer

ABSTRACT
The second section of the symposium on deliberative systems deals with three areas: the connection between deliberative actors through a network theory; the transmission of deliberative messages; and the institutional design of deliberative systems. In this short commentary, I shall review each one of the arguments and then present a critical balance between them.

The concept of deliberative systems is an important new development in the theory of deliberative democracy. Deliberative democracy is a critique of the aggregative view of democracy that dominated postwar democratic theory. Instead of aggregation through elections, deliberative democracy proposes different ways of improving the quality of democracy through public reasoning and argumentation (Rawls 1993, 72; Cohen 1997, 68). Deliberative systems theory shows that democratic theory currently faces a challenge that goes far beyond the institutional building of deliberation, that is, how to integrate new deliberative practices into the current political system (Parkinson and Mansbridge 2012).

Mansbridge and Parkinson presented the idea of deliberative systems as a way to overcome the current stalemate in both deliberative theory and deliberative practice. They define a deliberative system as '…a set of distinguishable, differentiated, but to some degree interdependent parts, often with distributed functions and a division of labour, connected in such a way as to form a complex whole' (Parkinson and Mansbridge 2012, 6). This definition is the starting point for thinking about deliberative systems as a form of integration through everyday talk and the formation of mini-publics (Parkinson and Mansbridge 2012). However, as the editorial introduction to this symposium points out 'despite its conceptual and practical appeal, the concept of deliberative systems also entails potential problems and raises several important questions. There are still ongoing scholarly debates over the relationship between the parts and the whole of the deliberative system, the prospects of its institutionalization, and the methodological choices as well as difficulties related to its empirical analysis'.

The second section of the symposium on deliberative systems offers important contributions coming both from Northern and Southern scholars in three areas: first, in the area of connection between deliberative actors through a network theory; second, in the area of transmission of deliberative messages; and third, in the area of the institutional design of deliberative systems. In this short comment, I will first briefly review each one of the argument and then make a critical balance of each one of the papers.

Deliberative networks or the connection of actors in a deliberative system

Deliberative systems involve an important change in perspective from the idea of abstract deliberative ideals to practical policy-making in real democracies. This is the point of departure of Andre Knops's article on deliberative networks. For him, a deliberative network involves a deliberative exchange and a relation between two exchanges. This approach seeks to make more concrete the relation among actors in a system. Knops proposed to deepen this approach by adding scope, strength, and transparency to the deliberative exchanges. According to the author, '…the decision of an earlier exchange is relevant to a later exchange… in terms of the reasons offered and the strength of the decision, those in a later exchange can vicariously accept the conclusion of the earlier exchange as a premise of the later deliberation'. This remark is very important to provide concreteness to deliberative democracy theory. The problem with the theory or even its systemic version is that, in the real world of policy-making institutions, arguments are not debated in a separate way. On the contrary, policy-making involves an accumulated set of debates and reasons that ground decisions. Knops important insight is that a deliberative systems theory need to ground deliberations on previous accumulated reason so that a criterion is created to evaluate a previous policy or to ground its critique.

A second important contribution of the paper 'Deliberative Networks' is a more concrete incorporation of the role played by institutions. The author proposes to incorporate institutions into a deliberative network by re-describing them '… as groups or associations, performing different roles and hence different aspects of the interactions involved in a single deliberative exchange…'. Again, the approach is very good because it incorporated real actors into deliberative systems theory.

The weakest point of the paper is the example of the operation of a deliberative network. The author exemplifies the network conception of deliberative system through the episode of the British government attempt to introduce a poll tax. The initial exchanges were the studies commissioned by two junior ministers of the Thatcher's administration. The first exchange was presented at a meeting attended by the prime minister and almost half of her cabinet. Knops points out the lack of transparency in between the initial exchange and the presentation of the report that could amount to a subsequent exchange. For him, the most explicit failure involved the lack of '…transparency about the partiality of the studies related to practical difficulties and costs'. Though I can agree that omission of details on policy implementation could be key in policy-making implementation, the example does not elaborate sufficiently on the strong lack of justice of the poll tax proposal and its political consequences. It would be more helpful to exemplify with a case that would not be explained by mainstream or more conventional frameworks. Yet, the framework presented is a real step forward in introducing policy-making considerations into the deliberative system's approach.

Transmission in deliberative systems

The deliberative system's theory assumes that there is transmission between parts of the system, that is to say, debates, arguments, and decisions are conveyed among the subparts of the system. However, how transmission takes place and what connects the different parts of the system remains unknown or in the words of Boswell, Hendricks, and Ercan, no literature so far 'encompasses the broad array of sites and institutions through which claims travel in a deliberative system'. In a fashion similar to the article on deliberative networks, the authors emphasize transmission in real world cases.

The authors give three examples of transmission, the case of honor killings in England and Germany, the case of energy policy debate in New South Wales, and the case of the obesity debate in Australia and the UK. In the case of 'honor killings', the debate emerged after killings that were widely publicized and triggered culture-based and gender-based debates. The authors show that in spite of strong public space debates in both countries, only in the case of Britain, institutional transmission mechanisms emerged in the intersection between the public apace and the state. This role performed by the Women's National Council opened the way for minority communities to articulate their concern and influence state policies. In addition to that, the House of Commons launched an inquiry that opened consultations with a series of key actors. All those characteristics were missing in Germany.

A second example by the authors is even more important because it tackles the issue of the lack of effectivity of mini-publics that play such a central role in the seminal work of Mansbridge and Parkinson. According to the authors of the paper Message Received: transmission in deliberative systems, '...empirical research suggests that in practice many mini-publics are poor transmitters because they lack any institutional or political connection to relevant and significant sites in empowered spaces, such as the media, elite committees and parliaments'. The argument on the limits of mini-publics that has been part of many criticisms on deliberative systems theory (Avritzer 2012) receives an important empirical confirmation in the authors' paper. The case of energy policy involved citizens reports that were incorporated in MP's recommendations. Thus, the authors advance an idea of an intentionally formed mini-public. The obesity case serves as a counter example in this direction. Being based almost exclusively on narrative, it lacks the intentional tool, that according to the authors, social actors need in order to make mini-publics more effective. Thus, the authors make a very important contribution on understanding transmission. However, the authors to not tackle the important issue about how to make representation and political institutions more sensitive to the claims made by social actors, an issue approached by the last paper in the special session.

Empirical test of the concept of deliberative system

Debora Rezende and Eleonora Cunha deepen the criticism of the deliberative system's theory and provide another important empirical insight on how concrete deliberations work. The authors' point of departure is slightly different from the two other pieces. They start with a criticism of a standard account of representation and propose a relational concept of representation described as '...spaces that reflect civil society representation ... and do not operate in an isolated manner, but rather belong to a group of deliberative spheres which have a close connection to specific arenas of public policy'. Thus, the authors raise two important points closely related to the Brazilian experience of deliberative systems: the first point is that deliberative systems should be though in terms of their relation to processes of representation; the second point is that civil society representation can link deliberative spaces with the political system.

The point of departure of the authors is a critique of the deliberative system approach of transmission. They claim in a similar fashion of Boswell, Hendricks, and Ercan that many authors lack the resources to be present in the representative arena. Instead of a weak conveyance of deliberation, they propose to figure out an institutional design that may guarantee a circulation of actors and proposals within the deliberative system.

For Rezende and Cunha, 'the design of the Brazilian participatory institutions, such as councils and conferences, in the phases of public policy establishes the level of decision-making, the way they interact with other forums, the forms of inclusion and authorization and mechanisms for accountability. A systemic articulation in these cases is shaped and regulated by a group of rules that creates and organizes these institutions'.

They exemplify their proposal with the analysis of the Brazilian social assistance policy. They enumerate and analyze this systemic process focusing on the national council, a mixed institution made of state and civil society actors; they continue describing the social assistance conference a space in which government officials and civil society representatives collaborate in the formulation of public policy. All these levels are considered part of SUAS – the integrated social assistance system. By analyzing SUAS in this way, the authors show a new connection between councils, conference, the political system, and society. Their point is that the rules of SUAS allow for the circulation of actors and generate a flow of information that places together representative and represented actors. Thus, a new form of connection between deliberative systems and the political system is proposed, one that starts with the connection through civil society representation of levels of the deliberative system that are later connected to the political system. Again as in the other papers presented above, the authors make a specific contribution to the theory of deliberative systems by showing how institutional design affects the capacity of civil society representatives to institutionalize their claims.

The contributions of empirical studies to theory

The three papers discussed in this special symposium point in the direction of important empirical contributions to the deliberative systems theory. Deliberative systems theory involved an important attempt to move forward in relation to the Habermasian theory on the role of societal influence on the political system. Habermas refrained to show how influence is transmitted from society to the political system (Habermas 1994). Deliberative system's theory is clearly a step forward in its attempt to connect 'arenas of formal and informal talk related to decisions on issues of common concern...' (Parkinson and Mansbridge 2012, 9). However, the specific form according to which these arenas are connected remained a problem for the deliberative system's theory.

The three papers throw light on how connection and transmission takes place. The deliberative network paper shows how deliberative networks connect themselves through process of differentiation through which different roles are played. It also points out that in policy arena, different deliberations need to be connected across time. In this sense, it is not enough to assume that communication takes place. It is necessary to show how in real world interaction occurs or fail to take place. The transmission paper is another step forward in the theory on deliberative systems because the paper explicitly shows how societal claims and the political system are connected. Again, the papers show both cases of successful transmission and cases of unsuccessful transmission. Finally, the paper on the Brazilian social assistance shows how to build through rules and norms a process of transmission of deliberation through civil society representation. The three papers point in the same direction, namely there is a pressing need to further elaborate on the empirical mechanism of a deliberative system. The next step in this process could be the integration of the frameworks presented here in order to advance the existing theory.

Disclosure statement

No potential conflict of interest was reported by the author.

References

Avritzer, L. 2012. "Democracy Beyond Aggregation: The Participatory Dimension of Public Deliberation." *Journal of Public Deliberation* 8 (2): 1–18.
Cohen, J. 1997. *Reflections on Deliberative Democracy*. Cambridge: MIT Press.
Habermas, J. 1994. "Three Deliberative Models of Democracy." *Constellation* 1 (1): 1–10. doi:10.1111/cons.1994.1.issue-1.
Parkinson, J., and J. Mansbridge. 2012. *Deliberative Systems*. Cambridge: Cambridge University Press.
Rawls, J. 1993. *Political Liberalism*. New York: Columbia University Press.

Index

Abers, R. 110
accountability 46, 93, 102–4, 106, 111–14, 134–5
activists 46–7
actors: circulation of, in SUAS 101, 109–13, 114; connection of 141
agency 25–6, 80, 92
agenda setting 56
aggregation 55
agonism 72
AIDS activism 61
Almeida, D. 9, 46, 99
Anderson, A. 63
anonymous public conversations 34
anti-globalization movement 29, 75
anti-whaling activists 28
apparent consensus 59
appropriate degree 21, 30n2
'Areopagos' deliberations 58, 68n5
assessors 133, 134
Australia, energy policy debate in 85–8
authorization 102, 104, 106, 111
Avritzer, L. 10, 140

Baker, K. 133, 135
Beatty, J. 59, 65
Benhabib, S. 34
blind deference 63, 64, 66
Bohman, J. 43, 55, 56, 62
Boswell, J. 9, 78
Boullier, D. 44–5
'Boundaries of a Deliberative System, The' (article) 73
Brazilian Social Assistance Policy 99–116
Brazilian Unified Health System (SUS) 115n2
Britain: 'honor killing', debate case in 81–5
British Columbia Citizens' Assembly 65
Brownlee, K. 25–6
bureaucrats 41–3

Castiglione, D. 103
Chambers, S. 6, 7, 20, 23, 34, 35, 43, 56, 58
Chequers meeting 131–2, 135–6
Christian Democratic Union (CDU) 82

citizens: assemblies 54; deliberation 66, 67, 75; experts and 75–6; representatives and 103
citizens' jury 86
civil disobedience, as deliberative disruption 25–7
civil society: in deliberative systems 9; leaders, in participatory institutions 110; representation, social assistance's deliberative system and 105–13
Clean Air Coalition 62
coercive power 55
Cohen, J. 3
collective decisions 17, 23
communication 16, 102; channels of 35, 104; between civil and political society 102; mediated 44; mode of 20, 24, 39
communicative power 5
conferences, relationship with councils 108, 112
connectivity inducers, in deliberative system 33–49; and mitigation of systemic dangers 39–47
consensus 58–9
Constitution (1988), of Brazil 105, 107
contestation, public scrutiny and 61–2
cooperative governance 24
Côrtes, S. V. 116n7
Council Tax 136
councils: hybrid characteristic of 109; institutional design of 105, 107; relationship with conferences 108, 112
Cuhna, Eleonora 9, 46
cultural pluralism 4
Cunha, E. S. 8, 99, 142–3

Dahl, Robert 68n1
de-centered politics 34
decisions 121–5, 130–1; collective 17, 23; legitimacy of 99–100; societal 17, 23
decision makers' discretionary powers: activists and 47; bureaucrats and 42; expansion of 37–8; media and 45; representation and 103
deforestation 27
Delborne, J. 63

INDEX

deliberation: among experts 58–61; integrated model of 35
deliberative acceptance 59–60, 65
deliberative action: conception of 19–22; dialogic feature 21; reflexivity 19–20; respectful of others 20
deliberative capacity 14, 17, 18, 23, 103
deliberative democracy, 140; bureaucracy's role in 41; discrete generational cohorts in 3; fourth generation of 1–10; representation and 101; systemic turn in 5–10; transformation across generations 3–5
deliberative elitism 65–7
deliberative equality 57
deliberative exchange: deliberative interaction 124; deliberative roles 124–5; evaluation of 127–8; partiality 132; scope of 125–6, 133–5; strength, membership and procedures 126–7, 133; transparency 127–8, 135–6
deliberative networks 128–30, 141; and deliberative systems 130–1
deliberative politics 5
deliberative polls 4, 54
deliberative principles 121–2
deliberative rhetoric 20
deliberative systems: alternative histories 71–2; approach/concept of, 1–2, 5, 33–5, 72, 122–3; boundaries of 14–30, 72–4; boundary problem 16–19; Brazilian Social Assistance Policy 99–116; civil disobedience as deliberative disruption 25–7; and civil society representation 105–13; connection of actors in 141; dangers and connectors 74–5; decision makers' discretionary powers, expansion of 37–8; defined 14, 103, 122, 140; deliberative action, conception 19–22; deliberative networks and 130–1; direct action as non-deliberative disruption 27–9; disruption in 22–9; and disruptive protest 9, 14–30; empirical test of 99–116, 142–3; everyday talk in 35, 72, 140; examining transmission in 78–95; experts and citizens 75–6; ideal of 7, 23–5; incompatible discursive dynamics 38–9; inducers of connectivity in 33–49; maintenance of 24; mitigation of systemic dangers 39–47; need for division of labor 6–7; outcome-functional definitions 123; political asymmetries creation 36–7; practical and theoretical problems 33–49; problem of expertise in 54–8; procedural-functional definitions 122; promoting deliberation on mass scale 6; recognizing 72–4; reflections on 71–6, 140–4; theory to empirical study 76; transmission in 142; two-track model 34, 79; use of non-deliberative rhetoric 24–5
deliberative theory: systemic turn on 34–5
democratic innovation 80
democratic legitimacy 3; of civil society's representation 103; of representation 100; systemic approach to 101–4

democratic representatives, authority for 102–3
Department of Health and Social Security (DHSS) 133
Department of the Environment 133, 135
Deveaux, M. 3–4
dialogic dimension of deliberative action 21, 73
direct action as non-deliberative disruption 27–9
discretionary power of decision makers 37–8, 103
discursive democracy 3
discursive transmission mechanisms, and obesity debate 88–91
disobedience, civil 25–7
displacement 66–7, 114
disruptive protest, deliberative systems and 14–30, 19
division of labor 6–7, 9, 54–6, 122, 128
domination 61
Dryzek, J. S. 3–4, 5, 9, 16, 71, 79–80, 104

elitism, deliberative 65–7
Elstub, Stephen 1, 2, 8
empowered/public spaces 16, 23, 80, 83, 104
empowerment to resist 62
energy policy debate: and innovative transmission mechanisms (case study) 85–8
environmental politics 3
environmentalism 29
Epstein, S. 61
equality 54, 57, 59
Ercan, S. 1, 9, 36, 78
Ettema, J. S. 43
everyday talk, in deliberative system 35, 72, 140
exclusion 37, 57, 63
expert consensus 58–9
expert deliberations 58–61
expertise, problem of locating: in deliberative politics 54–8
experts and citizens 75–6
external legitimacy 56

fairness and practicality, of poll tax 134
feminism 3
Ferejohn, J. 55–6
Fishkin, J. S. 4
Foster, C. 133
Foz do Chapecó Power Plant 36
Fraser, Nancy 61
function, epistemic 35
Fung, A. 28–9

Gastil, J. 43
Gavin, Neil 29
Germany: 'honor killing', debate case in 81–5; political parties in (*Parteinahe Stiftungen*) 84
Giddens, Lord 83
Gilbert, Margaret 59
Goodin, R. 6, 21, 34, 43, 62–3, 122
governance: cooperative 24; transnational 46
government agencies 82, 84–5

INDEX

government sponsored inquires 83, 84
Green Paper (1981) 132, 134
Greenpeace 26–7
Gutmann, A. 43

Habermas, J. 3–5, 34, 43, 79, 91, 122, 143
Health Councils, in Brazil 46
Hendriks, C. 9, 35, 78, 104, 105
Hoffmann, L. 133
'honor killing' debate, and institutional transmission mechanisms (case study) 81–5
House of Commons Home Affairs Select Committee 83

ideal deliberative procedure 121
impracticality 134–5
inclusion, in deliberative systems 17, 63, 88, 104, 106, 108–9, 111
income taxes 134
incompatible discursive dynamics: activists and 47; bureaucrats and 42–3; media and 45; negligence to 38–9
indeterminacy 18
inducers of connectivity, in deliberative system 33–49; activists 46–7; bureaucrats 41–3; media 43–6; and mitigation of systemic dangers 39–47
information proxies 63
innovative transmission mechanisms, and energy policy debate 85–8
institutional design, in SUAS 100, 106–9, 114
institutional transmission mechanisms, and 'honor killing' debates 81–5
institutionalization 113, 140
instrumentalization 4
interdependence 103
interest groups 133
intergovernmental commissions 105, 107
Intergovernmental Panel on Climate Change 59, 75
intermediary advocates 62
internal legitimacy 56
International Whaling Commission 28
interpersonal deliberation 19
intra-public discussions 35
iterative processes 55

Jasanoff, S. 61
Jenkin, Patrick 132, 135
Johnson, J. 59

Kashiwakura, Gabriella 116n12
Kleinman, D. 63
Knight, J. 59
Knops, Andrew 10, 120, 141
knowledge: associations 62; information and 20; of transmission 80

Lafont, C. 64–7
Lawson, Nigel 135

lay citizens 61, 76
Legislative Assemblies 105–6
Legislative Seminar 37
legitimacy 37; of civil society representation 108, 111; of decisions 99–100; democratic 3, 101–4; internal and external 56; of representative democracy 102; of women's organizations 85
Locatelli, C. 36
Lula administration 105

MacKenzie, M. M. 63–4
macro discursive spaces 105, 107
Major, John 136
manipulation 103
Mansbridge, J. 5, 7, 14, 16–18, 20, 34–5, 103, 140
media 85, 123; as inducer of connectivity in deliberative systems 43–6
mediated communication 44
mega-sports-events 44
Mendonça, R. F. 1, 8, 9, 33, 74–5, 103, 104
meta-consensus 65, 121, 137n2
meta-deliberation 54, 56, 62
micro discursive spaces 105, 107
middle democracy 80
Millennium Ecosystem Assessment 76
Milligan, T. 28
Minas Gerais State Legislature (Brazil) 37, 41
minipublics 4, 9, 16, 37, 72, 75, 142; as anticipatory public 93; debates on democratic innovations 85; as deliberative transmitters 85; and elites 86; as form of deliberative elitism 53–4; legitimacy of 35; as mode of scrutiny 62–7
Ministry of Social Development and Fight Against Hunger 113
mixed spheres, councils and conferences 105, 107
Moore, A. 9, 53, 59, 65, 75–6
moral diversity 121
multiculturalism 3
murders, culture- and gender-based frames of 81–5

National Council for Social Assistance 101, 108, 110, 115n3
National Social Assistance Policy 105
near unanimity 64–5
Neblo, M. 4, 7–8, 90
'network of deliberative exchanges' 10
Nike 76
non-deliberative disruption, direct action as 27–9
non-electoral representation 99–100
nonverbal modes of behavior 21
normative theorizing 3, 71
NSW Parliament: Public Accounts Committee (PAC) 86–7, 95n5

obesity debate: and discursive transmission mechanisms 88–91
operationalization 103

INDEX

Organic Law of Social Assistance (LOAS) 105, 115n4
oversight and scrutiny, of expert practices 61–2
Owen, D. 7, 19, 25, 103

Papadopoulos, Y. 24, 35
Parkinson, J. 6, 8, 19, 34–6, 43, 103–4, 122, 140
participants, in SUAS 101, 109–13, 114
participatory institutions, in Brazil 37, 47, 100, 104, 106–7, 110
partisan campaigning 14
party-affiliated organizations 84
persuasion 20
Peters, B. 44
Pitkin, H. F. 102
plebiscitary rhetoric 20
pluralism 121
policy community 107, 110, 116n7
policy councils 107
policymaking processes, deliberative action within 23–4, 120, 141
political asymmetries creation: activists and 47; advocacy of deliberative systems leading to 36–7; bureaucrats and 42; media and 45
political parties 84
political representation 99, 101–4
poll tax, in UK 10, 131–2, 134, 141
powers of prevention, exercise of 62
premisses of argument 125–6
property tax 134, 136
protest 26, 27; noncooperation and 62; social movement contestation and 66
proxies 63
Public Accounts Committee (PAC), of NSW Parliament 86–7, 95n5
public and empowered spaces 16, 23, 80, 83, 104
public contestation of discourses, un-individualistic conception of 34
public deliberation 5, 6, 35, 45, 57; expert knowledge and 58
public embarrassment 45
public reasons 56
public scrutiny, value of 61–2
public sphere: access to/influence over 14, 56; accountability in 104; 'critical' 57, 66–7; communication in 27, 43; deliberation in 74–5, 79; discourse in 4, 45; relationship with State institutions 114; 'wilder' 122
publicity 36, 55
'pure' publics 63

rainforest destruction 27
Rawls, J. 58
realism 8
reason-giving 19–20, 43, 54, 56
reasons 121, 125; exchange of 3, 37, 43, 124, 128; internal and external 56
Rees, Peter 135
reflexivity of deliberation 19–20, 73
regimes, regulatory 23

representation, political 99, 101–4
representatives 46–7
Rezende, Debora 142–3
rhetoric 16, 20, 24–5
Richardson, H. 62
Rothschild, Lord 133
Roundtable for Sustainable Palm Oil (RSPO) 27
Ruiz, Pollyanna 26

sales taxes 134
sanctions 20
Saward, M. 102
scientific consensus 58
scientific whaling 28
Scottish revaluation in 1984–1985 134
secluded deliberations, porousness of 56
secrecy, democratic justification of 55
self-interests 4, 14, 19
semiformal institutions 83, 84
sequencing of deliberative moments 6–7, 34, 55
service users, in social assistance 112
Smith, G. 7, 19, 25, 103
Smith, W. 9, 14, 73
Social Assistance Councils, in Brazil 46
Social Assistance Policy, in Brazil 105, 110
Social Assistance Unified System *see* SUAS (Brazilian Social Assistance Unified System)
social inequalities 4
social movements: in deliberative transmission 92; and knowledge associations 62; and State 110
societal decisions 17, 23
societal practices of contestation and critique 61
State: social movements and 110; society and 111
SUAS (Brazilian Social Assistance Unified System) 100–1, 116n5; actors, circulation of 101, 109–13; councils and conferences 107–8; creation in 2005 105; institutional design in 100, 106–9; relationship among spheres in 106
subaltern counter-publics 61
substantive deliberation 56
Supreme Court (US) 58, 74
Sürücü, Hatun: murder of 82

tacit consent 57–8
Talisse, R. 22
Tanjev, S. 44
technocracy 47, 57
Thatcher government: adoption of poll tax 131–2, 134, 141
Thompson, D. 7, 43, 54
Tories 132
transmission: amplifying 92–3; concept of 79–80; in deliberative systems 78–95, 142; discursive mechanisms, and obesity debate 88–91; enabling 91–2; innovative mechanisms, and energy policy debate 85–8; institutional mechanisms, and 'honor killing' debate 81–5; in practice 80–91; sustaining 93–4; theorizing 79–80

INDEX

transparency 24, 60, 127–8, 135–6
trust 63, 112, 125
Turner, S. P. 62
two-track model 34; of democratic legitimation 79

unanimity 64–5
unfairness 134
Unilever 27
Urbinati, N. 66–7
Urfalino, P. 58, 60

verbal exchange 21, 30n1
violence, against women 83
von Bülow, M. 110

Waldegrave, W. 133, 135
Wampler, B. 110
Warren, M. E. 57, 61, 63–4, 103
Weber, Max 41
Wessler, H. 43
Whitelaw, Lord 135
Wilson, Tom 133
Wimmel, A. 44
women, violence against 83
Women's National Council (WNC) 83, 94, 142
Working Groups 110

Yones, Heshu: murder of 82
Young, I. M. 4, 34

INDEX

transparence 24, 60, 129–9, 135–6
trust 6, 112, 122
tupper, S. P. 62
two-track model 4, of democratic legitimation 8

unanimity 4–5
utilitarianism 21
Lushever 27
Uni (rot), N. 66, 7
Untamed, F 58, 90

verbal exchanges 21, 30ff.
violence against women 85
von Billow, M. 110

Waldegrave, W. 134–135
Waugher, B. 110
Warren, M. E 57, 61, 63–4, 110
Weber, Max 41
Wickedness, 41
Winkler, Lord, 137 ff.
Will om firm 143
Wunder, A. 44
women, violence against 85
Women's National Caucus (WNC) 85, 98, 102
Working Groups 110

Yorke, Fresbtn murder of 87
Young, I. M. 150